ARMED FORCES AT THE ALTAR OF JUSTICE

Towards an Independent and Impartial Military Justice System:
Rethinking the Summary Court-Martial

Dr. Jyoti Puri

notionpress.com
INDIA · SINGAPORE · MALAYSIA

ISBN

Paperback 979-8-90540-340-8
Hardcase 979-8-90560-833-9

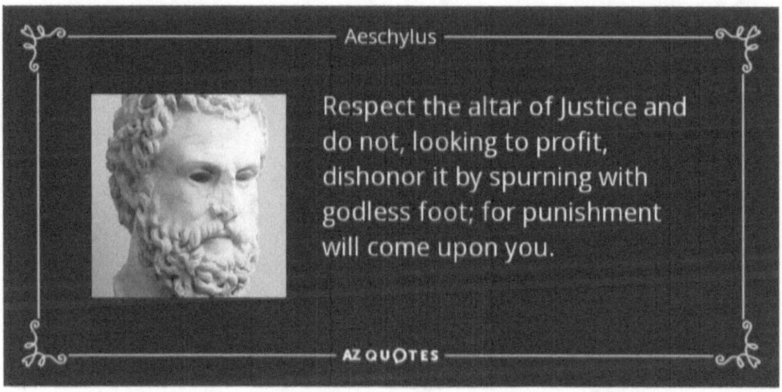

Dedicated to the Memory of

Late Captain (Retd.) K.M Saxena

Table of Contents

Acknowledgements

The genesis and fruition of this book are the result of the contributions of a great number of people who, in diverse ways, have supported this research and deserve special mention. It is a pleasure to convey my gratitude to them through this humble acknowledgement.

It gives me great pleasure to express my deep gratitude to Dr. Kavita Singh, for her unwavering encouragement, support, supervision, advice, and guidance from the very early stages of this research. Her mentorship has enriched this work immeasurably and provided me with invaluable learning experiences throughout the course of this study.

I am also indebted to Professor Dr. Ishwara Bhat, former Vice-Chancellor of the West Bengal National University of Juridical Sciences, whose intellectual guidance, passion for legal scholarship, and constant encouragement have profoundly influenced my growth as a student and researcher.

I am greatly indebted to my parents, friends, family, and colleagues for their support and encouragement. For academic feedback, I am particularly grateful to Late Captain (Retd.) K. M. Saxena, Advocate, for helping me understand the subtleties and frailties of the Indian Military Justice System. I also extend my sincere thanks to Late Colonel (Retd.) Y. R. Sharma, Advocate and former officer of the Judge Advocate General's Branch and Colonel Chandra Nath (retd.), an independent researcher in

Information Security, Privacy and Law, for providing valuable insights into the practical functioning of the Military Justice System and its legal framework.

I deeply appreciate the personal support of my husband, Colonel Surinder Puri, whose encouragement, intellectual companionship, and unwavering faith in my abilities have been a constant source of strength throughout this journey. His commitment to learning, integrity, and service has inspired me in countless ways.

I am equally grateful to my children, Squadron Leader Sheba (Retd.) and Captain Snehasish, serving in the Merchant Navy, whose achievements, affection, and encouragement have brought immense pride and motivation to my life. Finally, I acknowledge with gratitude all those who, directly or indirectly, contributed to the completion of this work. Any errors or shortcomings that remain are entirely my own.

Preface

I have spent more than four decades of my life within the extended family of the Armed Forces—first as a daughter, later as a wife, and ultimately as a mother. I entered the legal profession later in life following a prolonged legal struggle for the vindication of my rights, an experience that profoundly shaped my understanding of justice, due process, and institutional accountability.

It was after this experience, and my subsequent entry into the legal profession, that I began to observe a growing sense of dissatisfaction, frustration, and disillusionment among many members of the Armed Forces. Much of this sentiment appeared to stem from their perception of a justice system that did not always uphold the principles of independence, impartiality, and due process, particularly in the context of summary trials and disciplinary proceedings.

One may argue that my personal experiences could have influenced the perspective adopted in this work. Such a concern is understandable. However, I firmly believe that emotion and reason are not mutually exclusive. As Professor Amartya Sen aptly observes, if we are strongly moved by a particular emotion, it is worthwhile to examine what that emotion reveals and whether it withstands the scrutiny of reason.[1] Guided by

1 Amartaya Sen, The Idea of Justice, 39 (Allen Lane, an imprint of Penguin Books, 2009).

this approach, I have attempted to undertake this study with intellectual honesty, academic rigour, and an openness to competing viewpoints.

This work is not a critique of the Armed Forces as an institution. On the contrary, it is written with profound respect for the men and women who serve the nation under demanding and often extraordinary circumstances. The Armed Forces remain one of the most respected institutions in India, and rightly so. The purpose of this book is not to question the necessity of discipline, hierarchy, or operational effectiveness. Rather, it is to examine whether the mechanisms through which military justice is administered adequately reflect the constitutional values that those very institutions are sworn to defend.

The study seeks to explore the relationship between military discipline and the principles of justice. It examines whether the existing framework of military justice, particularly the institution of Summary Court Martial, provides sufficient safeguards to ensure fairness, impartiality, and accountability. Through an analysis of constitutional provisions, statutory frameworks, judicial decisions, comparative military law, and empirical observations, this work attempts to contribute to an informed discussion on the future of military justice in India.

The insights presented in this book are the result of years of research, professional legal experience, academic engagement, and interactions with serving and retired members of the Armed Forces. Together, these experiences have illuminated important questions concerning justice, discipline, command responsibility, and institutional legitimacy.

If this study contributes, even modestly, to a more meaningful discussion on the balance between military necessity and constitutional values, and if it encourages further reflection on the administration of justice within the Armed Forces, it will have achieved its purpose.

List of Abbreviations

Abbreviation	Meaning
AA	Army Act, 1950
ACHR	American Convention on Human Rights
AFT	Armed Forces Tribunal
AR	Army Rules, 1954
BNSS	Bharatiya Nagarik Suraksha Sanhita, 2023
CO	Commanding Officer
COAS	Chief of Army Staff
COI	Court of Inquiry
CrPC	Code of Criminal Procedure, 1973
DCM	District Court-Martial
ECHR	European Convention for the Protection of Human Rights and Fundamental Freedoms
GCM	General Court-Martial
GREF	General Reserve Engineering Force

Abbreviation	Meaning
ICCPR	International Covenant on Civil and Political Right
JAG	Judge Advocate General
JCO	Junior Commissioned Officer
LNK	Lance Naik
NCO	Non-Commissioned Officer
SCM	Summary Court-Martial
SGCM	Summary General Court-Martial
SOE	Summary of Evidence
SRO	Statutory Rules and Orders
UCMJ	Uniform Code of Military Justice
UDHR	Universal Declaration of Human Rights
WO	Warrant Officer

Table of Cases

Maj. Parvesh Chander Suri v. Union of India
Maneka Gandhi v. Union of India
Metropolitan Properties Co. (F.G.C.) Ltd. v. Lannon
Miranda v. Arizona

N
Naik Abhilash Singh Kushwah v. Union of India
Noyd v. Bond

O
O'Callahan v. Parker
Ous Kutilingal Achudan Nair and Others v. Union of India and Others

P
Piersack v. Belgium
Prosecutor v. Zigiranyirazo

R
R. Chatterjee v. Sub Area Commander
R. v. Généreux
R. Viswan and Others v. Union of India and Others
Ram Swarup v. Union of India
Ranjit Thakur v. Union of India and Others
Re Murchison v. United States
Reid v. Covert
Rex v. Sussex Justices, Ex parte McCarthy

S
S.N. Mukherjee v. Union of India
Sudhir Chandra v. Tata Iron and Steel Co. Ltd.
Sunil Batra v. Delhi Administration

CHAPTER 01

Ignorance is Definitely Not Bliss

Apart from the more than 1.5 million citizen soldiers who serve in our Armed Forces, most citizens who have never had any interaction with the Indian Military Justice System regard it as a self-contained mechanism equipped with adequate checks and balances. The rest remain in a blissful state of ignorance. During my recent stint as an educator, imparting the subtle nuances of criminal law to aspiring lawyers, I found that military law is virtually absent from mainstream legal discourse. The citizen soldiers who lay down their lives for us, protect the nation from external aggression, and live and fight in the harshest of conditions often remain nothing more than statistics or news headlines for the larger public. The least we can do is stand up for them when injustice is meted out to them. To do so, we must first become aware of their justice system and raise our collective voice to address and rectify its shortcomings.

Independence and impartiality constitute the essence of any court of law and form the cornerstone of every legal system. This principle finds expression in major international human rights instruments,[2] the Constitution of India, and our statutory

---

2 The International Covenant on Civil and Political Rights (hereinafter ICCPR) art. 14, 1966 (of which India is a signatory and is bound

framework.[3] A reading of these instruments confirms that a tribunal must, in all circumstances, be independent, impartial, and established by law.[4] The guarantee of an independent and impartial court operating under the rule of law, dispensing justice through fair trial procedures and adherence to due process at every stage, assures every litigant that his or her case will be adjudicated by a neutral judicial or quasi-judicial body.

In the context of the Indian Military Justice System, it may be argued that the framework is self-contained and incorporates adequate checks and balances. However, the wide discretionary powers vested in the Commanding Officer (hereinafter "CO")

---

by its provisions); The European Convention on Human Rights (hereinafter ECHR) art. 6 (1); The American Convention of Human Rights (hereinafter ACHR) art. 8 (1).

3 Art.14 (it states that the State shall not deny to any person equality before the law or the equal protection of the laws within the territory of India), Civil Procedure Code (hereinafter CPC) §327 (it states that for a trial to be fair, it must be an open court trial). *See also* CPC § 191 (it states that an accused shall be informed that he is entitled to have his case tried by another court. However, he has no right to select or determine by which other court the case is to be tried).

4 ICCPR art. 14 (it reads that all persons shall be equal before the courts and tribunals. In the determination of any criminal charge against him, or of his rights and obligations in a suit at law, everyone shall be entitled to a fair and public hearing by a competent, independent and impartial tribunal established by law). *See also* ECHR art.6 (it reads, In the determination of his civil rights and obligations or of any criminal charge against him, everyone is entitled to a fair and public hearing within a reasonable time by an independent and impartial tribunal established by law), The Universal Declaration of Human Rights (hereinafter UDHR) art. 10 (it says that everyone is entitled in full equality to a fair and public hearing by an independent and impartial tribunal, in the determination of his rights and obligations and of any criminal charge against him).

or the Convening Authority to determine which cases should be prosecuted effectively, place them in the position of dispensers of favour or fortune. Such powers inevitably affect both the perception and reality of impartiality and independence, thereby undermining public confidence and the confidence of the soldier in the fairness of the system. The establishment of the Armed Forces Tribunal (hereinafter "AFT") under the Armed Forces Tribunal Act, 2007, has undoubtedly provided service personnel with an additional avenue of redress. Nevertheless, the system would be far more effective if, from its very inception, it embodied both the subjective and objective elements of an independent and impartial tribunal established by law.

In 2015, late Mr. Manohar Parrikar, the then Defence Minister of India, initiated an important effort towards military justice reform through the constitution of a Committee of Experts. The Committee was primarily tasked with addressing the large volume of litigation involving the Ministry of Defence and the three Services, as well as improving the grievance redressal mechanism available to serving and retired personnel. Military justice reform, however, emerged as one of the Committee's most significant areas of inquiry.[5]

The Committee made several significant recommendations aimed at modernising the military justice system. These included the establishment of a permanent framework for courts-martial, measures to reduce the influence of the Convening Authority over military justice proceedings, specialised training programmes for Judge Advocate General (JAG) officers outside the traditional

5 N/A. (2023) 'Military justice reform: Developments & challenges', *Bar & Bench.* Available at: https://www.barandbench.com/columns/military-justice-reform-developments-challenges (Accessed on:, 26.10. 2024).

military environment, and the restricted use of Summary Courts Martial as an exceptional measure. While certain recommendations have witnessed partial implementation—most notably the introduction of external legal training programmes for JAG officers and the judicial endorsement of limiting the use of Summary Courts Martial in the Vishav Priya Singh case[6]—the more fundamental structural reforms remain unrealised.

Proposals relating to a permanent courts-martial framework and the dilution of the Convening Authority's pervasive influence over the administration of military justice continue to await legislative and institutional action. Consequently, despite the Committee's progressive vision and the acceptance in principle of several of its recommendations, the core concerns relating to the independence and impartiality of the military justice system remain largely unaddressed. This is despite the fact that they were made with the approval of the Prime Minister and that, in principle, the emerging issues identified by the Study Group were accepted by the then Defence Minister in 2016. The Minister had even directed that a report detailing the action taken be submitted within forty-five days.

More recently, the Government issued a Gazette Notification bringing into force the Inter-Services Organisations (Command, Control and Discipline) Act with effect from 10 May 2024. The Act empowers Commanders-in-Chief and Officers-in-Command of Inter-Services Organisations (ISOs) to exercise command and disciplinary control over service personnel under their authority, thereby facilitating effective administration and discipline while

6 Union of India & Ors vs Vishav Priya Singh (2016) AIR 2016 Supreme Court 3726. Available at: https://indiankanoon.org/doc/69192244/ (Accessed: 26 September 2024)

respecting the unique conditions of each Service. However, the legislation is essentially an enabling statute and does not seek to alter the existing Service Acts, Rules, or Regulations.[7]

When the public speaks of justice, it is generally understood as the principle of giving every individual his or her due. In the military context, however, the concept of justice is closely associated with procedural justice, which is achieved through decision-making processes that faithfully adhere to the requirements of due process. It is insufficient to argue that the overriding need to maintain discipline justifies a dilution of procedural safeguards and that any resulting illegality, arbitrariness, or capriciousness can subsequently be corrected by the Armed Forces Tribunal, the High Courts, or the Supreme Court.

The military, as an institution, must itself be just. A just institution fosters a sense of stability, belonging, satisfaction, and confidence among its members, while reducing perceptions of unfairness that may otherwise lead to resentment and disaffection. According to Michelle Maiese (2004), justice and fairness are central components of procedural justice. She argues that when adjudicatory procedures conform to the principles of a fair trial, individuals continue to repose faith in the adjudicators, even when the outcome is adverse to their interests.[8]

---

7 The Hindu (2023) 'Govt notifies Inter-Services Organizations Act through Gazette notification', *The Hindu*. Available at: https://www.thehindu.com/news/national/govt-notifies-inter-services-organisations-act-through-gazette-notification/article68161530.ece (Accessed: 26 September 2024).

8 Michelle Maiese, Procedural Justice *Beyond Intractability*, (Guy Burgess & Heidi Burgess eds. , University of Colorado, Boulder, 2004), available *at* <http://www.beyondintractability.org/bi-essay/procedural_justice/>. (last visited Mar. 5, 2012.).

It must be understood that discipline within the Armed Forces cannot be sustained solely through the authority of superiors to make or break the careers of their subordinates in cases of perceived disobedience. True discipline is nurtured when service personnel believe that the system governing them is fair, impartial, and just. Such confidence inspires a level of commitment whereby individuals willingly place their lives at the service of the nation. The mere fact that military personnel have voluntarily submitted themselves to the existing system, with all its imperfections, cannot justify the conclusion that reform is unnecessary.

Justice and discipline must coexist in proper balance. Unless that balance is achieved, members of the Armed Forces may continue to feel that they belong to a distinct and separate class rather than being equal citizens of India entitled to the same standards of fairness, dignity, and justice that the Constitution promises to all.

BRIEF INSIGHT INTO THE HISTORY AND DEVELOPMENT OF COURTS-MARTIAL[9]

The origins of the military justice system in India can be traced to the year 1754, when statutory provisions were introduced for the punishment of acts and omissions, particularly mutiny and desertion, committed by officers and soldiers serving in the troops of the Honourable East India Company. The Articles of War emerged from these provisions. Although these regulations

9 Law Commission of India (1999) *169th Report on Amendment of Army, Navy and Air Force Acts*, paras 2.1–2.8; Kumar, N. (2012) *Military Justice System in India: An Analysis*. New Delhi: Universal Law Publishing; Government of India (1950) *The Army Act, 1950 (Act No. 46 of 1950)*.

were primarily intended to govern troops other than native soldiers, in the absence of a separate disciplinary code, they were also applied to the native troops maintained by the Honourable East India Company.

In 1813, a distinct legal framework was enacted for governing natives serving in East India and within the territorial limits of the Company's Charter. Subsequently, in 1824, it was clarified that the Articles of War would apply universally, whether within or beyond His Majesty's dominions. This development led to the formulation of military codes by the Governments of the Presidency Towns of Fort William (Calcutta), Fort St. George (Madras), and Bombay. These codes largely followed the pattern of the Articles of War applicable to European officers and soldiers serving under the Honourable East India Company.

The enactment of the Government of India Act, 1833 marked a significant milestone in the evolution of military law in India. The Act vested legislative authority over the entire native army in the Governor-General in Council, thereby paving the way for a uniform military code. Consequently, the Articles of War (Act XX of 1845) became the first common military code applicable to the native armies of India. Act XX of 1845 was subsequently replaced by Act XIX of 1847, which in turn was repealed and replaced by Act XXIX of 1861. The latter statute was again repealed by Act V of 1869 and replaced by the Indian Articles of War. These Articles were further amended by Act XII of 1894.

A major legislative reform occurred in 1911 when the Indian Articles of War were repealed and replaced by the Indian Army Act, which came into force on 1 January 1912. This legislation continued to govern the Indian Army until it was repealed by Act

46 of 1950, namely the Army Act, 1950, which came into force on 22 July 1950 and remains the principal legislation governing the Indian Army.

The history of the various forms of courts-martial can be traced to the Indian Articles of War, 1894. At that time, five different types of courts-martial were recognised:

(a) General Court-Martial (hereinafter "GCM");

(b) District Court-Martial (hereinafter "DCM");

(c) Summary General Court-Martial (hereinafter "SGCM");

(d) Summary Court-Martial (hereinafter "SCM"); and

(e) Regimental Court-Martial (hereinafter "RCM").

In practice, Regimental Courts-Martial were rarely convened because the Summary Court-Martial proved to be a more effective and expedient mechanism for dealing with disciplinary matters. Owing to their infrequent use, Regimental Courts-Martial gradually fell into disuse and were eventually abolished. Consequently, the Indian Army Act, 1911 recognised only four categories of courts-martial.

The General Court-Martial and District Court-Martial broadly corresponded to the tribunals established under the British Army Act for troops of European origin. The tribunal previously known as the Field General Court-Martial under the earlier regime was redesignated as the Summary General Court-Martial under the Indian Army Act, 1911. A notable distinction, however, existed between the British and Indian systems. Under the British Army Act, the President of a Court-Martial was appointed by name, whereas under the Indian Army Act, 1911, the senior-most member of the court ordinarily functioned as the Presiding Officer.

The origins of the Summary Court-Martial are closely linked to the events following the Mutiny of the Bengal Army in 1857. It was observed that irregular formations, particularly the Punjab Irregular Force, maintained a higher degree of discipline and operational effectiveness than many regular units. This success was attributed largely to the unique position occupied by the Commanding Officer, who possessed the authority to deal swiftly and effectively with military offenders under his command.

This system mirrored the administrative structure then prevailing in certain frontier provinces, where political, military, and civil authority was concentrated in a single individual. Such concentration of authority enabled the Commanding Officer not only to try and sentence military offenders but also to ensure the execution of sentences through the cooperation of civil and prison authorities.

In the aftermath of the 1857 Mutiny, it was considered necessary to provide Commanding Officers with similar powers to deal promptly and effectively with disciplinary infractions. Consequently, by 1869, the Summary Court-Martial had emerged as one of the most important tribunals within the Indian military justice system. Following Independence, the legislature considered its retention essential for the maintenance of discipline and for the swift disposal of military offences. Accordingly, the Summary Court-Martial was retained under the Army Act, 1950. Over the years, it has continued to occupy a central position in the disciplinary framework of the Indian Army and has often been regarded as one of the principal instruments for the maintenance of military discipline.

EXISTING LAW

Following Independence on 15 August 1947, the need for a comprehensive revision of the Indian Army Act, 1911, the Indian Air Force Act, 1932, and the Indian Navy Discipline Act, 1934 was keenly felt. The objective was to create modern and self-sufficient codes of military discipline capable of meeting the unique requirements of the Armed Forces while preserving operational effectiveness and discipline. Although complete uniformity among the three Services was not considered necessary, efforts were made to eliminate glaring inconsistencies wherever possible. The revision of the naval legislation was delayed pending consideration of recommendations relating to the revision of the British Naval Code. Ultimately, the Indian Navy Bill received Parliamentary approval and Presidential assent on 27 December 1957, thereby completing the legislative framework governing the three Services.

The Narrative

The Indian Armed Forces, comprising more than 1.5 million citizen soldiers, represent one of the most disciplined and professional institutions in the country. Military discipline is sustained not merely through the coercive power of law but through a soldier's sense of duty, honour, self-respect, and commitment to the nation. Nevertheless, members of the Armed Forces remain citizens and are therefore entitled to legal protection whenever their rights are infringed or unlawfully curtailed. While certain constitutional rights may be restricted or abrogated in the interests of discipline and operational effectiveness, the administration of military justice must continue to satisfy the minimum requirements of fairness, legality, and due process.

At the heart of every credible justice system lies the guarantee of an independent and impartial tribunal established by law. A fair trial is not merely concerned with the correctness of the outcome but also with the integrity of the process by which that outcome is reached. Concerns have repeatedly been raised regarding the degree of independence enjoyed by military courts and the perception of fairness within the existing court-martial system. The central objective of this work is therefore to examine whether the present military justice framework adequately embodies the principles of independence and impartiality and, if not, how it may be reformed to align with contemporary constitutional standards and evolving international practices.

Articles 14 to 32 of the Constitution of India collectively seek to safeguard life, liberty, equality, and access to justice. Article 21 extends protection not merely to citizens but to every person. Equally significant is Article 39A, introduced through the Forty-Second Constitutional Amendment, which casts an obligation upon the State to promote equal access to justice and ensure that legal remedies are not denied on account of economic or social disadvantage. Against this constitutional backdrop, it becomes necessary to examine the extent to which military justice conforms to these fundamental values.

Article 33 of the Constitution empowers Parliament to restrict or abrogate certain fundamental rights of Armed Forces personnel to ensure the proper discharge of their duties and the maintenance of discipline. However, the Constitution does not define the precise contours of either "maintenance of discipline" or "proper discharge of duties." Over the years, these expressions have been interpreted by the Legislature, the Executive, the Judiciary, and the Armed Forces themselves. One of the objectives of this study is to explore the constitutional relationship between Articles 14, 21, 33, and 39A and to determine whether an appropriate balance has been struck between military necessity and individual rights.

Particular attention is devoted to the role of the Convening Authority within the Court-Martial process. The Convening Authority exercises substantial influence from the initiation of proceedings until their conclusion. Members of the court-martial are ordinarily subordinate in rank and remain subject to the overall command structure within which the Convening Authority operates. The Convening Authority also performs several functions that significantly affect the administration of military justice, including the convening of the court and the exercise of powers relating to confirmation and review. These features raise important questions concerning command influence, institutional independence, and the appearance of impartiality. The absence of judicial members on courts-martial, their ad hoc nature, and the limited role of the Judge Advocate—who acts only in an advisory capacity and does not participate in deliberations—further contribute to this debate.

This study also examines the Summary Court-Martial, a unique feature of the Army Act that finds no equivalent in either the Air Force Act or the Navy Act. Questions arise regarding its compatibility with Article 14 of the Constitution, particularly in relation to equality before law and equal protection of law. Although the establishment of the Armed Forces Tribunal has introduced a mechanism of appellate review, statutory limitations continue to restrict access to such remedies in certain cases. The procedural safeguards available in Summary Court-Martial proceedings, the proportionality of punishments imposed, and the continued necessity of such proceedings during peacetime merit careful examination.

The broader question underlying this work is whether the military justice system merely incorporates the language of fairness or whether justice is genuinely seen to be done. The relative absence of sustained parliamentary oversight and comprehensive legislative reform has contributed to the continuation of several long-standing structural issues. While incremental amendments have been introduced over time, the need for a more comprehensive review of military justice remains. In this context, Lord Hewart's celebrated dictum that "justice should not only be done, but should manifestly and undoubtedly be seen to be done"[10] assumes particular significance.

Ultimately, this work seeks to examine whether the Indian Military Justice System strikes an appropriate balance between the demands of discipline and the imperatives of justice. It further explores how military discipline can be effectively maintained while preserving the dignity of the individual soldier and ensuring compliance with the principles of fairness, independence, and due process. To this end, the study also undertakes a comparative examination of the military justice systems of the United Kingdom and the United States of America, both of which have undergone substantial reforms in response to changing constitutional expectations and evolving standards of fair trial.

---

10 Rex v. Sussex Justices *Ex parte* McCarthy [1923] All ER 233.

CHAPTER 02

Court-Martial Procedures in the Indian Armed Forces – From Inception to Conclusion

The Cornerstone of Military Discipline

Discipline is the foundation upon which every military organisation rests. Unlike civilian institutions, the Armed Forces are entrusted with the defence of the nation, often under circumstances that demand unquestioning obedience, cohesion, and operational readiness. To ensure the maintenance of such discipline, a distinct legal framework governs the conduct of military personnel. This framework, commonly referred to as Military Law, regulates not only the duties and obligations of service personnel but also the consequences of misconduct and indiscipline.

Military law is not merely an instrument of punishment. It seeks to balance the demands of discipline with the requirements of justice, ensuring that corrective and punitive measures are administered through a legally recognised process. The military justice system therefore serves a dual purpose: preserving discipline within the ranks while simultaneously safeguarding the rights of those subject to its jurisdiction.

This chapter examines the procedural framework governing Courts-Martial in the Indian Armed Forces. It traces the journey of a military case from its inception through investigation, hearing of charge, convening of the Court-Martial, trial, confirmation, and post-trial remedies. Understanding this process is essential before embarking upon an examination of the larger issues of independence, impartiality, and fairness that are discussed in the subsequent chapters.

Historical Foundations of Military Justice

Trial by Court-Martial is one aspect of military life that no soldier wishes to encounter. Throughout history, military tribunals have attracted both support and criticism. Their necessity has been justified on the grounds of maintaining discipline, while their procedures have often been scrutinised for departing from the safeguards ordinarily available in civilian courts.

One of the earliest and most forceful criticisms of military justice was voiced during the debates on the Mutiny Bill of 1749 in the British Parliament. Earl of Westmoreland, in a powerful speech, denounced the institution of trial by court-martial in the following words:

"What makes the people of this country more happy and secure than they are in any other, is that valuable privilege of being tried by their peers and by judges who understand the laws of their country, who are bound to be of counsel with the prisoner at the bar and who are as independent as it is possible for men to be made, consistent with the nature of mankind and the support of the Government; but by this bill, and indeed every former bill of the same kind, the Officers and soldiers of our army are entirely deprived of this valuable privilege. If any of them be accused of a military crime, they are to be tried by a law which admits of no jury, nor of any challenge, and by judges who understand nothing of the laws of their country............... A certain form must, it is true, be observed in putting any of them to death; but when an innocent man is condemned to die; the form and ceremony of trial is an aggravation of his misfortune; for I should choose to die by the order and bowstring of a bashaw rather than by the sentence of a Court-martial, from whom I should expect neither justice nor mercy."[11]

Although expressed in the eighteenth century, the concerns articulated by Earl of Westmoreland continue to resonate in contemporary debates on military justice. His criticism focused upon the absence of trial by jury, the limited role of legally trained adjudicators, and the perceived lack of independence of military tribunals.[12] While modern military justice systems have evolved considerably since that period, the central challenge remains unchanged: how to reconcile the requirements of military discipline with the principles of fairness, impartiality, and due process.

Following Independence, the need for a comprehensive revision of the Indian Army Act, 1911, the Indian Air Force Act, 1932,

---

11 14 William Cobbett, Cobbett's Parliamentary History of England: From Norman Conquest in 1066 to the Year1803 426, (Printed by T.C. Hansard, Peterborough Court, Fleet Street, 1813), *available at* http://books.google.co.in/books?id=2pc9AAAAcAAJ&pg=PA6&lpg=PA6&dq=mutiny+bill+1749+debate&source=bl&ots=-66TY5j89t&sig=zlw0qu8DmdI8Q3uHex5og48gssc&hl=en&sa=X (Accessed, Jan. 4, 2012).

12 Earl of Westmoreland (1749) *Speech on the Mutiny Bill.* London: Parliamentary Archives.

and the Indian Navy Discipline Act, 1934 was keenly felt. The objective was to establish modern and self-contained codes of military discipline capable of meeting the unique operational requirements of the Armed Forces while eliminating glaring inconsistencies among the three Services wherever possible. The revision of the naval legislation was delayed pending consideration of recommendations relating to the revision of the British Naval Code. Ultimately, the Indian Navy Bill was passed by Parliament and received Presidential assent on 27 December 1957, thereby completing the legislative framework governing the three Services.

The resulting statutory regime—comprising the Army Act, 1950, the Air Force Act, 1950, and the Navy Act, 1957—continues to form the bedrock of military discipline in India. These enactments created a comprehensive legal code governing offences, punishments, investigations, trials, and post-trial remedies within the Armed Forces.

In contemporary times, the military justice system functions within a constitutional framework that increasingly emphasises fairness, due process, and the protection of individual rights. While discipline remains the primary objective of military law, the legitimacy of the system ultimately depends upon the confidence that service personnel and the public repose in its procedures. The true test of any justice system lies not merely in its ability to punish wrongdoing but also in its capacity to ensure that justice is administered fairly and is seen to be administered fairly.

It is therefore necessary to understand not only the substantive provisions of military law but also the procedural mechanisms through which military justice is administered. The succeeding sections examine these procedures in detail, tracing the life cycle of a court-martial from the initial allegation of misconduct through investigation, hearing of charge, trial, confirmation, appellate review, and judicial scrutiny.

General Court Martial (GCM): The Pinnacle of Military Trials

The General Court-Martial (hereinafter "GCM") is the highest form of Court-Martial constituted under the Army Act, 1950. It possesses the widest jurisdiction and is empowered to try the most serious offences under military law. Given the gravity of the offences that may be brought before it and the severity of punishments that it may award, the law prescribes detailed provisions regarding its constitution, composition, and jurisdiction.

Convening Authority

The power to convene a GCM is vested in the Central Government, the Chief of the Army Staff (COAS), or such officers as may be empowered by warrant issued by the COAS. The authority to convene a General Court-Martial carries considerable responsibility, as the validity of the proceedings and the jurisdiction of the tribunal are dependent upon the lawful exercise of such authority.

A warrant is an order addressed to a person directing him to perform specified acts and conferring upon him the authority to exercise particular powers. Accordingly, the COAS issues what is commonly known as the A-1 Warrant,[13] empowering designated

13 Form of Warrant A-1, 752, MML 1983, vol III

officers, or those upon whom command may devolve during their absence, not being below the rank of a Field Officer, to convene a General Court-Martial for the trial of persons subject to military law who are charged with offences under the Army Act, 1950 and are liable to be tried by a GCM.

As a general rule, neither the Commanding Officer of the accused nor the officer who has investigated the allegations against the accused may convene the General Court-Martial for the trial of that individual.[14] Exceptions exist only in limited circumstances, such as trials conducted on board a ship or in special cases as may be determined by the Central Government.

The power to convene or confirm a General Court-Martial ordinarily extends only within the territorial limits of the officer's command. However, an officer holding a warrant to convene a GCM at a port of embarkation may authorise the officer commanding troops on board a ship to convene and confirm a District Court-Martial in respect of persons subject to the Army Act during the course of the voyage.[15]

The jurisdiction of a court-martial is derived from the convening order. Consequently, the convening order constitutes a foundational document in military justice proceedings. Any substantial defect in the convening order cannot ordinarily be cured by a subsequent certificate, and in many instances such defects may render the entire trial invalid. It is therefore imperative that the convening order is prepared with precision and in strict compliance with statutory requirements.[16]

---

14 RA 1987, ¶ 449 (b).

15 AA 1950, § 109, Note 5.

16 Army Orders(AOs) 213, 215/ 72

Composition of the General Court-Martial

A General Court-Martial must consist of not fewer than five officers, each of whom must have held a commission for a minimum period of three years. At least four members must hold a rank not below that of Captain. While five members constitute the statutory minimum, the Convening Authority may appoint a larger number of officers depending upon the nature, complexity, and anticipated duration of the proceedings.

As far as practicable, the composition of the court should consist of an odd number of members in order to facilitate majority decisions on findings and sentence. Officers who have served in any of the three services are eligible for counting their commissioned service towards the three-year requirement. However, seniority that precedes the commission is not counted for eligibility purposes[17]. Subject to the provisions of the Army Act, the GCM possesses jurisdiction to try any offence under the Act and may award any sentence authorised by law, except where statutory restrictions specifically apply.

Administrative Restrictions on Composition

According to Army Regulation (AR) 40, there are specific restrictions on the composition of the GCM. Officers from different Corps or departments should be appointed to the Court to avoid having officers exclusively from the same Corps or department as the accused[18]. To maintain impartiality, the

---

17 Army Act, 1950. Section 116. Available at: https://indianarmy.nic.in/writereaddata/documents/ARMYACTS190216.pdf (Accessed: 15 Aug 2024).

18 Army Regulation 40 Available at: https://thc.nic.in/Central%20Governmental%20Rules/Army%20Rules,1954.pdf (Accessed: 15 August 2024).

composition should ideally include officers from various Corps to avoid any biases. For the trial of an officer, all members should ideally be of a rank not lower than that of the accused officer unless the Convening Authority deems it impractical due to public service exigencies, in which case this should be noted in the convening order. Additionally, a Field Officer cannot be tried by a member below the rank of Captain[19].

Additional administrative restrictions include the following:

(a) Where a Colonel or an officer of higher rank is available to preside over the GCM, an officer of a lower rank should not ordinarily be appointed as President. In the absence of a Colonel, prior approval of the next superior authority should be obtained and recorded in the convening order.

(b) Where the accused is a Commanding Officer, it is desirable that as many members as practicable have held, or are holding, command appointments equivalent to that of the accused.

(c) In lengthy or complex trials, the court is generally constituted with more than the minimum number of members, and waiting members may also be detailed to address contingencies arising from challenges or disqualifications.

19 *Ibid*

Disqualification of Members

Army Regulation 39 prescribes circumstances in which an officer is disqualified from serving as a member of a General Court-Martial. These disqualifications are intended to preserve the integrity, impartiality, and fairness of the proceedings. An officer is disqualified if he:

(a) convened the court;

(b) is acting as the prosecutor or is a witness for the prosecution;[20]

(c) investigated the charges before trial;[21]

(d) recorded the Summary of Evidence (SOE);

(e) served as a member of a Court of Inquiry relating to the same allegations;

(f) conducted a preliminary inquiry into the case;

(g) was a member of a previous court-martial concerning the same offence;

(h) is the Commanding Officer of the accused or belongs to the Corps to which the accused belongs; or

(i) possesses any personal interest in the outcome of the proceedings.[22]

These restrictions are intended to ensure that the tribunal remains free from actual bias and that its proceedings inspire confidence in the administration of military justice.

---

20 *Ibid*

21 *Ibid*

22 AR 39. Available at: https://thc.nic.in/Central%20Governmental%20Rules/Army%20Rules,1954.pdf (Accessed: 16 Aug 2024).

Guardians of Impartiality: Who Cannot Sit in Judgment?

The legitimacy of any judicial or quasi-judicial body rests not merely upon its legal authority but also upon the impartiality of those who compose it. To preserve public confidence in the administration of military justice, certain categories of officers are expressly disqualified from being appointed or detailed as members of a General Court-Martial.

Among those who are ineligible to serve as members are:

(a) the Provost Marshal; and

(b) the Assistant Provost Marshal.

The rationale underlying these disqualifications is founded upon one of the oldest principles of natural justice—that no person should be a judge in his own cause.[23] Any individual possessing a personal interest in the proceedings, however slight or remote, stands disqualified from participating in the adjudicatory process. The object is not merely to prevent actual bias but also to eliminate any reasonable apprehension of bias in the minds of those subject to the military justice system.

The Judge Advocate: The Court's Legal Compass

The presence of a Judge Advocate is an indispensable requirement in the constitution of a General Court-Martial. As the principal legal adviser to the court, the Judge Advocate assists the members on questions of law, procedure, and sentencing, thereby ensuring

23 The principle that no one should judge their own case is enshrined in the Indian Armed Forces Act, 1950. For a comprehensive discussion on the principle of impartiality, refer to Smith, J. (2021). *The Principles of Equity*. Cambridge University Press.

that the proceedings remain within the bounds of legality and fairness.

The absence of the Judge Advocate renders the proceedings irregular and necessitates adjournment of the court. Where the appointed Judge Advocate dies, falls ill, or is otherwise unable to continue, another qualified officer must be appointed to perform those duties and enable the trial to proceed to its lawful conclusion.[24]

The Reach of Justice: Jurisdiction of the General Court-Martial

A General Court-Martial possesses the widest jurisdiction among all military tribunals constituted under the Army Act. It is empowered to try any person subject to the Army Act, irrespective of rank, for any offence punishable under the Act.

This jurisdiction, however, is not without limitation. A General Court-Martial ordinarily lacks jurisdiction to try offences of murder, culpable homicide not amounting to murder, or rape where the victim is not a person subject to Military, Naval, or Air Force law. Such offences ordinarily fall within the jurisdiction of the ordinary criminal courts.

An exception exists where the offence is committed while the accused is on active service or stationed at a frontier post or other place notified by the Central Government.[25] In such

24 The necessity of the Judge Advocate's presence and the procedure for their replacement is outlined in *Indian Armed Forces Act, 1950, Section 129 and Army Rule 82(4).*

25 The jurisdictional limitations for a GCM are specified in the *Indian Armed Forces Act, 1950, Section 125* (1950).

circumstances, the General Court-Martial may exercise jurisdiction notwithstanding the civilian status of the victim. These limitations reflect the legislative attempt to balance military necessity with the ordinary jurisdiction of the civil courts.

From Reprimand to Death: The Sentencing Powers of the General Court-Martial

The General Court-Martial is vested with the widest sentencing powers available under the military justice system. Upon conviction, it may award any punishment authorised by law, subject to the limitations prescribed by the Army Act, 1950. The range of punishments that may be imposed is enumerated in descending order of severity under Section 71 of the Army Act and constitutes the exclusive spectrum of punishments available for offences falling within Sections 34 to 68 of the Act.

In cases involving offences under Section 69 of the Army Act, which incorporates civil offences into military law, a General Court-Martial may award any punishment authorised by the corresponding civil law in force in India, with the exception of whipping.[26] This provision ensures that conduct constituting an offence under ordinary criminal law does not escape punishment merely because it is committed by a person subject to military law.

The most severe punishment that may be awarded by a General Court-Martial is the sentence of death. Recognising the irreversible nature of such a punishment, the law imposes an additional safeguard. A sentence of death may only be awarded

26 The powers and limitations regarding punishments that a GCM can impose are outlined in the *Indian Armed Forces Act, 1950, Section 71, 69* (1950).

when at least two-thirds of the members of the court concur in the finding and sentence. Such concurrence must be formally certified and recorded in the proceedings of the court.[27]

The extensive sentencing powers vested in a General Court-Martial reflect both the seriousness of the offences that may come before it and the paramount importance of discipline within the Armed Forces. The court is therefore empowered to impose punishments ranging from the mildest forms of censure and reprimand to the ultimate penalty of death, thereby ensuring that the punishment awarded is proportionate to the gravity of the offence and the demands of military discipline.

Summary General Court-Martial: Justice at the Edge of Necessity

Purpose and Convening

The Summary General Court-Martial (hereinafter "SGCM") was conceived as an exceptional tribunal designed to meet situations where the exigencies of military service render the convening of a General Court-Martial impracticable. It serves as a swift and effective judicial mechanism, particularly in operational environments, remote locations, and circumstances where the requisite number of officers necessary to constitute a General Court-Martial are unavailable.

Unlike a General Court-Martial, an SGCM may be convened without a warrant. Under the present statutory framework, SGCMs are rarely convened during peacetime, and the authority

27 The requirements for imposing a death sentence and the concurrence of GCM members are detailed in *Indian Armed Forces Act, 1950*, Section 132(2) (1950).

to convene them ordinarily rests with the Central Government or the Chief of the Army Staff (COAS). Given that an SGCM exercises powers comparable to those of a General Court-Martial, it is considered desirable that its proceedings be recorded in full rather than in the abbreviated form permitted under Army Rule 160, thereby ensuring procedural parity and maintaining confidence in the administration of military justice.

Authorities Empowered to Convene

Unlike the General Court-Martial and the District Court-Martial, the Summary General Court-Martial may be convened through a simple order and does not require the issuance of a warrant.

The authorities empowered to convene an SGCM include:

(a) an officer specifically authorised by an order of the Central Government or the Chief of the Army Staff;

(b) during active service, the officer commanding a force in the field or any officer empowered by him; and

(c) an officer commanding a detached portion of the regular Army while on active service, where it is impracticable to convene a General Court-Martial owing to disciplinary requirements and service exigencies.[28]

Composition of the Summary General Court-Martial

A Summary General Court-Martial must consist of not fewer than three officers. Unlike the General Court-Martial, there is no statutory requirement regarding the rank of the members or the

28 AA 1950,§ 112.

length of their commissioned service. Nevertheless, as a matter of sound administrative practice, officers with less than one year of commissioned service should not ordinarily be appointed as members. Preference is generally given to officers who have held commissions for at least three years.

Although smaller in composition, the SGCM possesses powers comparable to those of a General Court-Martial and may impose any punishment authorised by the Army Act, including death and imprisonment for life. Given the gravity of such punishments, a sentence of death may only be awarded where all members of the court unanimously concur in the sentence.

Ineligibility for Membership

To preserve the integrity and impartiality of the proceedings, certain categories of individuals are disqualified from serving as members of an SGCM. These include:

(a) the Provost Marshal;

(b) the Assistant Provost Marshal;

(c) any officer acting as prosecutor; and

(d) any person who is a witness for the prosecution.

A significant distinction between the SGCM and the GCM lies in the role of the Judge Advocate. While the presence of a Judge Advocate is mandatory in a General Court-Martial, there is no legal requirement for a Judge Advocate to be present during an SGCM. Consequently, the absence of a Judge Advocate does not affect the validity of the proceedings.

Jurisdiction of the Summary General Court-Martial

The SGCM possesses jurisdiction to try all persons subject to the Army Act for any offence punishable thereunder. However, like the General Court-Martial, it ordinarily lacks jurisdiction to try offences of murder, culpable homicide not amounting to murder, or rape where the victim is not subject to Military, Naval, or Air Force law.

This limitation does not apply where such offences are committed while the accused is on active service or at a frontier post or other place notified by the Central Government. In such circumstances, the SGCM may validly exercise jurisdiction over the offence.

The Reach of Its Punitive Powers

The Summary General Court-Martial may award any punishment authorised by the Army Act. Its sentencing powers extend from the least severe punishments available under military law to the gravest sanctions, including imprisonment for life and the death penalty.

Recognising the irreversible nature of a death sentence, the law requires unanimous concurrence of all members of the court before such a sentence may be imposed. This safeguard represents an important procedural protection within a tribunal specifically designed to function under exceptional circumstances.

District Court-Martial: Justice Within Narrower Bounds

The District Court-Martial (hereinafter "DCM") occupies a position below the General Court-Martial in the hierarchy of military tribunals. It was designed to deal with less serious offences and operates within a more restricted jurisdictional and sentencing framework.

The principal distinction between a General Court-Martial and a District Court-Martial lies not merely in their composition but also in the extent of punishment each tribunal is authorised to award.[29] As a result, the DCM is comparatively less frequently convened.

Authorities Empowered to Convene

Unlike GCMs and District Courts Martial (DCMs), SGCMs do not require a warrant and can be convened through a mere order from the Central Government or COAS. The authorities who can convene an SGCM include:

- An officer specifically empowered by an order from the Central Government or the COAS.
- On active service, the Officer Commanding a force in the field or any officer empowered by him.
- An Officer Commanding a detached portion of the regular army on active service, if it is impracticable to convene a GCM due to discipline and service exigencies.

Convening Authority

For the purpose of convening and confirming a District Court-Martial, the Chief of the Army Staff issues a B-1 Warrant in favour of an officer not below the rank of a Field Officer. Such warrants are generally issued to Sub-Area Commanders, Brigade Commanders, and equivalent authorities empowered under Section 108 of the Army Act.

---

29 Manual of Military Law (MML), vol III, 753.

Unlike a General Court-Martial, where separate warrants may be issued for convening and confirmation, the authority relating to a District Court-Martial is generally exercised through the B-1 Warrant itself.[30]

Composition of the District Court-Martial

A District Court-Martial must consist of not fewer than three officers, each of whom must have held a commission for not less than two complete years.[31]

There is no statutory requirement concerning the rank of the members. However, administrative restrictions contained in the Regulations for the Army seek to ensure that the tribunal possesses sufficient maturity and experience to discharge its judicial responsibilities effectively.[32]

The grounds of disqualification applicable to members of a General Court-Martial apply equally to members of a District Court-Martial.

Jurisdiction of the District Court-Martial

The jurisdiction of a District Court-Martial is considerably narrower than that of a General Court-Martial.

A DCM cannot try:

(a) an officer; or

(b) a Junior Commissioned Officer.[33]

---

30 Manual of Military Law (MML), vol III, 753.

31 AA1950, § 114.

32 RA 1987, ¶ 459 (c) and (d).

33 AA 1950, § 119.

Although it may try a Warrant Officer, its powers of punishment in such cases are limited, and it cannot sentence a Warrant Officer to imprisonment.[34]

Subject to these restrictions, the DCM may try offences falling within its statutory jurisdiction. However, it lacks the authority to deal effectively with offences carrying punishments beyond its sentencing powers.[35]

Limits of Punishment

The sentencing powers of a District Court-Martial are significantly restricted. It cannot award a sentence exceeding two years' rigorous imprisonment.

Consequently, offences such as murder, which may attract imprisonment for life or the death penalty, fall outside the practical jurisdiction of the DCM. Such offences must necessarily be tried by a tribunal possessing the requisite authority to impose the punishments prescribed by law.

The District Court-Martial thus represents a tribunal of limited jurisdiction, intended to provide a convenient and efficient mechanism for the trial of comparatively less serious military offences while preserving the more serious cases for adjudication by higher military courts.

Summary Court-Martial: Swift Justice, Enduring Controversy

The Summary Court-Martial (hereinafter "SCM") is the most frequently employed form of court-martial within the Indian

34 AA 1950, § 119.
35 AA 1950, § 119.

Army. It was conceived as a mechanism for the prompt and effective maintenance of discipline, enabling military authorities to deal expeditiously with comparatively less serious offences committed by personnel below the rank of Junior Commissioned Officer.

Unlike the General Court-Martial, Summary General Court-Martial, or District Court-Martial, an SCM is not convened through a formal convening order. It is held by virtue of the appointment of the Commanding Officer himself. Consequently, any officer who is the Commanding Officer of a Corps, Department, or Detachment is competent, by virtue of that appointment, to hold a Summary Court-Martial for the trial of persons serving under his command and subject to the Army Act.

The proceedings of an SCM are required to be attended throughout by two other persons, who may be officers, Junior Commissioned Officers, or one of each. However, unlike members of other courts-martial, they are neither sworn nor affirmed and do not constitute members of the court in the strict judicial sense.[36]

Following the commission of an offence, a Non-Commissioned Officer or other rank may be attached to another unit for the purpose of trial by Summary Court-Martial. Such attachment, however, should not be resorted to merely for the purpose of awarding a more severe punishment than might otherwise be imposed.[37] Similarly, deserters and absentees from units may be tried by Summary Court-Martial by the Commanding Officers

36 Army Act 1950, Sec 116.

37 Army Head Quarter letter No 42231/ AC/DV-1 dt. 22 May 1985.

of the respective Centres, Schools, or Group Headquarters to which they are attached or reported.[38]

Jurisdiction of the Summary Court-Martial

The jurisdiction of the Summary Court-Martial is limited in terms of the categories of personnel it may try. An SCM cannot try:

(a) an Officer;

(b) a Junior Commissioned Officer; or

(c) a Warrant Officer.[39]

It may, however, try any other person subject to the Army Act who is under the command of the officer holding the court. Subject to these restrictions, an SCM possesses jurisdiction to try offences under the Army Act, except those which by their very nature can only be committed by Officers, Junior Commissioned Officers, or Warrant Officers.

For example, the offence of "behaving in a manner unbecoming of his position and character" under Section 45 of the Army Act cannot be tried by an SCM because it is an offence specifically applicable to a class of persons outside its jurisdiction.

In respect of offences relating to the enemy under Section 34, mutiny under Section 37, and civil offences under Section 69 of the Army Act, the sanction of a superior authority is ordinarily required before trial by SCM.[40] This requirement may, however, be dispensed with where the Commanding Officer considers an immediate trial necessary in the interests of discipline.

---

38 RA 1987, ¶ 381.

39 AA 1950, § 120 (3).

40 AA 1950, § 120 (2).

It must nevertheless be remembered that there is no offence which a Commanding Officer is legally bound to refer to a court-martial. Every case must be considered on its own merits. Equally, a Commanding Officer should not dispose of a matter summarily where Section 120(2) of the Army Act requires reference to a superior authority or where the circumstances clearly warrant a punishment beyond the scope of his summary powers.[41]

Where an SCM is conducted without obtaining prior reference in a case that would not ordinarily be tried summarily, an explanatory memorandum should be attached to the proceedings recording the reasons for such action.[42] Conversely, where sanction has been obtained from the competent authority, the charge-sheet should bear an endorsement directing trial by SCM and be authenticated by the appropriate Staff Officer.

The Summary Court-Martial possesses no jurisdiction to try offences such as murder, where the only permissible punishments are death or imprisonment for life. Similarly, the restrictions imposed by Section 70 of the Army Act concerning offences of culpable homicide not amounting to murder and rape apply equally to proceedings before an SCM.

The Commanding Officer as Judge

One of the most distinctive features of the Summary Court-Martial is that the Commanding Officer who holds the court performs functions that, in ordinary criminal jurisprudence, would be distributed among several different actors. He presides over the proceedings, records the evidence, determines guilt or innocence, and awards sentence. This concentration of authority

41 RA1987, ¶ 405 (a).

42 AR1954, r 130.

has historically been justified on grounds of military necessity, speed, and the need to maintain discipline within a unit. At the same time, it has generated continuing debate regarding procedural safeguards, institutional independence, and the appearance of impartiality—issues which are examined in greater detail in subsequent chapters.

The Reach of Summary Punishment

Although designed as a summary procedure, the SCM possesses significant punitive powers. Where the officer holding the trial is of the rank of Lieutenant Colonel or above, he may award a sentence of imprisonment not exceeding one year, whether rigorous or simple. Where the officer holding the trial is below the rank of Lieutenant Colonel, the maximum sentence that may be imposed is three months' imprisonment, whether rigorous or simple.[43]

The comparatively swift nature of the SCM, coupled with the concentration of authority in the hands of the Commanding Officer, has ensured its enduring relevance within the military justice system. At the same time, these very characteristics have made it one of the most debated institutions in military law, standing at the intersection of two competing imperatives—discipline and justice.

Different Uniforms, Different Tribunals

The Law Regulating Discipline in the Indian Air Force

(The Air Force Act, 1950 – Act XLV of 1950)

The Air Force Act, 1950 closely follows the framework of the Army Act, 1950 in matters relating to military discipline and the

43 AA 1950, § 120 (5).

administration of military justice. The provisions governing the convening,[44] composition,[45] jurisdiction,[46] and powers of courts-martial are, in all material respects, substantially similar to those contained in the Army Act.

A notable distinction, however, lies in the absence of the Summary Court-Martial (SCM). Unlike the Army Act, which provides for four categories of courts-martial, the Air Force Act recognises only three forms of military tribunals,[47] namely:

(a) General Court-Martial (GCM);

(b) District Court-Martial (DCM); and

(c) Summary General Court-Martial (SGCM).

Thus, while the Air Force disciplinary system is founded upon principles similar to those governing the Army, it functions without recourse to the Summary Court-Martial. The significance of this distinction and its implications for military justice are examined in subsequent chapters.

The Law Regulating Discipline in the Indian Navy

(The Navy Act, 1957 – Act LXII of 1957)

Although the provisions of the Navy Act, 1957 are broadly based upon the principles embodied in the Army Act, 1950 and the Air Force Act, 1950, the legislation incorporates several modifications reflecting the unique conditions of naval service and long-established naval traditions.

---

44 Air Force Act 1950 (AFA 1950), §§110, 111, and 113.

45 AFA 1950§§ 114, 115, and 116.

46 AFA 1950, §§ 118 and 119.

47 AFA1950, § 109.

Unlike the Army Act and the Air Force Act, the Navy Act employs the broader concept of *Naval Tribunals*. A Naval Tribunal includes a Court-Martial constituted under Section 97 of the Navy Act and also encompasses a Disciplinary Court constituted under Section 96, a mechanism specifically intended for wartime and operational contingencies.

Another distinctive feature of the naval system is that officers of the Indian Naval Reserve Forces, when on active service, are eligible to serve as members of a Court-Martial.[48] This provision recognises the operational realities of naval deployments and the specialised nature of naval service.

Accordingly, while all three Service Acts share the common objective of maintaining discipline through specialised military tribunals, the Navy Act incorporates procedural variations designed to accommodate the distinctive operational environment and requirements of naval service.

The Naval Court-Martial: Justice Under the White Ensign

Authorities Empowered to Order a Court-Martial

The Navy Act, 1957 confers the power to order a Court-Martial[49] upon:

(a) the President;

(b) the Chief of the Naval Staff; and

(c) any officer empowered in this behalf by commission issued by the Chief of the Naval Staff.

---

48 Navy Act 1957 (NA 1957), § 3 (6).

49 NA 1957 § 97 (i).

The Act, however, incorporates certain unique provisions reflecting the operational realities of naval service. Where an officer superior to the holder of such commission is present or in command, the superior officer may order a Court-Martial notwithstanding the absence of a formal commission. Similarly, an officer officiating in place of a commission holder may exercise the same authority even though he does not personally hold such commission.[50]

Furthermore, where an officer empowered to order a Court-Martial detaches a portion of a fleet or squadron for independent service, he may authorise the Commanding Officer of the detached formation to order a Court-Martial by issuing a commission under his hand for the duration of such separate service.[51]

Composition of a Naval Court-Martial

A Court-Martial constituted under the Navy Act shall consist of not fewer than five and not more than nine members. Every member must be subject to Naval law, hold the rank of Lieutenant or above, and be at least twenty-one years of age.[52]

The Prosecutor, the Officer ordering the Court-martial, the CO of the ship to which the accused belonged at the time of the commission of the offence and the Officer investigating the offence are disqualified to be the Member of the Court-martial.[53]

50 NA 1957 § 97 (f).
51 NA 1957§ 97 (5).
52 NA 1957§ 97 (6 and 7).
53 NA 1957§ 97 (8 and 9).

The Navy Act further prescribes detailed requirements regarding the composition of the tribunal. No Court-Martial shall be deemed properly constituted unless:[54]

(a) the majority of the members, including the President, are drawn from the Executive Branch of the Naval Service;

(b) officers from branches other than the Executive Branch are included where required for trials involving offences under Sections 34, 35, 55 and 56 of the Act;

(c) members are drawn from at least two ships commanded by officers of the rank of Lieutenant or above;

(d) in the trial of a Flag Officer, the President is a Flag Officer and the remaining members are Captains or officers of higher rank;

(e) in the trial of a Captain, the President is a Captain or higher officer and the remaining members are Commanders or above;

(f) in the trial of a Commander, the President is a Commander or higher officer and at least three other members are Commanders or above; and

(g) in the trial of an officer below the rank of Commander, the President is a Commander (substantive or acting) or an officer of higher rank.

Unlike the Army and Air Force systems, where the senior-most member ordinarily acts as the Presiding Officer, the President of a Naval Court-Martial is specifically nominated by the authority ordering the Court-Martial. The nominated President

---

54 NA 1957§ 97 (10 , 11 and 13 to 16).

is thereafter responsible for summoning the remaining members of the tribunal.

Jurisdiction and Powers

A Naval Court-Martial may try any person subject to the Navy Act for any offence triable thereunder and may award any punishment authorised by law, subject to the limitations prescribed under Section 78 of the Act.[55]

The Disciplinary Court: A Wartime Tribunal

In addition to the Court-Martial, the Navy Act provides for a specialised tribunal known as the Disciplinary Court. This tribunal is primarily intended to operate in wartime and other exceptional operational circumstances.

A Disciplinary Court shall consist of not fewer than three and not more than five officers, the majority of whom must belong to the Executive Branch. At least one member must be senior in rank to the accused, and the President must in every case hold the rank of Commander (acting or substantive) or above. The members of the Court are nominated by the officer ordering its constitution.

Although more limited in scope than a Court-Martial, a Disciplinary Court may impose any punishment lower than detention in the scale of punishments prescribed under Section 81 of the Navy Act.

55 NA 1957 § 96 (1).

A Comparative Glimpse

A comparison of the three Service Acts reveals that while the Army and Air Force broadly follow a similar structure, the Navy adopts a distinct approach in certain respects. In the Army and Air Force, the senior-most member of the Court ordinarily acts as the Presiding Officer. Under the Navy Act, however, the President of the Court-Martial is specifically nominated by the authority ordering the tribunal, with due regard to the rank and status of the accused as well as the composition of the Court.[56]

These distinctions reflect the differing operational environments and traditions of the three Services while preserving the common objective of maintaining discipline through a specialised system of military justice.

From Allegation to Trial: The Journey Begins

Having examined the various forms of courts-martial under the Army Act, the Air Force Act, and the Navy Act, it becomes necessary to understand how a military prosecution actually commences. Before an accused can be brought before a Court-Martial, the military justice system must first determine whether sufficient material exists to justify formal proceedings.

The first significant step in this process is ordinarily the convening of a Court of Inquiry (COI), a fact-finding mechanism designed to investigate allegations, collect evidence, and ascertain whether a prima facie case exists. It is from this stage that the journey of a military case truly begins.

56 NA 1957 § 96 (1).

For this purpose, the procedural framework followed by the Indian Army—from the initial complaint to the culmination of the proceedings—shall be examined in detail. While the Air Force follows a substantially similar procedure, the Navy incorporates certain procedural variations arising from its distinct statutory framework and operational requirements.

CHAPTER 03

The Armed Forces Personnel Versus Article 33

INTRODUCTION

Having succeeded in compelling our British rulers to leave India on 15 August 1947, "*We, the People of India*"—then comprising nearly 35 crore sovereign individuals—embarked upon the historic task of framing a Constitution through our chosen representatives in the Constituent Assembly. This Constitution was intended to be a written record of the mutual compact entered into by "*We, the People of India.*" In this federation of sovereign citizens, members of the Armed Forces stood on the same footing as every other citizen, and their contribution as constituent sovereign individuals was no less significant than that of the civil populace.

"*We, the People of India*", speaking through the Resolution moved by Late Pt. Jawaharlal Nehru in the Constituent Assembly and adopted on 22 January 1947, laid the bedrock upon which the edifice of the future Republic was to be erected. As sovereign individuals, we possessed inherent rights, foremost among them the right to life and liberty, together with the natural right to protect that sovereignty from encroachment by any individual, institution, external power, or even our own creation—the Indian Union acting through its governmental agencies.

Accordingly, we imposed limitations upon the State through Part III of the Constitution, which enshrined the Fundamental Rights. Within the constitutional scheme, the State was ordained to function without unjustly encroaching upon the right to life and liberty. These rights occupied a paramount position, while the other rights enumerated under Articles 14 to 32 of the Constitution were incorporated as safeguards designed to secure and protect that very right to life and liberty from infringement by any person, authority, or even the State itself.

"*We, the People of India*" created no distinction amongst ourselves insofar as the protection of life and liberty was concerned. We recognised these rights as the inalienable possession of every human being, irrespective of caste, creed, colour, nationality, or social status. It is for this reason that Article 21 employs the expression "*person*" rather than "*citizen*" or any other restrictive description while guaranteeing protection of life and personal liberty.

Pursuant to the solemn Resolution of 22 January 1947, Article 13 was incorporated into the Constitution to circumscribe the limits within which any future Parliament could legislate.[57] It is noteworthy that Article 13(4) did not form part of the original Constitution which "*We, the People of India*" adopted, enacted, and gave unto ourselves on 26 November 1949.[58]

57 India Const. art. 13. (Article 13 lays down, laws Inconsistent with or in derogation of the fundamental rights:-- (1) All laws in force in the territory of India immediately before the commencement of this Constitution, in so far as they are inconsistent with the provisions of this Part, shall, to the extent of such inconsistency, be void.

58 India Const. art. 13(4) was inserted, *amended by* The Constitution (Twenty Fourth Amendment) Act, 1971, §2.

MILITARY JUSTICE SYSTEM UNDER THE CONSTITUTIONAL SCHEME

The Preamble to the Constitution declares that the primary objective of the Constitution of India is to secure to all its citizens Justice, Liberty, Equality, and Fraternity. The Fundamental Rights embodied in Part III constitute the principal mechanism through which these constitutional promises are sought to be realised. Article 13 reinforces this objective by prohibiting the State from making laws that abridge or take away the rights guaranteed under Part III and by rendering void any pre-Constitution laws that are inconsistent with those rights.

It may, however, be argued that the constitutional scheme treats these rights not merely as natural and inalienable attributes of every individual but as rights whose exercise may, in certain circumstances, be regulated or restricted by constitutional and legislative provisions. Consequently, a tension emerges between the concept of individual liberty and the authority vested in institutions created under the Constitution to regulate that liberty in the larger interests of the State. This tension assumes particular significance in the context of the Armed Forces.

Against this constitutional backdrop, Article 33 occupies a unique position. While Part III generally seeks to protect individual liberties, Article 33 empowers Parliament to restrict or even abrogate certain Fundamental Rights in their application to members of the Armed Forces and other specified categories of personnel. It is noteworthy that this far-reaching provision entered the Constitution without extensive debate in the Constituent Assembly, despite its profound implications for those who serve in uniform. The practical effect of Article 33 has been to place members of the Armed Forces in a constitutional position distinct from that of ordinary citizens.

As Austin (1999) observes,[59] the Indian constitutional framework seeks to balance the competing values of democracy, social revolution, and national integrity. Whenever these values come into conflict, a delicate balance must be maintained. The continuing challenge posed by Article 33 lies in determining whether that balance has been appropriately struck between military necessity and constitutional liberty.

For ease of reference, Article 33 is reproduced below:

"33. Power of Parliament to modify the rights conferred by this Part in their application to Forces etc.—Parliament may, by law, determine to what extent any of the rights conferred by this Part shall, in their application to:

> (a) the members of the Armed Forces; or
>
> (b) the members of the Forces charged with the maintenance of public order; or
>
> (c) persons employed in any bureau or other organisation established by the State for purposes of intelligence or counter-intelligence; or
>
> (d) persons employed in, or in connection with, the telecommunication systems set up for the purposes of any Force, bureau, or organisation referred to in clauses (a) to (c),

be restricted or abrogated so as to ensure the proper discharge of their duties and the maintenance of discipline among them."

---

59 Granville Austin, working of a Democratic Constitution: A History of the Indian Experience, 651 (Oxford University Press, New Delhi, 1999).

Amongst the Fundamental Rights, none occupies a more central position than the right to life and personal liberty guaranteed under Article 21 of the Constitution.[60] Deprivation of life or liberty can be justified only through a procedure established by law that is fair, just, and reasonable. The Supreme Court of India has repeatedly emphasised this principle in numerous decisions, including those concerning arbitrary, disproportionate, or unreasonable punishment imposed upon members of the Armed Forces.[61]

Concerns nevertheless arise regarding the practical operation of military justice. The limited availability of bail within the military justice system, coupled with the wide discretion vested in Commanding Officers regarding release from custody, raises important questions concerning procedural fairness and the safeguards contemplated under Article 21. The discretion given to the Commanding Officer to release the accused from custody smacks of arbitrariness and is liable to be misused.[62] The lack of legal aid provided to an accused is also against the guarantee given under Article 22 of our Constitution.[63]

---

60 India Const. art. 21 (it states that 'no person shall be deprived of his life and liberty except according to procedures established by law).

61 Ranjit Thakur vs Union of India and Ors, 1987, S.C, Available at: https://indiankanoon.org/doc/31796/ (Accessed: 5 October 2024).; Ex. Naik Sardar Singh vs Union of India and Others, 1991 S.C. Available at: https://indiankanoon.org/doc/1889118/ (Accessed: 5 October 2024).

62 U.C Jha, The Military Justice System in India: An Analysis (LexisNexis, Butterworths Wadwa, Nagpur, 2009) at p 36.

63 India Const. art 22 cl. 1, (it states that ' no person who is arrested shall be detained in custody without being informed, as seen as may be, of

The Constitution also protects individuals from being punished more than once for the same offence through the doctrine of double jeopardy embodied in Article 20(2).[64] Historically, this protection was not available to Air Force personnel under the Air Force Act, 1950,[65] although the Navy Act, 1957 contained such safeguards from its inception. Amendments introduced in the Army Act in 1992 removed provisions permitting successive trials by military and civil authorities. These legislative differences raise important constitutional questions concerning both Article 20(2) and the guarantee of equality before the law contained in Article 14.[66]

A significant development occurred with the enactment of the Armed Forces Tribunal Act, 2007. For the first time, members of the Armed Forces were provided with a statutory appellate mechanism against orders passed by courts-martial.[67] Prior

---

the grounds for such arrest nor shall he be denied the right to consult, and be defended by, a legal practitioner of his choice.').

64 India Const. art 20 cl. 2, (it states that, 'no person shall be prosecuted and punished for the same offence more than once).

65 AFA 1950, § 126 (it provides that a person convicted or acquitted by a Court-martial may, with the previous sanction of the Central Government, be tried again by a criminal Court for the same offence, or on the same facts).

66 India Const. art. 14 (it enunciates equality before law and equal protection of law, and which in the above scenario where only the Air Force Personnel have to undergo Double Jeopardy and not their fellow soldiers and counterparts in the Army and the Navy, does not seem to be the case and is in utter violation of Article 14 of the Indian Constitution).

67 India Const. art. 136 cl. 2 (Article 136 of the Indian Constitution lays down special leave to appeal by the Supreme Court but in clause 2 it specifically mentions that 'nothing in clause (i) shall apply to any judgment, determination, sentence or order passed or made by any

thereto, challenges to court-martial proceedings largely depended upon the exercise of discretionary constitutional jurisdiction by the superior courts in exceptional cases. It is also pertinent to note that Article 227(4) of the Constitution[68] excludes the power of superintendence of the High Courts over courts or tribunals constituted under laws relating to the Armed Forces,[69] thereby creating a distinctive constitutional framework for military justice.

JUDICIAL PRONOUNCEMENTS ON ARTICLE 33 OF THE INDIAN CONSTITUTION

It may be strongly argued that Article 33, as presently interpreted and applied, raises serious questions in relation to the basic structure of the Constitution. The provision undoubtedly creates an exception to the otherwise broad guarantees contained in Part III and has frequently been invoked to justify restrictions upon rights available to members of the Armed Forces. Critics of the provision contend that it dilutes the spirit of the Preamble and the constitutional guarantees embodied in Articles 13, 14, 21 and 22, while its proponents maintain that it is an indispensable mechanism for ensuring discipline and operational effectiveness within the Armed Forces.

Court or Tribunal constituted by or under any law relating to the Armed Forces).

68 India Const. art. 227 cl. 4 (Article 227 lays down High Court power of superintendence over all Courts but in clause 4 it is mentioned that 'nothing in this Article shall be deemed to confer on a High Court power of superintendence over any Court or Tribunal constituted by or under any law relating to the Armed Forces).

69 *See* Jha, *supra* note 62, at p 62

Over the years, Article 33 has come before the Supreme Court and various High Courts in a variety of contexts. In some cases, the provision has been referred to incidentally, while in others it has formed the foundation of the controversy itself. Several judicial pronouncements have also examined whether actions taken under military law satisfy the requirements of fairness, reasonableness, and due process contemplated under Article 21 of the Constitution. An examination of these decisions is therefore necessary to understand the judicial approach towards Article 33 and its impact upon the constitutional rights of Armed Forces personnel.

R. Chatterjee v. Sub Area Commander

Facts

One of the earliest judicial references to Article 33 is found in *R. Chatterjee v. Sub Area Commander*.[70] The petitioner, Lieutenant R. Chatterjee, a Short Service Commissioned Officer of the Indian Army, was alleged to have deserted service. He had joined military service prior to the coming into force of the Army Act, 1950. Subsequent to his retirement or release from service, he was taken into military custody and tried by a Court-Martial on charges of remaining absent from his station for a period of one month without proper authorisation.

The petitioner challenged the competence of the military authorities to try him by Court-Martial after he had allegedly ceased to be subject to military law. He further contended that, having joined service pursuant to a Short Service Commission

70 R Chatterjee v. Sub Area Commander, AIR 1951 MAD 777 Available at, https://indiankanoon.org/doc/364881/ (Accessed: 5 October 2024).

advertisement, the provisions of the Army Act, 1950 were not applicable to him.

Issue

The principal issue before the Court was whether the military authorities possessed jurisdiction to try the petitioner by Court-Martial after his release from service and, more importantly for present purposes, the extent to which Fundamental Rights applied to members of the Armed Forces in the absence of specific legislation enacted under Article 33 of the Constitution.

Decision

While Article 33 itself was not directly challenged in the proceedings, the Court was required to consider its effect. The Court observed that Article 33 empowers Parliament to determine the extent to which the Fundamental Rights guaranteed under Part III may be restricted or abrogated in their application to members of the Armed Forces.

The Court held that until Parliament specifically determined the extent of such restriction or abrogation, the law as it existed prior to the conferment of Fundamental Rights would continue to apply to Armed Forces personnel. Accordingly, Article 33 was treated as an enabling provision requiring legislative action before any modification of Fundamental Rights could take effect.

Analysis

The significance of *R. Chatterjee* lies not in any direct challenge to Article 33 but in the Court's recognition that the provision is not self-executing. The judgment acknowledges that Parliament must actively determine the extent to which Fundamental Rights are to be restricted in their application to Armed Forces personnel.

The decision is important because it implicitly recognises that members of the Armed Forces do not stand entirely outside the constitutional framework of Fundamental Rights merely by virtue of military service. Restrictions upon those rights require constitutional and legislative justification. Although the Court did not undertake a detailed examination of Article 33, the judgment remains significant as one of the earliest judicial discussions of the provision and laid the foundation for subsequent debates concerning the relationship between military discipline and constitutional liberty.

Ram Swarup v. Union of India

Facts

In *Ram Swarup v. Union of India*,[71] the petitioner, a Sepoy in the Indian Army, was convicted by a General Court-Martial and sentenced to death on charges of killing two Sepoys and one Havildar. Following confirmation of the sentence, he approached the Supreme Court by way of a writ petition.

Among the various grounds raised, the petitioner contended that he had been denied the assistance of a legal practitioner of his choice during the General Court-Martial proceedings, thereby violating the guarantee contained in Article 22(1) of the Constitution. He further argued that Parliament, while

71 Ram Swarup v. Union of India, AIR 1965 SC 247, Available at https://indiankanoon.org/doc/234020/ (Accessed: 5 October 2024).

exercising its powers under Article 33 of the Constitution, had enacted Section 21 of the Army Act, empowering the Central Government to frame rules restricting certain rights of Armed Forces personnel. Since the matters specified therein did not expressly include the Fundamental Rights guaranteed under Articles 14, 20, and 22 of the Constitution, it was contended that Parliament had not intended to modify those rights.

Issue

The principal issue before the Court was whether the provisions of the Army Act could be challenged on the ground that they infringed Fundamental Rights guaranteed under Part III of the Constitution and whether the petitioner had been denied the protection afforded by Article 22(1).

Decision

The Supreme Court accepted the arguments advanced by the Attorney General and held that every provision of the Army Act constituted a law enacted by Parliament. Consequently, if any provision of the Act affected a Fundamental Right guaranteed under Part III, such provision would not become void merely on that account. The Court observed that Parliament, by enacting the Army Act, must be deemed to have exercised its powers under Article 33 and thereby effected the necessary modification of the relevant Fundamental Rights in their application to members of the Armed Forces.

The challenge was accordingly rejected.

Analysis

The significance of *Ram Swarup* lies in the broad interpretation accorded by the Supreme Court to Article 33. The Court effectively held that whenever Parliament enacts legislation governing the Armed Forces, any resulting restriction upon Fundamental Rights may be treated as a permissible exercise of the power conferred by Article 33.

It may, however, be argued that the judgment did not sufficiently examine whether the denial of legal representation in a capital case was consistent with the principles of fairness and due process. Effective legal assistance from a counsel of one's choice is widely regarded as an essential component of a fair trial and does not, by itself, impede military discipline or the proper discharge of military duties.

The Court appears to have attached significance to the fact that the accused had not specifically requested legal representation. Yet the absence of an express request does not necessarily imply a conscious waiver of such a valuable right. The educational background, social circumstances, and legal awareness of the accused are relevant considerations, particularly where the proceedings involve charges carrying the ultimate penalty of death. A soldier facing a capital charge may not fully appreciate either the gravity of the proceedings or the legal protections available to him.

Viewed from this perspective, *Ram Swarup* represents one of the earliest instances in which Article 33 was interpreted in a manner that accorded substantial deference to military legislation, while leaving unresolved the broader question of how far constitutional guarantees relating to fair trial and legal representation may be curtailed in the name of military discipline.

Ous Kutilingal Achudan Nair and Others v. Union of India and Others

Facts

In this case,[72] a challenge was made to Section 21 of the Army Act, 1950 read with Rules 19, 20, and 21 of the Army Rules, which prohibit participation in unauthorised associations and the formation of unions. The petitioners were office bearers of staff unions in newly constituted employee unions and challenged their dismissal and other disciplinary action initiated against them by their employers.

The petitioners contended that the restrictions imposed upon them infringed their right to form associations and unions. However, the constitutional validity of Article 33 itself was not challenged.

Issue

The principal issue before the Supreme Court was whether civilian employees attached to or accompanying the Armed Forces could be subjected to restrictions upon their Fundamental Right to form associations under Article 19(1)(c) by virtue of Article 33 of the Constitution and Section 21 of the Army Act.

Decision

The Supreme Court upheld the validity of the restrictions and, while relying upon Article 33 of the Constitution, observed:

72 Ous Kutilingal Achudan Nair and Others, v. Union of India and Others, AIR 1976 SC 1179, Available at: https://indiankanoon.org/doc/1959294/ (Accessed: 5 October 2024).

"Article 33 of the Constitution provides an exception to the preceding articles in Part III including Article 19 (1)(c). By Article 33, Parliament is empowered to enact law determining to what extent any of the rights conferred by Part III shall, in their application, to the members of the armed forces or forces charged with the maintenance of public order, be restricted or abrogated so as to ensure the proper discharge of their duties and the maintenance of discipline among them. In enacting the Army Act, 1950, in so far as it restricts or abrogates any of the fundamental rights of the members of the armed forces, Parliament derives its competence from Articles 33 of the Constitution. Section 2(1) of the Act enumerates the persons who are subject to the operation of this Act. According to sub-clause (i) of this section, persons governed by the Act, include persons not otherwise subject to military law who, on active service, in camp, on the march or at any frontier post specified by the Central Government by notification in this behalf, are employed by, or are in the service of, or are followers of, or accompany any portion of the regular army. The members of the unions represented by the appellants obviously fall within this category. It is their duty to follow or accompany the armed personnel on active service or in camp or on the march. Although they are non-combatants and are in some matters governed by the Civil Service Regulation, yet they are integral to the armed forces. They answer the description of the 'members of the armed forces' within the contemplation of Article 33. Consequently by virtue of Section 21 of the Army Act, the Central Government was competent by notification to make rules restricting or curtailing their fundamental rights under Article 19(1)(c)...."

The appeal was accordingly dismissed.

Analysis

The significance of this decision lies in the expansive interpretation accorded by the Supreme Court to Article 33. The Court extended the reach of Article 33 beyond combat personnel and applied its rationale to civilian employees who accompanied or served with the Armed Forces in operational circumstances.

It is discernible from the above extract that the Court considered such civilian employees to be sufficiently integrated with the Armed Forces to justify restrictions upon their Fundamental Right to form associations under Article 19(1)(c). Consequently, the restrictions imposed through Section 21 of the Army Act read with Rules 19, 20, and 21 of the Army Rules were upheld.

It may, however, be argued that the judgment considerably broadened the scope of Article 33 by permitting restrictions upon a class of persons who were not combatants in the conventional sense. The practical effect of the decision was that individuals otherwise governed by civilian service regulations could, by reason of their association with the Armed Forces, be denied rights ordinarily available to civilian employees, including the right to organise themselves into associations or unions.

The case is therefore significant not merely for what it decided, but for the breadth of the principle it endorsed. By treating such civilian employees as falling within the contemplation of Article 33, the Court reinforced a judicial trend favouring a wide construction of the provision and a correspondingly broad power in the State to restrict Fundamental Rights in the interest of military discipline and operational efficiency.

Lt. Col. Prithi Pal Singh Bedi v. Union of India

Facts

In this case,[73] the petitioners, who were facing trial by a General Court-Martial (GCM) for alleged breaches of military discipline, challenged the legality and validity of the order convening the Court-Martial, particularly its composition.

In the writ petitions filed under Article 32 of the Constitution, it was contended on behalf of the petitioners that, in order to satisfy the requirements of Article 33, any restriction or abrogation of Fundamental Rights must be expressly provided by a specific law enacted by Parliament. It was further argued that Rule 40 of the Army Rules ought to be construed in a manner that advances the mandate of Article 21 and strikes a fair balance between the requirements of military discipline and the personal liberty of individual members of the Armed Forces. The petitioners also urged that the principles of natural justice should be observed even in proceedings before military tribunals.

Issue

The principal issue before the Supreme Court was whether Article 33 requires Parliament to specifically identify and expressly restrict each Fundamental Right sought to be modified in its application to members of the Armed Forces and whether military law should be interpreted in a manner consistent with the principles of natural justice and personal liberty.

---

73 Lt. Col. Prithi Pal Singh Bedi Etc vs Union of India & Others, 1982 S.C, Available at: https://indiankanoon.org/doc/278740/ (Accessed: 5 October 2024).

Decision

Dismissing the petitions, the Supreme Court held:

"The dominant purpose in construing a statute is to ascertain the intention of Parliament. One of the well-recognised canons of construction is that the legislature speaks its mind by use of correct expression and unless there is any ambiguity in the language of the provision, the Court should adopt literal construction if it does not lead to an absurdity. To ascertain the literal meaning it is equally necessary first to ascertain the juxtaposition in which the rule is placed, the Purpose for which it is enacted and the object which it is required to sub-serve and the authority by which the rule is framed. Article 33 of the Constitution which confers power on Parliament to determine to what extent any of the rights conferred by Part III shall in their application to the members of armed forces be restricted or abrogated does not obligate that Parliament must specifically adumbrate each fundamental right and specify in the law the degree of restriction or total abrogation of each right. That would be reading into Article 33 a requirement which it does not enjoin. The power to legislate in respect of any item must be referable to an entry in the relevant legislative list. The law has to be enacted by Parliament subject to the requirement of Part III read with Art. 33 which itself forms part of Part III. Therefore if any provision of the Army Act is in conflict with fundamental rights it shall have to be read subject to Art. 33 as being enacted with a view to either restricting or abrogating the fundamental rights to the extent of inconsistency or repugnancy between Part III and the Army Act."

The Court accordingly rejected the contention that Parliament was required to specifically enumerate each Fundamental Right and expressly state the degree to which it stood restricted or abrogated.

Analysis

The decision in *Prithi Pal Singh Bedi* marks a significant stage in the judicial interpretation of Article 33. The Supreme Court adopted a broad construction of the provision and held that Parliament need not specifically identify each Fundamental Right that stands restricted in its application to members of the Armed Forces. According to the Court, once Parliament enacts legislation governing the Armed Forces, any inconsistency between that legislation and the rights guaranteed under Part III must be read in the light of Article 33.

The practical consequence of this interpretation is that restrictions upon Fundamental Rights may arise by implication from military legislation without Parliament expressly declaring which right is being restricted and to what extent. This approach substantially enlarges the scope of Article 33 and accords considerable deference to legislative judgment in matters relating to military discipline.

It may, however, be argued that a more restrictive interpretation would have been more consistent with the exceptional nature of Article 33. Since the provision authorises restrictions upon rights that are otherwise regarded as fundamental, one possible view is that Parliament should expressly identify the rights sought to be curtailed and clearly define the extent of such curtailment. Such an approach would provide greater transparency and ensure closer constitutional scrutiny of limitations imposed upon members of the Armed Forces.

At the same time, it is noteworthy that the petitioners' reliance upon Article 21 and the principles of natural justice was not entirely rejected as a matter of principle. The judgment implicitly recognised the need to balance military discipline with individual liberty, although the balance in this case was ultimately struck in favour of military necessity. The decision therefore remains an important authority both for its expansive interpretation of Article 33 and for its acknowledgment that military justice must continue to operate within a constitutional framework.

R. Viswan and Others v. Union of India and Others

Facts

In this case,[74] all twenty-four petitioners were civilian employees of the General Reserve Engineering Force (GREF), who had been brought within the ambit of the Army Act, 1950 by virtue of Central Government Notifications Nos. SRO 329 and 330 dated 23 September 1960.

Two of the petitioners had proceeded on leave and, following a practice not uncommon among civilian employees posted in remote border and tribal areas, failed to rejoin their duties within the stipulated period. For the first time in the history of the GREF, the provisions of the Army Act, 1950 were invoked against them. The remaining twenty-two petitioners were charged under Section 63 of the Army Act for acts amounting to demonstrations and collective insubordination. They were tried by Court-Martial and, upon conviction, were dismissed from service.

74 R. Viswan and Others v. Union of India and Other, AIR 1983 SC 658, Available at: https://indiankanoon.org/doc/374187/ (Accessed: 9 October 2024).

The petitioners challenged the legality of their dismissal before the Supreme Court on several grounds, namely:

(a) that GREF was not a force raised and maintained under the authority of the Central Government;

(b) that Statutory Regulations and Orders (SROs) Nos. 329 and 330 dated 23 September 1960 were ultra vires Sections 4(1) and 4(4) of the Army Act, 1950;

(c) that the application of Section 21 of the Army Act, 1950 read with Rules 19, 20 and 21 of the Army Rules, 1954 was unconstitutional since the members of GREF were neither members of the Armed Forces nor members of a force charged with the maintenance of public order within the meaning of Article 33;

(d) that Parliament alone was empowered under Article 33 to determine the extent to which Fundamental Rights could be restricted or abrogated and that such power could not be delegated to the Central Government through Section 21 of the Army Act; and

(e) that the petitioners were entitled to exercise their Fundamental Rights under Article 19(1)(a), (b), and (c) without the restrictions imposed by Rules 19 to 21 of the Army Rules and that their convictions under Section 63 of the Army Act were consequently illegal and void.

Issue

The principal issues before the Court were whether the members of GREF could be treated as falling within the ambit of Article 33 and whether Parliament could validly authorise the Central Government to impose restrictions upon Fundamental Rights through Section 21 of the Army Act and the Rules framed thereunder.

Decision

The Supreme Court rejected all the contentions advanced by the petitioners and upheld the validity of the impugned provisions.

The Court held that the members of GREF formed an integral part of the organisational structure supporting the Armed Forces and could therefore be subjected to restrictions permissible under Article 33. The Court further upheld the validity of the statutory framework through which such restrictions had been imposed.

In the course of its judgment, the Court observed:

"Article 33 carves out an exception in so far as applicability of Fundamental Rights to the members of the armed forces is concerned. Parliament itself can of course enact a law restricting or abrogating any of the Fundamental Rights.....the extent of restriction would depend necessarily on the prevailing situation at a given point of time and it would be inadvisable to encase it in statutory formula...."

Accordingly, the Court held that the notifications, the application of the Army Act to GREF personnel, and the disciplinary action taken against the petitioners were all protected by the operation of Article 33 of the Constitution.

Analysis

The decision in *R. Viswan* represents one of the most expansive judicial interpretations of Article 33. The Supreme Court not only upheld the application of military law to civilian employees of the GREF but also accepted that restrictions upon Fundamental Rights could be imposed through a statutory framework that vested considerable discretion in the executive authorities.

Particularly significant was the Court's acceptance of the proposition that the extent of restrictions under Article 33 need not be exhaustively defined by Parliament and could vary according to the prevailing circumstances. This approach afforded substantial flexibility to the State in matters concerning military discipline and operational requirements.

The judgment also reinforced the trend visible in *Ram Sarup* and *Prithi Pal Singh Bedi*, namely, a judicial preference for interpreting Article 33 broadly and for according considerable deference to legislative and executive assessments of military necessity.

From a constitutional perspective, however, the decision raises important questions concerning the limits of delegation and the degree to which restrictions upon Fundamental Rights should be expressly determined by Parliament itself. It may be argued that where constitutional liberties are sought to be curtailed, greater legislative specificity would provide stronger safeguards against arbitrary exercise of power and ensure closer constitutional scrutiny.

Viewed in hindsight, the case might also have provided an opportunity for a direct challenge to the constitutional validity of Article 33 itself. Such a challenge would have required the Court to examine whether the breadth of the power conferred by Article 33 is fully compatible with the larger constitutional commitment to liberty, equality, and the protection of Fundamental Rights. However, since the vires of Article 33 was not directly assailed, that question remained unanswered.

Ajmer Singh and Others v. Union of India and Others

Facts

The appellants, who had been convicted by a General Court-Martial for offences under the Army Act and were undergoing sentences of imprisonment, claimed the benefit of the set-off provision contained in Section 428 of the Code of Criminal Procedure, 1973. They approached the Supreme Court contending that the Army Act was silent regarding the date from which a sentence of imprisonment was to be reckoned and that, in the absence of any specific provision to the contrary, the provisions of the Code of Criminal Procedure ought to apply.

It was argued on their behalf that Section 5 of the Code merely provided that nothing contained therein would affect any special or local law. Since the Army Act did not expressly deal with the matter of set-off, the benefit available under Section 428 of the Code should be extended to persons convicted by Court-Martial.

Issue

The principal issue before the Supreme Court was whether the benefit of set-off under Section 428 of the Code of Criminal Procedure could be claimed by persons convicted and sentenced by a Court-Martial.

Decision

Dismissing the appeals, the Supreme Court held:

"The provision for set off contained in s. 428 of the Code of Criminal Procedure is not attracted in the case of persons convicted and sentenced by Court-Martial to undergo imprisonment. The Army Act, the Navy Act and the Air Force

Act constitute special laws in force conferring special jurisdiction and powers on Courts-Martial. They embody a completely self-contained comprehensive code specifying the various offences and prescribing the procedure for detention, custody, investigation and trial of the offenders, the punishment to be awarded, confirmation and revision of the sentences imposed the execution of such sentences and the grant of pardons, remissions and suspensions in respect of such sentences. Section 5 of the Code renders the provisions of the Code inapplicable in respect of all matters covered by such special law. .... The distinction made in s. 475 of the Code between 'trial by a Court to which this Code applies' and by a Court-Martial' conclusively indicates that Parliament intended to treat the Court-Martial as a forum to the proceedings before which the provisions of the Code will have no application."[75]

The Court accordingly held that Section 428 of the Code of Criminal Procedure had no application to persons convicted and sentenced by Courts-Martial.

Analysis

The significance of *Ajmer Singh* lies in the Supreme Court's emphatic characterisation of the Army Act, the Navy Act, and the Air Force Act as constituting a "completely self-contained comprehensive code." This formulation has subsequently been relied upon in numerous cases to justify the exclusion of ordinary criminal procedural safeguards from the military justice system.

---

75 Ajmer Singh and Others v. Union of India and Others, AIR 1987 SC 1646; Available at: https://indiankanoon.org/doc/27649/, Also in F.R. Jesuratnam v. Chief of Air Staff, (1976) Cri. L.J. 65, Available at: https://indiankanoon.org/doc/16191/(Accessed: 9 October 2024).

The judgment reinforces the principle that Courts-Martial are not merely specialised criminal courts operating alongside the ordinary judicial system but are tribunals functioning under an independent statutory framework with their own procedures, punishments, and mechanisms for review and confirmation.

From the perspective of military discipline, such an approach ensures procedural autonomy and preserves the distinct character of military justice. From the standpoint of constitutional rights, however, the decision raises a broader question: whether the classification of military law as a self-contained code should automatically exclude procedural benefits that Parliament has considered necessary for the protection of personal liberty in the ordinary criminal justice system.

The case is therefore important not only for its ruling on Section 428 of the Code of Criminal Procedure but also because it strengthened the judicial doctrine that military law operates as a separate and largely autonomous legal system. That doctrine, when read together with Article 33, has often been invoked to justify departures from procedural safeguards otherwise available to civilians under the ordinary law of the land.

Major G. S. Sodhi v. Union of India[76]

Facts

The petitioner, Major G. S. Sodhi, was charge-sheeted and tried by Court-Martial on allegations of having used physical assault. Upon being found guilty, he was awarded the punishment of removal from service.

---

76 Major G.S Sodhi v. Union of India, AIR 1991 SC 1617 Available at: https://indiankanoon.org/doc/260960/ (Accessed: 13 October 2024).

The petitioner challenged the Court-Martial proceedings and the punishment imposed upon him on various grounds. Among the issues raised was the legality of recording an Additional Summary of Evidence after the Summary of Evidence had already been completed.

Issue

The principal issue before the Supreme Court was whether the recording of an Additional Summary of Evidence was permissible under the Army Rules and whether alleged violations of Rules 22 to 25 of the Army Rules vitiated the subsequent Court-Martial proceedings.

Decision

The Supreme Court referred to its earlier decision in *Lt. Col. Prithi Pal Singh Bedi v. Union of India*[77] and reiterated:

"The Parliament in its wisdom in exercise of its powers under Article 33 has enacted this law and the officers are to be guided by factors like exigencies of service, maintenance of discipline in the army, speedier trial, the nature of the offence and the person against whom the offence is committed."

The Court further observed:

"The next submission is that the additional summary of evidence is not contemplated under law and therefore the proceedings in relation to such additional summary of evidence is vitiated. It must be remembered that it is only an additional recording of summary of evidence for which no special provision is necessary because it is only in addition to the summary of evidence already

77 Lt. Col. P.P.S Bedi, *supra* note 73.

commenced and once the SOE is permitted under rule the additional SOE is its necessary concomitant. We may, however, point out that the entire proceedings contemplated under Rule 22 to 25 are only preliminary and it is meant for the purpose of Commanding Officer satisfying himself whether court-martial should be ordered or not. We must also observe that the main thrust of the argument in this case is only about the violation of Rule 22 to 25. But we are unable to find any flagrant violation of these rules. Even otherwise if there are some minor irregularities they do not in any way affect the proceedings in the General Court-Martial during which a regular trial was conducted." The Court accordingly upheld the proceedings

Analysis

The importance of *Major G. S. Sodhi* lies not merely in its outcome but in the observations made by the Supreme Court regarding the nature of proceedings under Rules 22 to 25 of the Army Rules and the permissibility of recording Additional Summary of Evidence.

With the utmost respect to the Hon'ble Supreme Court, it may be argued that certain aspects of the judgment merit reconsideration.

First, the Court appears not to have fully appreciated that the procedure prescribed under Rules 22 to 25 consists of distinct stages serving different purposes. Proceedings under Rule 22 are akin to the process contemplated under Section 204 of the Code of Criminal Procedure, 1973 (now Section 227 of the Bharatiya Nagarik Suraksha Sanhita, 2023), where the authority concerned determines whether sufficient grounds exist for proceeding further. At this stage, the Commanding Officer performs a function that is judicial in character and not merely administrative.

Secondly, Rules 23 and 24 perform a role comparable to the committal proceedings previously contemplated under Section 209 of the Code of Criminal Procedure and its successor provisions. These proceedings are not mere formalities. They involve the recording of prosecution evidence, the opportunity to cross-examine witnesses, and the right of the accused to present a defence. Once the prosecution has concluded its evidence and the accused has been called upon to disclose his defence, the prosecution ordinarily has no right in criminal jurisprudence to reopen its case merely because weaknesses have been exposed by the defence.

Thirdly, it may be questioned whether Additional Summary of Evidence can properly be regarded as a "necessary concomitant" of the Summary of Evidence. There can be little objection to the prosecution producing all available evidence before the accused is called upon to enter his defence. However, once the accused has been cautioned under Rule 23(3) and invited to disclose his defence, the subsequent introduction of additional prosecution evidence raises concerns regarding procedural fairness. Such a course may create the appearance that the prosecution is being afforded an opportunity to strengthen or improve its case after obtaining knowledge of the defence strategy.

Fourthly, the observation that proceedings under Rules 22 to 25 are "only preliminary" may require closer scrutiny. While these proceedings undoubtedly precede the actual Court-Martial, they nevertheless involve the exercise of judicial discretion affecting the rights of the accused. The Commanding Officer is required to act impartially between the prosecution and the accused and to determine whether the matter should proceed to trial. In that sense, the proceedings possess important judicial attributes.

Finally, the Court's observation that "minor irregularities" would not affect the validity of the subsequent Court-Martial may be viewed as controversial. It may be argued that where procedural safeguards exist for the protection of the accused, the distinction between a minor irregularity and a substantial violation should be approached with caution. Procedural fairness derives its significance precisely from the requirement that the rules of the process be observed consistently and impartially.

The broader significance of *Major G. S. Sodhi* therefore lies in the judicial characterisation of Rules 22 to 25 as preliminary proceedings and in its acceptance of Additional Summary of Evidence. Unless revisited by a larger Bench or reconsidered in a future case, the decision continues to govern the legality of Additional Summary of Evidence within the military justice system and is likely to be cited whenever such proceedings are challenged.

Union of India v. L.D. Balam Singh

Facts

In *Union of India v. L.D. Balam Singh,*[78] the issue before the Supreme Court arose from proceedings involving military personnel who were being tried by Court-Martial for offences

78 AIRONLINE 2002 SC 153, Avaialable at; https://indiankanoon.org/doc/414510/ (Accessed: 30 October 2024), also at; Singh, N. (2023). *Military Justice Reform - Developments and Challenges.* Available at: https://www.barandbench.com/columns/military-justice-reform-developments-challenges. (Accessed: 30 October 2024).

under the Narcotic Drugs and Psychotropic Substances Act, 1985 (NDPS Act). The question was whether the procedural safeguards and protections provided under the NDPS Act were equally applicable to members of the Armed Forces facing trial before a Court-Martial.

The Punjab and Haryana High Court had held that the procedural requirements prescribed under the NDPS Act were applicable even in cases where military personnel were tried under the military justice system. Aggrieved by this decision, the Union of India approached the Supreme Court.

Issue

The principal issue before the Court was whether members of the Armed Forces, when tried by Court-Martial for offences under a special statute such as the NDPS Act, were entitled to the procedural safeguards contained in that statute or whether such safeguards stood excluded by reason of military law and Article 33 of the Constitution.

Decision

The Supreme Court affirmed the judgment of the Punjab and Haryana High Court and held that the procedural protections embodied in the NDPS Act were equally applicable to military personnel facing trial before a Court-Martial.

While recognising the importance of discipline within the Armed Forces and acknowledging the power conferred upon Parliament under Article 33 of the Constitution, the Court emphasised that members of the Armed Forces do not thereby cease to be citizens entitled to constitutional protection.

The Court observed that military personnel cannot be regarded as a separate class of citizens standing outside the constitutional framework. To hold otherwise would be inconsistent with the fundamental principles underlying the Constitution. Accordingly, the procedural safeguards prescribed by the NDPS Act were held to be applicable even in military trials.

Analysis

The significance of *L.D. Balam Singh* lies in its reaffirmation that Article 33 does not place members of the Armed Forces beyond the protection of the Constitution. While recognising the necessity of military discipline, the Supreme Court made it clear that military personnel do not surrender their status as citizens upon joining the Armed Forces.

Unlike several earlier decisions that emphasised the exceptional nature of Article 33 and the autonomy of military law, this judgment underscores an equally important constitutional principle—that restrictions imposed in the interest of discipline cannot be interpreted so broadly as to deprive service personnel of statutory and constitutional safeguards otherwise available under law.

The decision is therefore noteworthy for restoring balance to the constitutional discourse surrounding military justice. It recognises that while discipline is indispensable to the effectiveness of the Armed Forces, members of the military remain citizens of India and continue to enjoy constitutional protections except to the extent that such rights have been lawfully restricted in accordance with Article 33.

Viewed in this light, *L.D. Balam Singh* stands as an important reminder that Article 33 was never intended to create a class of citizens excluded from constitutional guarantees, but merely to permit such restrictions as are necessary for the proper discharge of military duties and the maintenance of discipline.

Union of India and Others v. Ex. Flt. Lt. G.S. Bajwa

Facts

In *Union of India and Others v. Ex. Flt. Lt. G.S. Bajwa*,[79] the respondent challenged the legality of his Court-Martial proceedings on several grounds relating to procedural fairness and the denial of a reasonable opportunity to defend himself. The Supreme Court has ruled that the legality of the provisions of the Air Force Act 1950, cannot be challenged on grounds of being violative of Fundamental Rights of armed forces personnel as the restriction imposed were mandated by the Constitution itself.[80] The respondent contended:

(a) that the denial of his request to be represented by an advocate resulted in a miscarriage of justice, particularly when the prosecution itself had alleged that he was suffering from psychological difficulties to some extent;

(b) that he had submitted two lists of defence witnesses but was required to disclose the relevance of each witness and the purpose for which the witness was to be examined, thereby compelling him to reveal his line of defence to the prejudice of his case;

79 Union of India and Others v. Ex. Flt. Lt. G.S Bajwa, MIL LJ 2003 SC 129 Available at: https://indiankanoon.org/doc/681931/ (Accessed: 13 October 2024).

80 Jha, *supra* note 62 at 48.

(c) that despite repeated requests, he was not supplied copies of the proceedings recorded on a day-to-day basis and that such non-supply amounted to denial of a reasonable opportunity to defend himself and violated the principles of natural justice; and

(d) that the Prosecutor, Judge Advocate, and members of the General Court-Martial had met behind closed doors and altered portions of the recorded proceedings and evidence, deleting material favourable to him and modifying depositions to suit the prosecution case.

Issue

The principal issue before the Supreme Court was whether the procedural safeguards demanded by the respondent formed an essential component of a fair military trial and whether the provisions of the Air Force Act and the procedures followed during the Court-Martial infringed any Fundamental Rights available to members of the Armed Forces.

Decision

The Supreme Court rejected the respondent's contentions and upheld the validity of the proceedings.

In doing so, the Court relied upon its earlier decision in *Ram Swarup v. Union of India* and reiterated:

"We agree that each and every provision of the Act is a law made by Parliament and that if any such provision tends to affect the fundamental rights under Part III of the Constitution, that provision does not, on that account, become void, as it must be taken that Parliament has thereby, in the exercise of its power under Article 33 of the Constitution, made the requisite modification to affect the respective fundamental right."

The Court thus reaffirmed the principle that restrictions arising from military legislation are protected by Article 33 and cannot ordinarily be challenged on the ground that they affect Fundamental Rights available to Armed Forces personnel.

Analysis

The judgment in *Ex. Flt. Lt. G.S. Bajwa* is significant because it illustrates the practical implications of the broad interpretation accorded to Article 33 in earlier decisions.

With due respect to the Hon'ble Supreme Court, it may be argued that the concerns raised by the respondent merited closer examination from the perspective of procedural fairness. One of the cardinal principles of criminal jurisprudence is that the defence is entitled to withhold its strategy until the prosecution has concluded its case and disclosed all evidence relied upon against the accused. Requiring an accused to reveal the relevance of defence witnesses before their examination may create a legitimate apprehension that the prosecution could anticipate, counter, or otherwise neutralise the proposed defence.

This concern assumes even greater significance within the military environment, where witnesses, the prosecution, and the accused frequently belong to the same organisation and remain subject to the same chain of command. The issue is not necessarily whether witnesses would in fact be influenced, but whether a reasonable person standing trial could apprehend that such influence was possible. In matters affecting the perception of fairness, such apprehensions cannot be lightly dismissed.

Equally important was the grievance regarding the non-supply of day-to-day copies of proceedings. Although military law permits the accused to inspect the proceedings at specified stages, it may be argued that inspection alone is not always an adequate substitute for contemporaneous access to documentary records. Copies of witness depositions and proceedings serve an important function in enabling effective cross-examination and ensuring that inconsistencies can be identified and confronted while the trial is still in progress.

The respondent's complaint was not merely that he wished to examine the proceedings after their completion, but that access to the material during the trial was necessary to effectively defend himself. From this perspective, the issue touches upon broader principles of natural justice and the accused's ability to participate meaningfully in his own defence.

The judgment is also noteworthy because it once again derives support from the reasoning adopted in *Ram Swarup*,[81] namely that legislation enacted for the Armed Forces is protected by Article 33 even where its provisions affect rights otherwise guaranteed under Part III of the Constitution. In that sense, *Ex. Flt. Lt. G.S. Bajwa* reinforces the judicial trend of according a broad protective ambit to Article 33 and military legislation enacted thereunder.

Viewed collectively, the decisions discussed thus far reveal that, for more than half a century after the Constitution came into force, challenges before the superior courts generally focused upon the validity of specific provisions of military law rather than upon the constitutional validity of Article 33 itself. As a result, the broader constitutional implications of Article 33 and its impact upon the Fundamental Rights of Armed Forces personnel remained largely unexplored.

81 Ram Sarup, *supra* note 71.

Few Strides Towards the Modernisation of the Indian Military Justice System

The judicial pronouncements discussed thus far reveal a consistent pattern of deference towards military legislation enacted under the authority of Article 33 of the Constitution. While the courts generally upheld restrictions imposed upon members of the Armed Forces, the closing years of the twentieth century and the beginning of the twenty-first witnessed the emergence of important reform initiatives aimed at making the military justice system more transparent, accountable, and compatible with contemporary constitutional standards.

In 1992, Parliament enacted the Army (Amendment) Act, 1992 (Act No. 37 of 1992), introducing amendments to several provisions of the Army Act, 1950. However, these amendments did not substantially incorporate the recommendations made by the Supreme Court in *Lt. Col. Prithi Pal Singh Bedi v. Union of India.*[82] It is also noteworthy that corresponding reforms were not simultaneously introduced into the military justice systems governed by the Air Force Act, 1950 and the Navy Act, 1957.

The absence of meaningful legislative response to the concerns expressed by the Supreme Court, coupled with the extensive reforms already undertaken in jurisdictions such as the United Kingdom and the United States, prompted the Law Commission of India to undertake a *suo - motu* review of the existing military justice framework.[83]

---

82 Prithi Pal Singh *supra note* at 73.

83 Law Commission of India. (1999). *169th Report on Amendment in the Army, Navy and Air Force Acts*. Available at: https://cdnbbsr.s3waas.gov.in/s3ca0daec69b5adc880fb464895726dbdf/uploads/2022/08/2022081024.pdf, (Accessed: 30 October 2024).

A significant constitutional reaffirmation came in *Union of India v. L.D. Balam Singh* (2002),[84] where the Supreme Court observed:

"While it is true that army personnel ought to be subjected to strictest form of discipline and Article 33 of the Constitution has conferred powers on to Parliament to abridge the rights conferred under Part III of the Constitution in respect of the members of the armed forces, but does that mean and imply that the army personnel would be denuded of the constitutional privileges as guaranteed under the Constitution? Can it be said that the army personnel form a class of citizens not entitled to the Constitution's benefits and are outside the purview of the Constitution? To answer the above in the affirmative would be a violent departure from the basic tenets of the Constitution. An army personnel is as much a citizen as any other individual citizen of this country. Incidentally, the provision as contained in Article 33 does not by itself abrogate any rights and its applicability is dependent on parliamentary legislation."

This observation marked an important departure from the perception that military personnel exist outside the constitutional framework. It reaffirmed the principle that members of the Armed Forces remain citizens entitled to constitutional protection, subject only to such restrictions as may be lawfully imposed under Article 33.

Two noteworthy developments followed in the sphere of military justice reform. The first was the establishment of the Armed Forces Tribunal under the Armed Forces Tribunal Act, 2007. For the first time, Armed Forces personnel were provided

84 LD Balam, *supra note* at 78.

with a specialised appellate forum empowered to undertake a merits review of Court-Martial proceedings. This represented a significant advance over the earlier position, where judicial intervention was largely confined to the limited scope of constitutional review.

The second development was the introduction of a requirement that Courts-Martial provide brief reasons in support of their findings. Though modest in appearance, this reform represented an important step towards greater transparency and accountability in military adjudication.

The 169th Report of the Law Commission of India played a significant role in stimulating debate on military justice reform and ultimately contributed to the creation of the Armed Forces Tribunal. Nevertheless, several aspects of the proposed reform framework attracted criticism. In particular, concerns were expressed regarding the composition of the proposed appellate mechanism, which included a substantial military component alongside judicial members. Critics argued that such a structure could give rise to apprehensions regarding institutional independence and impartiality.

Similarly, proposals for creating a separate Service Tribunal generated debate because of concerns that the exclusion of ordinary constitutional remedies under Article 226 might restrict access to justice rather than enhance it.

The continuing tension between military discipline and individual liberty remains the central challenge confronting military justice reform in India. Any meaningful reform must strike a careful balance between preserving the discipline essential to operational effectiveness and safeguarding the constitutional rights of those who serve in uniform.[85]

A major initiative in this direction was undertaken in 2015 by the late Mr. Manohar Parrikar, then Defence Minister of India, through the constitution of a Committee of Experts to examine military justice reform. Among its important recommendations were the creation of a permanent framework for Courts-Martial, measures to reduce the influence of the Convening Authority upon military justice, specialised training programmes for Judge Advocate General (JAG) officers outside the military environment, the use of Summary Court-Martial only in exceptional circumstances, and the establishment of a dedicated study group to initiate progressive legislative reforms.

While the recommendation relating to external legal training for JAG officers has been implemented, most of the structural reforms proposed by the Committee continue to await legislative action. Nevertheless, the appointment of the Chief of Defence Staff in December 2019 and the continuing movement towards greater integration of the three Services present a valuable opportunity to revisit the idea of a unified military justice code applicable across the Army, Navy, and Air Force.

Encouragingly, recent judicial pronouncements demonstrate an increasing willingness to scrutinise military procedures through the lens of constitutional fairness and due process. Some of these decisions reflect a more progressive approach

---

85 Bhanu, P.N. (2023). *Analysis on 169th Law Commission Report - Amendment of Army, Navy and Air Force Act*. Available at, https://legalvidhiya.com/analysis-on-169th-law-commission-report-amendment-of-army-navy-and-air-force-act/ (Accessed: 31 October 2024).

towards balancing military discipline with individual rights and are examined in the following section.

Naik Abhilash Singh Kushwah v. Union of India (2015)

Facts

In this case,[86] Naik Abhilash Singh Kushwah was discharged from service on the ground that he was suffering from Alcohol Dependency Syndrome. The applicant challenged the discharge on the ground that the finding had not been affirmed by a competent Medical Board and that the discharge had been ordered primarily on the basis of red ink entries without compliance with the mandatory procedural safeguards prescribed by the relevant Army Orders.

The controversy centred upon Army Order dated 28 December 1988, which requires a preliminary inquiry before any decision is taken to discharge a service member from the Army. The Order specifically provides that adverse entries alone are insufficient to justify discharge. The competent authority is required to assess and record the necessity for such action, conduct an inquiry, furnish a copy of the inquiry report to the affected individual, afford an opportunity to respond, and thereafter obtain approval from the higher authority before passing a discharge order.

The applicant contended that these safeguards had not been observed and that the discharge order was therefore arbitrary

86 Naik Abhilash Singh Kushwah versus Union of India, AFT, regional bench, Lucknow Original Application No. 168 of 2013 this the 23rd day of Sep 2015, Available at; https://aftlko.up.nic.in/AFR/AFR%20 2015/OA%20168%20of%20%202013%20-Abhilash(Discharge)%20 AFR.pdf (Accessed: 31 October 2024).

and contrary to the requirements of fairness embodied in Articles 14 and 21 of the Constitution.

Issue

The principal issue before the Tribunal was whether the procedural safeguards prescribed by the Army Order dated 28 December 1988 were mandatory and whether non-compliance with those safeguards would vitiate the discharge proceedings.

Decision

The Tribunal held that the Army Order dated 28 December 1988 had been issued under the authority of Rule 13(2A) of the Army Rules[87] and, having been promulgated by the Chief of the Army Staff in exercise of statutory powers, possessed binding legal force.

The Tribunal observed that compliance with the procedure prescribed in the Army Order was mandatory and that any departure from its requirements could invalidate the resulting proceedings or punishment. The Tribunal further held that such procedural safeguards were intended to ensure fairness in decision-making and were consistent with the constitutional guarantees embodied in Articles 14 and 21 of the Constitution.

The Tribunal recognised that while the Government possesses the authority to restrict certain rights of Armed Forces personnel in the interest of discipline, such restrictions must operate within the framework of law and cannot disregard the procedural protections established by valid statutory instruments.

---

87 *Ibid.*

Analysis

The significance of *Naik Abhilash Singh Kushwah* lies in its reaffirmation that military discipline and procedural fairness are not mutually exclusive concepts. The decision recognises that the maintenance of discipline within the Armed Forces does not justify the abandonment of fair procedures, particularly where a service member's career and livelihood are at stake.

Of particular importance is the Tribunal's recognition that Army Orders issued under statutory authority are not mere administrative guidelines but possess binding legal force. Consequently, authorities exercising disciplinary powers cannot selectively disregard procedures intended to protect service personnel from arbitrary action.

The Tribunal's observations on morale and justice are equally noteworthy. It emphasised that arbitrary or autocratic treatment of Armed Forces personnel has the potential to undermine morale and foster resentment within the ranks. The maintenance of discipline ultimately depends not merely upon command authority but also upon the confidence of service personnel that they will be treated fairly and in accordance with law.

The decision further acknowledged that members of the Armed Forces remain beneficiaries of constitutional protections, particularly those flowing from Articles 14 and 21, except to the extent lawfully restricted under Article 33. In doing so, the Tribunal moved away from a purely disciplinary approach and towards a model that seeks to balance military necessity with constitutional fairness.

Viewed in this light, *Naik Abhilash Singh Kushwah* represents an important step in the gradual evolution of Indian military justice. It reinforces the principle that adherence to procedure is not an obstacle to discipline but one of the means by which discipline acquires legitimacy. A soldier who believes that he has been treated fairly is far more likely to accept an adverse decision than one who perceives the process itself to be unjust.

Union of India v. Vishav Priya Singh (2016)

Facts

In *Union of India v. Vishav Priya Singh*,[88] the Supreme Court was called upon to examine an appeal arising from a judgment of the Delhi High Court concerning the validity of Summary Court-Martial (SCM) proceedings.

The High Court had undertaken a detailed examination of the historical origins, purpose, and scope of the Summary Court-Martial mechanism under the Army Act. It observed that the SCM was not conceived as an ordinary mode of military trial but had its roots in the circumstances that followed the Revolt of 1857. The procedure was designed to enable Commanding Officers to deal swiftly and effectively with situations requiring immediate disciplinary intervention and was therefore intended to operate as an exceptional mechanism rather than as a routine form of trial.

The High Court consequently held that the extraordinary powers vested in a Commanding Officer under the SCM framework

88 Union of India vs. Vishav Priya Singh, AIR 2016, S.C 3726, Available at https://indiankanoon.org/doc/69192244/ (Accessed: 30 October 2024), also at; Singh, N. (2023). *Military Justice Reform - Developments and Challenges*. Available at: https://www.barandbench.com/columns/military-justice-reform-developments-challenges. (Accessed: 30 October 2024).

ought to be exercised only in circumstances demonstrating genuine urgency and necessity.

Issue

The principal issue before the Supreme Court was whether the Summary Court-Martial procedure could be invoked as a matter of routine or whether it was intended to operate only as an exceptional mechanism justified by circumstances requiring immediate disciplinary action.

Decision

The Supreme Court affirmed the approach adopted by the Delhi High Court and endorsed its understanding of the nature and purpose of the Summary Court-Martial.

The Court observed:

"We completely support and affirm the High Court's perspective that SCM is an exception, requiring a clear justification for the urgency of action. The rationale for convening an SCM should be well-articulated, or the records must sufficiently explain the necessity for this approach."

Accordingly, the Supreme Court held that the invocation of the Summary Court-Martial procedure must be supported by circumstances demonstrating urgency and that the reasons for adopting such an exceptional procedure must either be expressly recorded or be clearly discernible from the record.

Analysis

The significance of *Vishav Priya Singh* extends far beyond the facts of the individual case. For perhaps the first time, the Supreme Court unequivocally recognised that the Summary Court-Martial is not intended to function as a routine disciplinary mechanism but as an exceptional procedure justified only by circumstances demanding immediate action.

This observation assumes particular importance because the Summary Court-Martial differs fundamentally from other forms of Court-Martial. The Commanding Officer performs multiple roles within the process and the procedural safeguards available in General Court-Martial and Summary General Court-Martial proceedings are considerably reduced. It is precisely for this reason that the Supreme Court emphasised the need for demonstrable urgency before resorting to such a procedure.

The judgment also lends substantial judicial support to the long-standing criticism that the Summary Court-Martial has often been employed in situations for which it was never originally intended. By tracing its origins to the extraordinary circumstances following the Revolt of 1857, the Court underscored the exceptional nature of the power and cautioned against its routine use in ordinary disciplinary matters.

Equally significant is the fact that the decision resonates with the recommendations of the Committee of Experts on Military Justice Reform, which had also recommended that Summary Court-Martial proceedings should be used only in exceptional cases. The judgment therefore represents an important convergence between judicial thinking and contemporary reform proposals.

Viewed from the perspective of military justice reform, *Vishav Priya Singh* marks a notable shift in judicial approach. Unlike earlier decisions that largely emphasised military necessity and deference to command authority, this judgment insists upon justification, transparency, and accountability before extraordinary disciplinary powers can be exercised. It thereby strengthens the principle that even within the military justice system, exceptional procedures must remain the exception and not become the norm.

Wing Commander Shyam Naithani v. Union of India and Others (2022)

Facts

In *Wing Commander Shyam Naithani v. Union of India and Others*,[89] the Delhi High Court was called upon to examine an important constitutional question arising from the establishment of the Armed Forces Tribunal (AFT) and the scope of judicial review available against its decisions.

The central issue was whether the power of judicial review vested in the High Courts under Articles 226 and 227 of the Constitution had been completely excluded following the decision of the Supreme Court in *Union of India v. Major General Shri Kant Sharma* (2015) 6 SCC 773.[90] The matter assumed

89 Available at, https://indiankanoon.org/doc/25175570/ (Accessed: 29 October 2024).

90 Available at, https://indiankanoon.org/doc/83270443/ (Accessed: 29 October 2024). Held: If the High Court hears a petition under Article 226 against an order from the Armed Forces Tribunal, bypassing the statutory provisions of Sections 30 and 31, it could create an anomalous situation for the aggrieved party seeking relief. Section 30 allows appeals to the Supreme Court, but Article 136(2) excludes appellate jurisdiction over Armed Forces Tribunal decisions if the party goes to High Court. Consequently, if the High Court rules on the petition, the aggrieved person cannot appeal both the Tribunal's order and the High Court's order in a single appeal. This situation could prevent them from pursuing remedies under the relevant sections of the Armed Forces Act. Thus, it is advisable for the High Court to adhere

significance because if such an interpretation were accepted, litigants aggrieved by decisions of the Armed Forces Tribunal would effectively be left with only the limited appellate remedy provided under Sections 30 and 31 of the Armed Forces Tribunal Act, 2007.

Issue

The principal issue before the Delhi High Court was whether members of the Armed Forces retained the right to invoke the writ jurisdiction of the High Courts under Articles 226 and 227 of the Constitution against decisions of the Armed Forces Tribunal, or whether such jurisdiction stood excluded by the Armed Forces Tribunal Act, 2007 and the decision in *Major General Shri Kant Sharma.*

Decision

The Delhi High Court reaffirmed the constitutional significance of judicial review and held that Article 33 of the Constitution does not restrict or prohibit members of the Armed Forces from invoking the writ jurisdiction of the High Courts.

The Court observed that Article 33 merely empowers Parliament to impose restrictions upon certain activities of Armed Forces personnel in the interests of discipline and operational effectiveness. The Army Act, Air Force Act, and Navy Act contain restrictions relating primarily to political activities, associations, and similar matters. None of these enactments prohibit a member of the Armed Forces from approaching a constitutional court under Articles 226 and 227.

---

to the law established by the Supreme Court, as mandated by Article 141, allowing the aggrieved party to utilize the remedies provided under the Act.

The Court further held that the existence of a statutory appeal to the Supreme Court under Sections 30 and 31 of the Armed Forces Tribunal Act cannot be construed as excluding the constitutional jurisdiction of the High Courts. It noted that appeals to the Supreme Court under the Act are maintainable only when a point of law of general public importance arises. Consequently, the constitutional remedy under Article 226 continues to remain available in appropriate cases. . In Ex. Lac Yogesh Pathania,[91] the Supreme Court emphasized that appeals under this Act are considered solely when such a point is involved. When reviewing a Tribunal's decision, the Writ Court engages in judicial review, focusing on the decision-making process and intervening only to correct jurisdictional errors or obvious mistakes, or if the Tribunal acts unlawfully.

The Court also clarified that while Article 227(4) limits the administrative superintendence of High Courts over tribunals constituted under laws relating to the Armed Forces, it does not extinguish the power of judicial review. Such review remains available to correct jurisdictional errors, patent illegality, violations of natural justice, and instances of manifest injustice.

Analysis

The significance of *Wing Commander Shyam Naithani* extends well beyond the immediate controversy before the Court. The judgment reaffirms one of the foundational principles of Indian constitutional law—that judicial review forms part of the basic structure of the Constitution and cannot be excluded except by express constitutional mandate.

---

91 Available at, https://indiankanoon.org/doc/189569179/ (Accessed: 30 October 2024).

Of particular importance is the Court's clear recognition that Article 33 does not place members of the Armed Forces outside the protection of constitutional remedies. The judgment rejects any suggestion that service personnel constitute a separate class of citizens deprived of access to constitutional courts. Instead, it affirms that restrictions imposed under Article 33 are limited to those expressly authorised by Parliament and cannot be expanded by implication to curtail constitutional remedies.

The decision also clarifies an issue that had generated considerable uncertainty after the establishment of the Armed Forces Tribunal. By holding that the writ jurisdiction of the High Courts survives notwithstanding the appellate provisions of the Armed Forces Tribunal Act, the Court preserved an essential constitutional safeguard against arbitrary or unlawful exercise of power.

Equally significant is the Court's recognition that military justice, though distinct in many respects, remains subject to constitutional supervision. The Armed Forces Tribunal is undoubtedly a specialised adjudicatory body, but it is not insulated from judicial review. Its decisions remain open to scrutiny where jurisdictional error, procedural unfairness, violation of natural justice, or manifest illegality is demonstrated.

Viewed in the broader context of military justice reform, *Wing Commander Shyam Naithani* represents an important constitutional milestone. Earlier judicial decisions often focused upon the breadth of Parliament's power under Article 33 and the necessity of preserving military discipline. This judgment, while fully acknowledging those concerns, emphasises an equally important principle—that military justice must ultimately remain accountable to the Constitution.

The decision therefore stands as a powerful reminder that the Armed Forces, the Armed Forces Tribunal, and the military justice system itself operate within the constitutional framework created by "We the People of India." Discipline may justify certain restrictions, but it cannot extinguish the constitutional guarantee that unlawful action remains subject to judicial scrutiny. The judgment thus reflects the continuing evolution of Indian military jurisprudence towards a more balanced accommodation of military necessity and constitutional liberty.

Conclusion

Article 33 occupies a unique and controversial position within the constitutional framework of India. While Part III of the Constitution guarantees Fundamental Rights to all persons, Article 33 permits Parliament to restrict or even abrogate those rights in their application to members of the Armed Forces so as to ensure the proper discharge of duties and the maintenance of discipline. The difficulty, however, lies in the fact that neither the Constitution nor subsequent legislation has clearly defined the limits of the expression "maintenance of discipline." Consequently, its interpretation has largely been left to the Legislature, the Executive, and the Judiciary.

The judicial decisions examined in this chapter reveal a gradual evolution in constitutional thinking. Earlier judgments generally adopted a broad interpretation of Article 33, often upholding restrictions on the rights of service personnel in the interest of military necessity and discipline. Decisions such as *Ram Sarup*, *Prithi Pal Singh Bedi*, *R. Viswan*, and *Ex. Flt. Lt. G.S. Bajwa* demonstrate the judiciary's willingness to accord wide latitude to Parliament and the Executive in matters relating to military affairs. Over time, however, courts increasingly began to recognise that members of the Armed Forces do not cease to be citizens upon donning the uniform. Decisions such as *L.D. Balam Singh*, *Naik Abhilash Singh Kushwah*, *Vishav Priya Singh*, and *Wing Commander Shyam Naithani* reflect a growing emphasis on procedural fairness, accountability, constitutional safeguards, and meaningful judicial review within the military justice system.

The central challenge, therefore, is not whether discipline should be maintained in the Armed Forces—few would dispute its necessity—but rather how discipline is to be balanced with constitutional liberty. A military justice system commands respect not merely because it enforces discipline, but because it inspires confidence that justice is administered fairly, impartially, and in accordance with law.

The experiences of jurisdictions such as the United Kingdom and the United States demonstrate that military effectiveness and robust procedural safeguards are not mutually exclusive. Indeed, modern military justice systems increasingly recognise that fairness strengthens discipline rather than weakens it. The reforms introduced in those jurisdictions and the gradual judicial shift visible in India suggest that military justice must continue to evolve alongside constitutional values and contemporary notions of human rights.

The establishment of the Armed Forces Tribunal, the recommendations of the Law Commission, the Committee of Experts on Military Justice Reform, and recent judicial pronouncements represent important steps in that direction. Yet many structural concerns remain unresolved. The continuing debate surrounding the role of the Convening Authority, the use of Summary Court-Martial, the concentration of powers within the military justice system, the scope of Article 33, and access to meaningful judicial review indicates that the journey towards a more balanced military justice system is far from complete.

Perhaps one reason why Article 33 escaped sustained constitutional scrutiny for decades is that its impact was felt most acutely by those occupying the lowest ranks of the Armed Forces. Many affected personnel lacked the financial resources, legal assistance, and institutional support necessary to challenge adverse actions before constitutional courts. As Justice V.R. Krishna Iyer poignantly observed, they were often "priced out from the market of justice."[92] The gradual expansion of judicial review and the establishment of the Armed Forces Tribunal have undoubtedly improved access to remedies, but the larger constitutional questions surrounding Article 33 continue to await fuller examination.

The Supreme Court in *Sunil Batra v. Delhi Administration*[93] reminded us that a prisoner does not shed his Fundamental Rights at the prison gate. The same constitutional philosophy must inform military justice. A soldier may accept restrictions necessary for discipline, but he does not surrender his dignity, humanity, or entitlement to fairness under the law. Discipline and justice are not opposing ideals; rather, enduring discipline derives its legitimacy from justice.

More than two centuries ago, William Blackstone observed:

"How much therefore is it to be regretted that a set of men, whose bravery has so often preserved the liberties of their country,

92 Sunil Batra v Delhi Administration II, AIR 1980 SC 1579.

93 *Ibid.*

should be reduced to a state of servitude in the midst of a nation of freemen!....."[94]

Those words continue to resonate today. The men and women of the Armed Forces stand as guardians of the sovereignty, liberty, and constitutional values of the nation. The challenge before lawmakers, judges, scholars, and military leaders is not merely to preserve discipline, but to ensure that the constitutional promise of justice remains equally available to those who defend it. Ultimately, the true measure of any military justice system lies not only in its ability to maintain discipline, but also in its capacity to assure every soldier, sailor, and air warrior that justice will be done and will manifestly be seen to be done. The constitutional promise of justice, liberty, equality, and dignity belongs no less to those who defend the Republic than to the citizens whom they serve and protect.

94 William Blackstone, Commentaries on the Laws of England: A Facsimile of the First Edition of 1765-1769, (Chicago: University of Chicago Press, 1979), *available at* http://presspubs.uchicago.edu/founders/documents/a1_8_16s2.html (last visited on Jun. 14, 2012).

CHAPTER 04

Justice and its Access in the Indian Military Justice System

"Justice ought to bear rule everywhere, and especially in armies; it is the only means to settle order there, and there it ought to be executed with as much exactness as in the best governed cities of the kingdom, if it be intended that the soldiers should be kept in their duty and obedience".[95]

INTRODUCTION

Armed Forces personnel are citizens of India, notwithstanding the unique nature of their service and working conditions. While military service necessarily entails certain restrictions and obligations not applicable to civilian life, it does not follow that service personnel constitute a separate society requiring a wholly distinct conception of justice. Such a proposition would sit uneasily with the Rule of Law, which demands that all citizens remain subject to the same constitutional framework. This raises

95 Louis De Gaya, The Art of War (1678), *reprinted in* Francis A. Gilligan & , Fredric I. Lederer, Court-Martial Procedure V (1991), *reproduced in*, Fredric I. Lederer and Barbara S. Hundley, *Needed: An Independent Military Judiciary- A Proposal to Amend the Uniform Code of Military Justice,* 3 Wm & Mary Bill of Rts. J, 629 (1994), *available at* http://scholarship.law.edu/wmborj/vol3/iss2/5(Accessed on 29.06. 2012).

a number of fundamental questions: Are the Armed Forces a distinct society requiring a separate system of justice apart from the ordinary legal system? What is the true purpose of the Military Justice System? Do service personnel enjoy genuine access to justice? Is military justice complementary to discipline, or does it exist primarily to enforce it? What constitutes a fair trial in the military context? Are service personnel afforded adequate due process protections and tried by an independent and impartial tribunal?

Indian Military Law, as it emerged after Independence, was substantially derived from the pre-existing British Indian Army Act, 1911. Designed primarily as an instrument for maintaining discipline, it reflected the prevailing standards of its time. The system was command-oriented and contained only limited procedural safeguards by contemporary standards. Consequently, while it served the objective of maintaining discipline, its structure and processes often remained out of step with evolving notions of social justice, due process, and judicial independence.

The military justice framework has remained largely unchanged for decades. This institutional stagnation prompted the Supreme Court of India to observe in 1982 that "the winds of change blowing over the country have not permeated the closed and sacrosanct precincts of the Army."[96] Although a significant step was taken through the enactment of the Armed Forces Tribunal Act, 2007, which for the first time provided a statutory appellate mechanism against Court-martial verdicts, the structure of the Court-martial system itself has undergone little substantive reform. Questions therefore continue to arise

96 Lt. Col. P.P.S Bedi, *supra* note 73.

regarding the independence and impartiality of those entrusted with administering military justice. While military courts are undoubtedly better placed than civilian courts to appreciate the demands of military discipline and operational effectiveness, the more important question remains whether accused personnel receive a fair trial and whether victims receive meaningful redress.

In the United States, a leading judicial pronouncement observed that "Courts-martial as an institution are singularly inept in dealing with the nice subtleties of constitutional law."[97] Such criticism, according to David Schlueter (1991, p. 10), is neither destructive nor unwarranted; rather, it is both necessary and healthy.[98] Those who participate in a legal system, particularly those who operate within it, must be willing to identify deficiencies and advocate reform wherever required. In military parlance, those within the system must remain "proactive" rather than merely "reactive." It is in this spirit that the present chapter examines the concepts of justice, access to justice, due process, fair trial, and judicial independence within the Indian Military Justice System.

---

97 O' Callahan v. Parker, 395 U.S. 258, 265 (1969) (determining that only service connected offenses were subject to court-martial jurisdiction), *available at* http://caselaw.lp.findlaw.com/scripts/getcase.pl?navby=case&court=us&vol=395&invol=258 (Accessed on 01.01.2012).

98 David A. Schlueter, *The Twentieth Annual Kenneth J. Hodson Lecture: Military Justice for the 1990's-A Legal System Looking for Respect*, 133 Military Law Review 10, (1991), *available at* http://www.loc.gov/rr/frd/Military_Law/Military_Law_Review/pdf-files/27647D~1.pdf (Accessed on 21. 07.2012)

PURPOSE OF INDIAN MILITARY JUSTICE SYSTEM: JUSTICE OR DISCIPLINE?

It may be argued that Indian Military Law, whose primary objective has traditionally been the maintenance of discipline and operational readiness within the Armed Forces, is concerned more with discipline than with justice. To examine this proposition, it is necessary to analyse the competing models of military justice identified by Gaya (1678) (cited in Lederer & Hundley, 1994).[99] According to Gaya, those who advocate a discipline-based system view military law principally as an instrument for securing prompt and unquestioning obedience through the deterrent effect of punishment. Conversely, proponents of a justice-based system maintain that military personnel should be punished only for offences that have been fairly established and proven, and not for derelictions they did not commit. Both approaches possess distinct advantages and shortcomings.

Gaya further observes that most commanders would naturally favour a discipline-based system because it operates swiftly, efficiently, and economically. Its principal weakness, however, lies in the perception of unfairness. Where discipline is regarded as arbitrary or unjust, personnel are likely to lose confidence in their superiors and develop diminished institutional loyalty. In extreme situations, this may result in resentment, disobedience, or even mutiny.[100]

A justice-based system, on the other hand, places emphasis on individual accountability and procedural fairness. Under such a system, punishment is imposed only where guilt has been

99 Gaya, *supra*, note 95.
100 *Id.*

established through a fair process and the sanction imposed is proportionate to the offence committed. The resulting perception of fairness strengthens both individual responsibility and institutional loyalty. The disadvantage, however, is that accuracy and fairness require procedural safeguards, which inevitably make the process slower, more complex, and more expensive. Depending upon the standard of proof employed, such a system may also result in the acquittal of guilty individuals, thereby attracting criticism and potentially undermining deterrence.

The relationship between justice and discipline within the military framework is therefore neither simple nor antagonistic. While discipline remains indispensable to military effectiveness, it must be administered in a manner that is perceived as fair and just. This principle was eloquently articulated in the 1960 Powell Report (cited in Gibson, 2012) submitted to the Honourable Wilber M. Brucker, Secretary of the Army, on the Uniform Code of Military Justice and the maintenance of good order and discipline within the Armed Forces. The Report observed:

"Discipline—a state of mind which leads to a willingness to obey an order no matter how unpleasant or dangerous the task to be performed—is not a characteristic of a civilian community. Development of this state of mind among soldiers is a command responsibility and a necessity. In the development of discipline, correction of individuals is indispensable; in correction, fairness or justice is indispensable. Thus, it is a mistake to talk of balancing discipline and justice—the two are inseparable."[101]

101 United States Department of Defence, *Report to the Honourable Wilber M. Brucker, Secretary of the Army, by Committee on the Uniform Code of Military Justice, Good Order and Discipline in the Army,* cited in

The Powell Report rightly recognised that military personnel must have confidence in the fairness of the justice system that governs them. Such confidence is essential for maintaining morale, cohesion, and institutional legitimacy. A military justice system that is perceived as fair reinforces discipline, whereas one perceived as arbitrary weakens the very discipline it seeks to enforce.

The purpose of the Military Justice System, therefore, extends beyond the mere punishment of offenders. Its broader objective is to preserve discipline, maintain morale, ensure accountability, and promote confidence in the rule of law within the Armed Forces. Justice and discipline are not competing objectives; rather, each depends upon the other.

The practical significance of this relationship may be illustrated by the example given by Schlueter (1991).[102] Suppose a soldier, Sepoy Bhoop Singh, is charged with possession of narcotic drugs. A conviction would reinforce the standards expected of military personnel and demonstrate the consequences of conduct that undermines operational readiness and discipline. Conversely, an acquittal, if perceived as unjustified, might raise questions regarding the effectiveness of command and the integrity of the military justice process. Similar concerns arise in cases involving wilful disobedience of lawful orders, mutinous conduct, or incitement to disorder, where the authority of command itself is directly implicated.

Michael Gibson, *Canada's Military Justice System*, 12, no 2, Canadian Military Journal 61, 64, (2012), *available at* http://www.journal.forces.gc.ca/vol12/no2/61-gibson-eng.asp (Accessed on Jul. 20, 2012).

102 Schlueter, *supra*, note 98.

Public and institutional perceptions of offences may also differ significantly. Certain offences, such as child abuse or drug trafficking, may attract widespread public condemnation, whereas offences such as absence without leave (AWOL) or insubordination may be viewed primarily through the lens of military discipline. Nevertheless, every offence has the potential to affect morale, cohesion, and operational effectiveness if not dealt with appropriately. The Military Justice System must therefore ensure not only that discipline is maintained, but also that justice is visibly and fairly administered.[103]

One of the enduring challenges of military justice is that it seeks to address both disciplinary and criminal misconduct within a single framework. This may sometimes create the perception that the system is excessively punitive or insufficiently responsive to the differing nature of various offences. A distinction between purely disciplinary infractions and conduct amounting to ordinary criminal wrongdoing may therefore permit a more nuanced and proportionate approach to military justice.

Janet Walker (1994, p. 16) [104]argues that service personnel, because of the unique obligations and risks associated with military service, are entitled to the highest standards of procedural protection. Ensuring rigorous adherence to due process enhances both the legitimacy of military justice and public confidence in its outcomes. A system that is fair in procedure is more likely to

103 *Id*, at p 12.

104 Janet Walker, *Military Justice: From Oxymoron to Aspiration*, 33, no 1, Osgoode Hall Law Journal, 16 (1994), *available at* http://osgoode.yorku.ca/osgmedia.nsf/0/FEEA84324A73051985256F1F0070901A/$FILE/mil%20just.pdf (Accessed on Dec. 12, 2012).

command respect, even where its decisions are adverse to the individual concerned.

Ultimately, the legitimacy of the Military Justice System depends upon its ability to reconcile discipline with justice. A system that successfully combines operational effectiveness with procedural fairness will not only maintain discipline but will also foster trust, morale, and cohesion within the ranks—qualities that are indispensable to an effective fighting force.

ACCESS TO JUSTICE AND THE RIGHT TO A FAIR TRIAL IN INTERNATIONAL LAW

Access to justice is a cornerstone of the Rule of Law. It ensures that every individual, including members of the Armed Forces, has the ability to seek legal redress, obtain effective legal representation, and have disputes adjudicated fairly by an impartial tribunal. The principle rests upon the belief that justice must be accessible, equitable, and free from arbitrary interference, irrespective of a person's status or occupation.

Within the Indian constitutional framework, Article 39A emphasises the importance of equal justice and access to legal aid, while the Preamble reflects the constitutional commitment to securing justice for all citizens. The right to a fair trial is therefore not merely a procedural guarantee; it is an essential safeguard against arbitrary action and a fundamental requirement for maintaining public confidence in the legal system.

For Armed Forces personnel, the unique demands of military service cannot be permitted to diminish these protections. Just as civilians are entitled to effective legal representation and procedural safeguards, service personnel must also have meaningful access to justice. Practical difficulties arising from military service, operational commitments, or institutional structures should not become grounds for restricting fundamental guarantees of fairness. Rather, legal systems must be designed to accommodate such challenges while preserving the rights of those subject to them.[105]

Access to justice extends far beyond the mere ability to approach a court or secure legal assistance. It incorporates the broader Principle of Legality, which requires that disputes be adjudicated according to established legal rules and procedures rather than arbitrary discretion. It also presupposes the existence of independent institutions capable of administering justice free from improper influence. A judicial system must therefore possess institutional autonomy, procedural fairness, accountability, and adherence to recognised human rights standards. Equally important is the absence of corruption and executive interference, both of which undermine confidence in the administration of justice.

Against this backdrop, it becomes necessary to examine the extent to which military courts and tribunals remain independent of executive influence and command structures, and whether service personnel have sufficient confidence in the

---

105 Max Planck Institute for Comparative Public Law and International Law (MPIL), (2005), *Max Planck Manual on Fair Trial Standards In the Afghan Constitution, the Afghan Interim Criminal Code for Courts, the Afghan Penal Code and other Afghan Laws as well as in the International Covenant on Civil and Political Rights*, Heidelberg, Germany, *available at* http://siteresources.worldbank.org/INTLAWJUSTINST/Resources/maxplanckfairtrialmanual2edengl.pdf (Accessed on Aug. 5, 2012).

military justice system to regard it as capable of delivering fair and effective justice.

The right to a fair trial has been recognised in numerous international instruments and has emerged as one of the most fundamental guarantees of modern legal systems. For the purposes of this study, particular attention is drawn to Article 14 of the International Covenant on Civil and Political Rights, 1966 (ICCPR);[106] Article 6 of the European Convention for the Protection of Human Rights and Fundamental Freedoms, 1950

---

106 *See* ICCPR, *supra* note 5, (It enunciates that all persons shall be equal before the courts and tribunals and in a criminal offence, everyone shall be entitled to a fair and public hearing by a competent, independent and impartial tribunal established by law. They shall have the right to be presumed innocent until proved guilty according to law and everyone shall be entitled to the following minimum guarantees, in full equality: (a) To be informed promptly and in detail in a language which he understands of the nature and cause of the charge against him;
(b) To have adequate time and facilities for the preparation of his defence and to communicate with counsel of his own choosing;
(c) To be tried without undue delay;
(d) To be tried in his presence, and to defend himself in person or through legal assistance of his own choosing; to be informed, if he does not have legal assistance, of this right; and to have legal assistance assigned to him, in any case where the interests of justice so require, and without payment by him in any such case if he does not have sufficient means to pay for it;
(e) To examine, or have examined, the witnesses against him and to obtain the attendance and examination of witnesses on his behalf under the same conditions as witnesses against him;
(f) To have the free assistance of an interpreter if he cannot understand or speak the language used in court;
(g) Not to be compelled to testify against himself or to confess guilt), *available at* http://www2.ohchr.org/english/law/ccpr.htm (Accessed on 05.07.2012).

(ECHR);[107] Article 8 of the American Convention on Human Rights, 1969 (ACHR);[108] Article 26 of the African Charter on Human and Peoples' Rights, 1981 (Banjul Charter);[109] and Article 10 of the Universal Declaration of Human Rights (UDHR).[110] Collectively, these instruments establish internationally accepted standards relating to fair trial, due process, judicial independence, and access to justice.

---

107 ECHR art. 6, 1950 (also states that in the determination of his civil rights and obligations or of any criminal charge against him, everyone is entitled to a fair and public hearing within a reasonable time by an independent and impartial tribunal established by law. The minimum rights being on the lines as given under the ICCPR Articles for minimum guarantee), *available at* http://www.hri.org/docs/ECHR50.html#C.Art6 (Accessed on 06.07. 2012).

108 ACHR art. 8, 1969, (reads that every person has the right to a hearing, with due guarantees and within a reasonable time, by a competent, independent, and impartial tribunal, previously established by law, in the substantiation of any accusation of a criminal nature made against him or for the determination of his rights and obligations of a civil, labour, fiscal, or any other nature. During the proceedings, every person is entitled, with full equality with minimum guarantees...), *available at* http://www.hrcr.org/docs/American_Convention/oashr.html. (Accessed on 07.07. 2012).

109 African Charter on Human and Peoples' Rights ('Banjul Charter') art. 26, 1981, (it states that State parties to the present Charter shall have the duty to guarantee the independence of the Courts and shall allow the establishment and improvement of appropriate national institutions entrusted with the promotion and protection of the rights and freedoms guaranteed by the present Charter), *available at* http://www1.umn.edu/humanrts/instree/z1afchar.htm (Accessed on 08.07. 2012).

110 UDHR art. 10 (states that everyone is entitled in full equality to a fair and public hearing by an independent and impartial tribunal, in the determination of his rights and obligations and of any criminal charge against him), *available at* http://www.un.org/en/documents/udhr/index.shtml#a10 (Accessed on 07.07. 2012).

India, as a State Party to the ICCPR, is under an international obligation to uphold the rights guaranteed under the Covenant, including the right to a fair trial. These obligations cannot be avoided by reliance upon domestic legislation, including military laws. The right to a fair trial has attained such significance that it is widely regarded not merely as a treaty obligation but also as a principle of customary international law. Consequently, all States are expected to respect and protect this right irrespective of their domestic legal arrangements.

For Armed Forces personnel, these obligations assume particular importance. Fair trial guarantees form the foundation of due process and protect individuals against arbitrary, biased, or unjust treatment. Access to justice is therefore not merely a theoretical ideal but a practical necessity that directly affects the rights, liberties, careers, and reputations of service personnel.

In the military context, fair trial guarantees require that service personnel be tried before independent and impartial tribunals operating according to established legal procedures. Adequate legal representation, transparency in proceedings, equality of arms, and freedom from unlawful command influence are essential components of such a system. Failure to provide these safeguards risks undermining confidence in military justice and may adversely affect morale, cohesion, and discipline within the Armed Forces.

India's commitment to the principles embodied in the ICCPR therefore requires that its military justice system conform, as far as practicable, to internationally recognised standards of fairness, impartiality, and due process. By ensuring effective legal representation, independent adjudication, and transparent procedures, the military justice system not only fulfils international obligations but also strengthens its own legitimacy and credibility.[111]

Fair trial guarantees thus constitute an indispensable element of both due process and access to justice. Their application to members of the Armed Forces, and the extent to which they are reflected in the Indian Military Justice System, shall be examined in the following sections.

DUE PROCESS, PROCEDURAL FAIRNESS AND FAIR TRIAL

In a constitutional democracy such as India, the true measure of the Rule of Law lies in the availability of procedural due process protections to all persons, including members of the Armed Forces. A violation of due process occurs when the State, through its actions, deprives an individual of rights, liberty, or livelihood without adhering to legally established procedures. Such departures from prescribed legal safeguards strike at the very foundation of the Rule of Law.

The omission of the phrase "due process of law" from Article 21 of the Constitution was a conscious choice made by the framers. Nevertheless, beginning in the late 1970s, the Supreme Court of India expanded the scope of Article 21 through judicial interpretation and infused into it substantive requirements

111 International Commission of Jurists (ICJ) (2007), *International Principles on the Independence and Accountability of Judges, Lawyers and Prosecutors, Practitioners Guide No. 1*, Switzerland, Geneva, *available at* http://www.icj.org/dwn/database/PG-J&L-ENG.pdf (Accessed on 05.07. 2012).

of fairness, reasonableness, and justice.[112] This development fundamentally transformed Indian constitutional jurisprudence.

The landmark decision in *Maneka Gandhi v. Union of India*[113] marked a turning point in this evolution. The Supreme Court held that any procedure affecting the life or personal liberty of an individual must be "just, fair and reasonable" and not arbitrary, fanciful, or oppressive. Article 21 was thus interpreted as embodying the essential principles of due process. Since then, procedural fairness has become an indispensable component of constitutional governance and a safeguard against arbitrary State action.

The Indian Constitution further reinforces these protections through Article 14, which guarantees equality before the law and equal protection of the laws. Moreover, the Code of Criminal Procedure mandates that trials must be conducted in open court to uphold the tenets of fairness.[114] Criminal trials are ordinarily required to be conducted in open court to ensure transparency and fairness. Article 22 guarantees the right of an accused person to consult and be defended by a legal practitioner of his choice.[115] Articles 20(3) and 22(1) provide protection against compulsory

---

112 Manoj Mate, *The Origins of Due Process in India: The Role of Borrowing in Personal Liberty and Preventive Detention Cases*, 28:1 Berkeley Journal of International Law 216, 260 (2010), *available at* http://www.boalt.org/bjil/docs/BJIL28.1_Mate.pdf (accessed on 26.08.2012l).

113 Maneka Gandhi v. Union of India, AIR 1978, SC 597.

114 Code of Criminal Procedure, Sec 327.

115 Khatri (II) v. State of Bihar (1981)1 SCC 627. *See also*, Hussainara Khatoon & Ors. V. Home Secretary, Bihar, Patna, (1980) 1 SCC 98, (the Supreme Court Held: "the right to free legal service is clearly an essential ingredient to a reasonable, fair and just procedure for a person accused of an offence and it must be held implicit in the guarantee of Article 21 and the status under constitutional mandate to

self-incrimination and secure the right to a fair and expeditious trial. Similarly, Section 164 of the Code of Criminal Procedure requires a Magistrate to satisfy himself that any confession made by an accused is voluntary and free from coercion, inducement, or intimidation.

Collectively, these constitutional and statutory safeguards establish a robust framework designed to protect individual rights within the criminal justice system. By guaranteeing equality before the law, legal representation, protection against coercion, and adherence to fair procedures, these provisions strengthen public confidence in the administration of justice and ensure that justice is not only done but is also seen to be done.[116]

Within the military justice system, due process is principally reflected through the procedures governing Courts-Martial. These procedures are intended to ensure that an accused person receives a fair and public hearing before a competent tribunal and is afforded a meaningful opportunity to defend himself. Although the Indian Military Justice System incorporates several elements of due process and fair trial, there remains a significant gap between the theoretical framework and its practical implementation.

For any procedure to be regarded as fair, it must be administered by impartial decision-makers who adhere strictly to established legal norms. Consistency in application, equal treatment of all parties, meaningful participation, and transparency are indispensable elements of procedural fairness. The legitimacy

---

provide a lawyer to an accused person if the circumstances of the case and the needs of justice so required")

116 Maiese, *supra* note 8.

of any justice system depends not merely upon the existence of procedural safeguards but upon their faithful implementation.

According to Buttram et al. (1995, p. 273):

"Unbiased decision-makers must carry out the procedures to reach a fair and accurate conclusion. Those involved should believe that the intentions of third-party authorities are benevolent, that they want to treat people fairly and take the viewpoint and needs of interested parties into account."[117]

Despite these principles, due process protections within the Indian Military Justice System are not always observed in their fullest spirit. Some of the principal concerns are discussed below.

Right to be Informed of Charges

The accused is ordinarily informed of the charges against him. However, difficulties arise because the initial charge-sheet supplied is often described as a "Tentative Charge-sheet." At the stage of trial, the charges may be modified or substituted, potentially requiring the accused to defend allegations materially different from those originally communicated. Such a practice may undermine the accused's ability to prepare an effective defence.

As observed by Wayn and Scott (2010, pp. 588–589), criminal jurisprudence is founded upon the presumption of innocence. An accused person must therefore be afforded adequate time and

117 Robert T. Buttram, Robert Folger & B.H. Sheppard, Equity, Equality and Need: Three Faces of Social Justice, *in Conflict, Cooperation, and Justice: Essays Inspired by the Work of Morton Deutsch*, at 273 (B.B. Bunker & Morton Deutsch eds, 1995, Jossey-Bass Inc. Publishers, San Francisco).

opportunity to prepare a defence to every charge brought against him. Where additional factual allegations emerge that may form the basis of conviction, they ought to be reflected through a fresh or amended charge and be subjected to the same procedural safeguards applicable to the original charge.[118]

In *Prosecutor v. Zigiranyirazo*, it was held that:

"According to any Fair Trial standard it is not permissible to delay disclosure of the factual component of the offence until the disclosure of prosecution's pre-trial brief or the service of evidence."[119]

The tentative nature of charges in military proceedings may therefore fail to provide the level of specificity and certainty required by contemporary standards of due process and fair trial.

Right to Speedy Trial

The Military Justice System is often praised for its ability to conduct trials expeditiously. In practice, however, significant delays may occur before charges are formally preferred and cases brought to trial. It is not uncommon for proceedings to take two or three years, and sometimes longer, before reaching conclusion.

---

118 Jordash Wayn & Martin Scott, *Due Process and Fair Trial Rights at the Special Court: How the Desire for Accountability Outweighed the of Justice the Special Court of Sierra Leone*, 23 Leider Journal of International Law, 585,608 (2010), *available at* www.doughtystreet.co.uk/files/Due%20Process%20FairTrial%20Rights%20SCSL.pdf, (Accessed on 30.08.2012).

119 Case no ICTR 2001-73 PT, 30 September 2005, Para 2, *available at* www.unictr.org/Portals10/Cases%5CEnglish%5CZigiranyirazo%5Cdecisions%5C300905b.pdf,(Accessed on 30.08.2012).

During this period, service personnel may face various administrative restrictions imposed in the name of discipline or vigilance. They may be removed from their appointments, transferred away from their units, denied career opportunities, or subjected to other adverse administrative consequences based solely upon suspicion. Such measures can have profound effects upon both professional advancement and financial stability.

Unlike civilians, whose liberty is generally curtailed only through recognised legal restraints, military personnel may experience prolonged uncertainty while effectively bearing the burden of a presumption of guilt before any formal adjudication. Although military trials may ultimately conclude more rapidly than many civilian proceedings, the hardships endured during the pre-trial phase can be substantial. This highlights the need to balance the requirements of military discipline with the rights and welfare of accused personnel.

Right Not to Be Compelled to Incriminate Oneself and Exclusion of Involuntary Confessions

The privilege against self-incrimination and the exclusion of involuntary confessions are fundamental aspects of due process. Yet concerns persist regarding their practical implementation within military proceedings.

Instances have been reported where senior officers conducting Courts of Inquiry exert pressure upon junior personnel to admit wrongdoing or accept responsibility for acts they may not have committed. Witnesses may likewise feel compelled to align their testimony with the expectations of superior officers, particularly where career advancement and future postings depend upon favourable assessments from the chain of command.

Where proceedings are founded upon coerced confessions or improperly influenced testimony, the fairness and legitimacy of the entire process is called into question. As Colonel T. G. Becker (1998, p. 31)[120] observed:

"The status of a procedural violation as being so fundamental that it continues on infringement of Military Due Process may be critical to the ultimate fate of the prosecution."

The importance of protecting individuals from compelled self-incrimination cannot therefore be overstated. Procedural safeguards in this regard are essential to preserving the integrity of military justice.

Right to Counsel of One's Choice

The right to legal representation of one's choice is recognised in principle but remains

significantly restricted in practice. This concern is particularly acute in Summary Court-Martial proceedings, which are unique to the Indian Army and may result in serious consequences, including imprisonment or dismissal from service.

At the pre-trial stage, access to legal assistance is often limited. During trial, the Convening Authority retains discretion to refuse permission for representation by a civilian advocate on the ground that such representation is not considered expedient.[121]

120 Colonel Thomas G Becker, *Games Lawyers Play: Pre- Preferral Delay, Due Process and the Myth of Speedy Trial in the Military Justice System*, 45 Air Force Law Review 1, 31(1998), *available at* www.afjag.afmil/shared/media/document/AFD081204034.pdf (Accessed on 31.07.2012).

121 AR 1954, r 96.

Although the accused is provided with a Defending Officer or a "Friend of the Accused," these individuals frequently lack formal legal training and may be ill-equipped to provide effective legal assistance.

Financial constraints further compound the problem. Many service personnel below officer rank are unable to afford private legal representation. In addition, accused persons are often transferred from the place of occurrence and subsequently moved again to the location where the trial is conducted, frequently in remote areas where experienced legal practitioners may be unavailable.

Even in capital cases, where legal aid is theoretically available, the remuneration provided to appointed counsel has historically been nominal,[122] raising legitimate concerns regarding the quality and effectiveness of such representation.

The cumulative effect of these limitations places the accused at a significant disadvantage and raises concerns regarding compliance with the principle of "equality of arms," which forms an essential component of a fair trial. In *Dombo Beheer BV v. The Netherlands*,[123] the European Court emphasised that each party must be afforded a reasonable opportunity to present its case without being placed at a substantial disadvantage vis-à-vis its opponent. The same principle is equally relevant within the military justice context.

---

122 RA1987, vol I, ¶ 479(c).

123 App No, 14448/ 88, Judgment of, 27th October 1993, *available at* http://www.humanrights.is/the-human-rightsproject/humanrightscasesandmaterials/cases/regionalcases/europeancourtofhumanrights/nr/485 (Accessed on 09.08.2012).

Right to Present a Defence

The accused in military proceedings is entitled to call witnesses in his defence, and the Court-Martial is empowered to facilitate the attendance of such witnesses. However, practical difficulties may arise where the accused is required to disclose in advance the purpose for which each witness is being called. Such a requirement may compel the accused to reveal the nature and strategy of his defence before it is presented at trial.

Further concerns arise from the fact that many defence witnesses are themselves members of the Armed Forces and remain subject to the same chain of command. Where their identity and proposed evidence become known in advance, there exists a perception—whether justified or not—that such witnesses may be susceptible to influence or pressure. This places the accused at a potential disadvantage when compared to the prosecution and may undermine the fairness of the proceedings.

The right to present a defence is meaningful only when the accused is able to do so freely, effectively, and without fear that the process itself may compromise the integrity of the evidence to be led on his behalf.

INDEPENDENT AND IMPARTIAL JUSTICE SYSTEM

For a court to render just and legitimate decisions, its adjudicators must be free from every form of external influence, particularly interference from the executive. Judicial decision-making must remain independent, uninfluenced by personal, institutional, or command pressures. Equally important is the perception of independence. There should be no reasonable basis for an informed and prudent observer to conclude that the position, integrity, or impartiality of the adjudicators has been compromised or is susceptible to compromise. In the military justice context, the mere formal independence of a tribunal is insufficient; the Presiding Officer and the members of the Court-Martial must also be perceived as objective, neutral, and impartial.

The importance of institutional independence was emphasised by the European Court of Human Rights in *Findlay v. The United Kingdom*,[124] wherein the Court observed that, in determining whether a tribunal can be regarded as "independent," regard must be had to a number of factors, including the manner of appointment of its members, the duration of their tenure, the existence of safeguards against external pressure, and whether the tribunal presents an appearance of independence.

Impartiality, however, extends beyond institutional arrangements. It contains both a subjective and an objective dimension. The subjective aspect concerns the personal conviction and conduct of the adjudicator and requires the absence of actual prejudice or

---

124 Findlay v. The United Kingdom, 110/1995/616/706, Council of Europe: European Court of Human Rights, 25 February 1997, *available at* http://www.unhcr.org/refworld/docid/3ae6b66d1c.html (Accessed on 08.10. 2011), (the European Court of Human Rights observed that;
'...in order to establish whether a tribunal can be considered "independent", regard must be had, *inter alia,* to the manner of appointment of its members and their term of office, the existence of guarantees against outside pressure and to the question whether the body presents an appearance of independence...')
See also, Grieves v. The United Kingdom, App No. 57065/00, Judgment on 16th December, 2003, *available at*
http://www20.gencat.cat/docs/Departament_de_la_Presidencia/GJ/Document/Arxiu/12213585.pdf (Accessed on 20.05. 2012).

bias. The objective aspect seeks to determine whether there exist sufficient guarantees to exclude any legitimate doubt regarding impartiality.

This distinction was clearly articulated by the European Court in *Piersack v. Belgium,*[125] where impartiality was defined as the absence of bias or prejudice. The Court drew a distinction between subjective impartiality, which focuses on the personal state of mind of the decision-maker, and objective impartiality, which considers whether the circumstances of the case create an appearance of bias. In that case, although there was no evidence of actual prejudice on the part of the judge, the fact that he had previously served as a Public Prosecutor in the same judicial district was sufficient to give rise to legitimate concerns regarding impartiality. The appearance of possible bias was therefore enough to fail the objective test.

125 App. No 8692/ 79, Judgment of 1st October 1982, (wherein the European Court defined "impartiality" as 'the absence of prejudice or bias..... A distinction can be drawn in this context between a subjective approach, that is endeavouring to ascertain the personal conviction of a given judge in a given case, and an objective approach, that is determining whether he offered guarantees sufficient to exclude any legitimate doubt in this respect'). *available at* http://www.humanrights.is/the-human-rights project/humanrightscasesandmaterials/cases/regionalcases/europeancourtofhumanrights/nr/621 (Accessed on 08.08. 2012) *See also*, Hauschildt v. Denmark, App. No. 10486/ 83, Judgment of 24TH May, 1989, *available at* http://www.humanrights.is/the-human-rights
project/humanrightscasesandmaterials/cases/regionalcases/european courtofhumanrights/nr/518 (Accessed on 09.08. 2012).

Similarly, in *Re Murchison v. United States,*[126] the Supreme Court of the United States reaffirmed that due process requires an impartial decision-maker and observed that a fair trial before a fair tribunal is a basic requirement of justice. The Court recognised that the legitimacy of any judicial process depends not only upon actual fairness but also upon public confidence in the fairness of the tribunal.

The right to an independent and impartial court therefore encompasses both objective and subjective elements. The objective element is largely institutional and derives from the doctrine of separation of powers, which seeks to protect adjudicators from executive, legislative, or other external influence. The subjective element requires that judges and adjudicators refrain from any conduct, attitude, or expression that may reasonably create an apprehension of bias in the minds of litigants or informed observers.

The significance of these principles is reflected in the *Basic Principles on the Independence of the Judiciary* (1985),[127] which

---

126 349 U.S. 133 (1955), *available at* http://laws.findlaw.com/us/349/133.html (last visited on Jul. 1, 2012). *See also,* Weiss v. United States, Military App No 92-1482, Judgment for 19th January 1994, *available at* http://laws.findlaw.com/us/510/163.html (Accessed on 01.07.12).

127 The 1985 Basic Principles on the Independence of the Judiciary (provide:
1. The independence of the judiciary shall be guaranteed by the State and enshrined in the Constitution or the law of the country. It is the duty of all governmental and other institutions to respect and observe the independence of the judiciary.
2. The judiciary shall decide matters before them impartially, based on facts and according to law, without any restrictions, improper influences, inducements, pressures, threats or interferences, direct or indirect, from any quarter or for any reason.

remain one of the most important international instruments concerning the administration of justice. The Principles emphasise that judicial independence must be guaranteed by the State and enshrined in law, and that judges must be able to decide matters before them impartially, on the basis of facts and law, free

---

3. The judiciary shall have jurisdiction over all issues of a judicial nature and shall have exclusive authority to decide whether an issue submitted for its decision is within its competence as defined by law.
4. There shall not be any inappropriate or unwarranted interference with the judicial process, nor shall judicial decisions by the courts be subject to revision. This principle is without prejudice to judicial review or to mitigation or commutation by competent authorities of sentences imposed by the judiciary, in accordance with the law.
5. Everyone shall have the right to be tried by ordinary courts or tribunals using established legal procedures. Tribunals that do not use the duly established procedures of the legal process shall not be created to displace the jurisdiction belonging to the ordinary courts or judicial tribunals.
6. The principle of the independence of the judiciary entitles and requires the judiciary to ensure that judicial proceedings are conducted fairly and that the rights of the parties are respected....
10. Persons selected for judicial office shall be individuals of integrity and ability with appropriate training or qualifications in law. Any method of judicial selection shall safeguard against judicial appointments for improper motives. In the selection of judges, there shall be no discrimination against a person on the grounds of race, colour, sex, religion, political or other opinion, national or social origin, property, birth or status, except that a requirement, that a candidate for judicial office must a national of the country concerned, shall not be considered discriminatory).
(also it should be noted that Paragraphs 11–12 and 17–20 of the Basic Principles add conditions that ensure security of tenure of judges so that they will not be under pressure to decide a case in a way that is not impartial), *available at* http://www.icrc.org/customary-ihl/eng/docs/v2_cha_chapter32_rule100_sectionb (Accessed on 08,.08. 2012).

from restrictions, improper influences, inducements, pressures, threats, or interferences, whether direct or indirect.

These principles are of particular relevance in the military justice system, where adjudicators often function within a hierarchical command structure. The existence of such a structure makes it imperative that both institutional safeguards and procedural protections operate effectively to ensure that justice is not only done but is manifestly seen to be done.

IS THE INDIAN MILITARY JUSTICE SYSTEM INDEPENDENT AND IMPARTIAL?

The Indian Military Justice System is a creature of statute, established by Parliament in exercise of powers conferred by the Constitution. Within this framework, Courts-Martial are recognised as duly constituted tribunals entrusted with the responsibility of maintaining discipline within the Armed Forces. Nevertheless, the constitutional legitimacy of any military justice system ultimately depends upon its ability to provide an accused person with a fair trial before an independent and impartial tribunal. While Article 33 of the Constitution empowers Parliament to restrict certain rights of service personnel in the interests of discipline and the proper discharge of duties, it does not authorise the denial of the fundamental requirements of a fair trial.

The importance of perceived independence was emphasised in *R. v. Genereux*, where the Court observed:

"An individual who challenges the independence of a tribunal under S 11(d) need not prove an actual lack of independence. The question is whether a reasonable person familiar with the constitution and structure of a General Court-martial would perceive the tribunal as independent…"[128]

The significance of this principle lies in the fact that independence is judged not solely by the personal integrity of the adjudicators but also by the institutional framework within which they function. In the Indian Military Justice System, questions arise regarding the objective appearance of independence because the Presiding Officer and members of the Court-Martial are appointed by the Convening Authority, who remains an integral part of the command structure. Although there may be no reason to doubt the personal honesty or integrity of individual officers serving on a Court-Martial, the appearance of independence is equally important in maintaining public confidence in the administration of justice.

The dangers posed by command influence have been recognised in other military jurisdictions as well. In *Harvey*, the Court reaffirmed that:

"The military judge is the last sentinel in the trial process to protect a court-martial from unlawful command influence... everyone involved in both unit command and in military justice must exercise constant vigilance to protect against command influence becoming unlawful."[129]

---

128 *R. v. Généreux, [1992] 1 S.C.R. 259, Available at*, https://decisions.scc-csc.ca/scc-csc/scc-csc/en/item/836/index.do (Accessed on 03.11.2024).

129 United States v. Harvey, 64 M.J. 13 (C.A.A.F. 2006), *available at* http://www.armfor.uscourts.gov/opinions/2006Term/040801.pdf, also available at: http://court-martial.com/unlawful-command-influence/ (Accessed on 07.08. 2012)

While the Indian Military Justice System incorporates several procedural safeguards, concerns continue to be raised regarding whether the tribunal itself satisfies the objective requirements of independence and impartiality. In her analysis of the implications of the *Findlay* decision,[130] Lyon (2002) observed:

"There was certainly an appearance of a lack of complete independence of the court from the convening officer... A reasonable man would most certainly conclude that there was a real possibility that a member of the court might be unconsciously influenced by his military and subordinate relationship to the convening officer, that this unconscious influence would prevent him from considering the evidence before him solely on its merits, and that there was a real danger of that unconscious influence causing injustice to the accused, even if there was no evidence of any actual lack of impartiality or of any attempt by the convening officer to influence the court."[131]

This observation is particularly relevant when examining the structure of the Indian Military Justice System. Although independence and impartiality are conceptually distinct, the latter cannot realistically exist without the former. A tribunal that

---

130 Findlay, *supra*, note 124.

131 Ann Lyon, After Findlay: A consideration of some aspects of the military justice system, *in* Evolving Military Justice (Eugene R. Fidell & Dwight H. Sullivan, eds., Annapolis, MD: Naval Institute Press), *available at* http://books.google.co.in/books?id=G3tYljWV_zEC&printsec=frontcover&source=gbs_ge_summary_r&cad=0#v=onepage&q&f=false, *also available at* http://www.aph.gov.au/Parliamentary_Business/Committees/Senate_Committees?url=fadt_ctte/miljustice/report/c05.htm (Accessed on 01.03.2012).

does not appear independent is unlikely to inspire confidence in its impartiality. The concentration of authority in the hands of the Convening Authority therefore becomes a matter of legitimate concern.

The Convening Authority occupies a uniquely influential position within the military justice process. Acting under powers conferred by statute, the Convening Authority decides whether a matter should proceed to trial, determines the nature of the charges to be prosecuted, appoints the Prosecutor, constitutes the Court-Martial, and selects its members. Those appointed as members of the Court-Martial frequently serve within the same command hierarchy and may, directly or indirectly, remain subordinate to the Convening Authority.

The Convening Authority also plays a significant role in the post-trial process. Traditionally, the findings and sentences of the Court-Martial required confirmation by an authority within the same command structure. The Convening Authority may seek advice from the Judge Advocate General's Branch, direct the appointment of a Defending Officer, and exercise powers relating to remission, mitigation, suspension, or review of punishments. In certain circumstances, the Court-Martial may be reassembled for reconsideration of findings or sentence.

Such extensive involvement at multiple stages of the process inevitably raises concerns regarding the separation between prosecutorial, administrative, and adjudicatory functions. Even where no actual interference occurs, the concentration of powers in a single authority may create an appearance of command influence that undermines confidence in the fairness of the proceedings.

Further concerns arise from the traditional confirmation and review process, which takes place within the offices of the competent military authorities. The accused is ordinarily not present during these proceedings, is not afforded an opportunity to respond to any advice tendered, and is generally unaware of the nature of the legal opinions that may influence the final decision. Such procedures stand in contrast to contemporary notions of transparency and participatory justice.

As Judge J. W. Rant observed:

"The ad hoc nature of a court-martial is inconsistent with the established view that a fixed term of office is a crucial guarantee of a tribunal's independence."[132]

This criticism draws attention to the absence of institutional safeguards commonly associated with judicial independence.

The importance of such safeguards was emphasised in *Valente v. The Queen*,[133] a leading decision of the Supreme Court of Canada, where judicial independence was said to rest upon three essential elements: security of tenure, financial security, and institutional independence in matters bearing directly upon the exercise of judicial functions.

When these criteria are applied to the Indian Military Justice System, certain difficulties become apparent. Members of a

132 Judge J W Rant, *The British Courts-Martial System: It Ain't Broke, But It Needs Fixing*, 152 Military Law Review, 179, 188 (1996), *available at* http://www.loc.gov/rr/frd/Military_Law/Military_Law_Review/pdf-files/276C79~1.pdf (Accessed on 01.05.2012).

133 [1985] 2 S.C.R. 673, *available at* http://www.judicialethics.umontreal.ca/en/jurisprudence/documents/VALENTE_ANGLAIS.pdf (Accessed on 01.08.2012).

Court-Martial do not enjoy security of tenure in their judicial capacity. They are appointed on an ad hoc basis from within the command structure and return to their ordinary military duties upon completion of the proceedings. Nor do they possess separate financial security associated with an independent judicial office. They continue to function as serving officers whose career progression remains linked to the military hierarchy.

The requirement of institutional independence likewise presents challenges. Officers serving as adjudicators remain subject to the command structure of the Armed Forces and do not function within a separate judicial institution. Consequently, a perception may arise that compliance with command expectations could consciously or unconsciously influence decision-making. Whether such influence actually exists is less important than the fact that a reasonably informed observer may perceive such a possibility.

The issue, therefore, is not one of questioning the personal integrity of military officers who serve as members of Courts-Martial. Rather, it concerns whether the institutional framework within which they operate satisfies the objective standards of independence and impartiality recognised in modern jurisprudence. Measured against the principles articulated in *Findlay*, *Genereux*, *Piersack*, *Murchison*, and *Valente*, the structure of the Indian Military Justice System continues to invite debate regarding whether justice is not only done, but is manifestly and undoubtedly seen to be done.

CONCLUSION

An examination of the need for a distinct military justice system reveals that military law serves a purpose that extends beyond the traditional objectives of criminal law. While criminal law seeks both to prevent and rehabilitate antisocial conduct, military law is additionally designed to foster discipline, loyalty, cohesion, and an unwavering commitment to duty. As Nicholas (1971, p. 482) observed, "Criminal Law has a preventive as well as rehabilitative function; it restricts antisocial behaviour to enable people to coexist within accepted social patterns."[134] Military service, however, demands a level of obedience, sacrifice, and collective responsibility that is rarely required in civilian life. It is this unique requirement that provides the principal justification for a separate military justice system.

The existence of a distinct system of military justice, however, does not diminish the obligation to ensure fairness. History demonstrates that laws perceived as unequal, arbitrary, or oppressive inevitably lose moral authority and invite resistance rather than respect. A disciplinary system can command loyalty only when it is regarded as legitimate by those who are subject to it. The challenge, therefore, lies in striking a proper balance between the operational requirements of an effective fighting force and the rights and dignity of service personnel.

The Indian Military Justice System possesses several strengths. It is self-contained, specialised, and capable of responding swiftly to matters affecting discipline and operational effectiveness. Nevertheless, concerns remain regarding the extent to which it satisfies contemporary standards of due process, judicial independence, and impartiality. A system that carries penal consequences must place the right to legal representation, procedural fairness, and access to justice at the forefront of its

---

134 Louis B. Nichols, *The Justice of Military Justice*, 12 Wm. & Mary L. Rev. 482 (1971), *available at* http://scholarship.law.wm.edu/wmlr/vol12/iss3/3 (Accessed on 09.08.2012).

functioning. Equally important is the need for adjudicators to be perceived as independent, impartial, and free from actual or apparent external influence.

The analysis undertaken in this chapter suggests that piecemeal reform is unlikely to address the deeper structural concerns affecting the system. Questions relating to command influence, institutional independence, access to counsel, procedural safeguards, and the composition of Courts-Martial require careful and comprehensive consideration. Reform should not await constitutional challenge or judicial intervention; rather, it should arise from a conscious recognition that military effectiveness and fair trial guarantees are complementary rather than competing objectives.[135]

Ultimately, discipline derives its legitimacy from justice. A military justice system commands respect not merely because it possesses the authority to punish, but because those subject to it have confidence that their cases will be heard and determined fairly, impartially, and in accordance with law. It is therefore imperative that the military justice system continues to evolve in harmony with contemporary standards of due process and fair trial, while preserving the discipline essential to military effectiveness.

The observation of Justice Ginsburg in *Weiss* captures this principle with remarkable clarity:

"...men and women in the Armed Forces do not leave constitutional safeguards and judicial protection behind when

135 Weiss v. United States, Military App No 92-1482, Judgment for 19th January 1994, *available at* http://laws.findlaw.com/us/510/163.html (last visited on 01.07.12)..

they enter military service..... A member of the Armed Forces is entitled to equal justice under law not as conceived by the generosity of a commander but as written in the Constitution."[136]

That statement encapsulates the enduring challenge facing every modern military justice system: to maintain discipline without sacrificing justice, and to ensure that those who defend the Constitution remain protected by it1s guarantees.

136 *Id.*

CHAPTER 05

Summary Court-Martial: Swift Discipline or Constitutional Justice?

INTRODUCTION

In 1823, Sir William Blackstone characterised summary proceedings as "hearings in which an accused may be convicted of various offences without any formal process or jury, at the discretion of judges appointed by Act of Parliament or common law."[137] The concept of summary justice has historically been justified on grounds of expediency and necessity, particularly where swift disciplinary action is considered essential to maintaining order and authority.

Within the Indian Army, the Summary Court-Martial (SCM) represents the most expeditious form of military trial. Although the statutory provisions governing SCM proceedings appear

137 4Sir William Blackstone, Commentaries on the laws of England: Book the Fourth, 280 (A Strahan & W. Woodfall, Law Printers to the King, 1791), *available at* http://books.google.co.in/books?id=Q1ozAAAAIAAJ&jtp=280#v=onepage&q&f=false (Accessed on 23.08.2012); *also cited* in Claire Newhouse, Summary Proceedings Within the Australian Military Justice System: How and Why Are They Inherently Unjust? (October 31, 2005) (Unpublished Honour thesis for Faculty of Law, The Australia National University), *available at*: www.scribd.com/doc/50489718/10/II Summary-Proceedings-An-'Exceptional-Proceedings (Accessed on 29.02.2012).

to incorporate several safeguards associated with a fair trial, questions arise as to whether these safeguards are consistently applied in practice. The central concern is whether a procedure that permits deprivation of liberty, dismissal from service, and long-term adverse consequences can legitimately operate with a reduced degree of procedural protection.

Proponents of the SCM system contend that a lesser application of due process is justified by the unique demands of military discipline and operational effectiveness. Critics, however, argue that the curtailment of procedural safeguards undermines the principles of natural justice, due process, and the Rule of Law. The debate becomes even more significant when one considers that, notwithstanding the establishment of the Armed Forces Tribunal, personnel awarded imprisonment of less than three months continue to be denied a statutory right of appeal.[138]

The SCM procedure is unique to the Indian Army and is designed for the trial of service personnel accused of offences under the Army Act. Historically, summary forms of military justice have found greater acceptance during periods of active operations, war, or in remote locations where access to regular courts is either impracticable or impossible. In such circumstances, operational necessity may justify a degree of procedural flexibility. During peacetime, however, the requirements of constitutional governance, the Rule of Law, and the principles of

138 Staff Reporter, *Bench of Armed Forces Tribunal Opened,* The Hindu, Dec. 7, 2009, *available at* http://www.hindu.com/2009/12/07/stories/2009120759840300.htm (Accessed on 24.01.2012).

fundamental justice demand closer scrutiny of procedures that curtail individual liberty.[139]

The consequences of an SCM conviction are often far from trivial. A service member may face imprisonment, dismissal from service, adverse entries in service records, loss of pensionary benefits, and long-term damage to future employment prospects. Yet, despite these serious consequences, the accused is ordinarily denied legal representation during the proceedings. The resulting tension between military discipline and procedural fairness raises important constitutional questions concerning Articles 14 and 21 of the Constitution of India.

This chapter draws substantially upon the work of Claire Newhouse[140] and the theoretical framework developed by the socio-legal scholar Dr. Doreen McBarnet.[141] Their analysis of summary justice systems provides a useful lens through which to examine whether the reduced procedural safeguards characteristic of SCM proceedings can be justified when weighed against the seriousness of the penalties imposed.

---

139 Bill C- 41, Supporting the Troops: Fairness for Canada's Soldiers (BCCL, 2011)
available at http://bccla.org/wp-content/uploads/2012/03/20110311-BCCLA-Policy-Bill-C41.pdf (posted on Mar.11, 2011) (Accessed on 27.06.2012).

140 Newhouse, C. (2005) *Summary Proceedings Within the Australian Military Justice System: How and Why Are They Inherently Unjust?* Unpublished Honours Thesis. Faculty of Law, Australian National University, Canberra. Available at: Scribd (Accessed: 29 February 2012).

141 DJ McBarnet, Conviction, Law, the State and the Construction of Justice (Macmillan, London, 1989), *cited in,* Newhouse, *supra* note 140

Despite its widespread use and significant impact upon the lives and careers of service personnel, the Summary Court-Martial has received comparatively little academic attention. This may be attributable to a perception that the offences involved are minor or that the procedure itself raises few complex legal issues. Yet the deprivation of liberty, livelihood, and reputation through a process involving reduced procedural protections raises questions that go to the very heart of constitutional justice. It is these questions that this chapter seeks to examine.

ORIGIN

The Summary Court-Martial (SCM) was introduced into the regular army following the Mutiny of the Bengal Army in 1857.[142] The British administration believed that one of the principal causes of the uprising was the inability of Commanding Officers to deal swiftly and effectively with acts of indiscipline, disobedience, and incipient mutiny. The existing system did not empower Commanding Officers to impose immediate punishment upon errant soldiers, thereby limiting their ability to suppress dissent at its earliest stage.[143]

The situation, however, was markedly different in the Punjab Irregular Force, where the Commanding Officer enjoyed extensive powers to deal summarily with military offenders and

142 Divi Jain, *Summary Court Martial and the Indian Judiciary*, Legal Service India.com (Oct. 5, 2007), *available at* http://www.legalserviceindia.com/article/l30-Summary-Court-Marital-And-The-Indian
Judiciary.html (Accessed on 08.03.2012).

143 Pragmatic, *Army Act-A Sad Remnant From 1857*, Pragmatic Euphony Blog (Jan. 26, 2008), *available at* http://pragmatic.nationalinterest.nic.in (Accessed on 26.03.2012).

to reward commendable conduct.[144] The perceived effectiveness of this model led the British authorities to conclude that wider powers should be vested in Commanding Officers throughout the army.

Under this system, the adjudicator effectively combined the roles of Deputy Commissioner, Political Officer, and Military Commandant.[145] The Commanding Officer possessed the authority not only to convict and sentence a military offender but also, in his capacity as a Magistrate, to execute the sentence. Such orders were recognised and enforced by the civil and prison authorities alike.[146] In order to prevent future uprisings and to ensure prompt disciplinary control, wide powers were vested in Commanding Officers, and the Summary Court-Martial was formally introduced in 1869.[147]

The procedures governing SCM were contained in Articles 93–97 and 107 of the Indian Articles of War, 1869.[148] The institution was subsequently retained under the Indian Army Act, 1911, and, following Independence, was continued under the Army Act, 1950, which came into force on 22 July 1950. Despite significant constitutional and legal developments since Independence, the essential structure of the SCM has remained substantially unchanged to this day.[149]

144 Manual of Military Law, *available at* http://indarmy.nic.in (Accessed on 26.03.2012).

145 Jain, *supra* note 142.

146 *Id.*

147 *Id, at p 24.*

148 Manual of Military Law, *supra* note 144.

149 G.K.Sharma & M.S.Jaswal, Study and Practice of Military Law, 607 (Deep & Deep Publications Pvt. Ltd., New Delhi, 2010).

PURPOSE AND NATURE

The Summary Court-Martial was conceived as a swift and effective mechanism for dealing with disciplinary offences within the Army. Its primary objective is the maintenance of discipline through the prompt disposal of cases and the immediate punishment of offenders where circumstances so require. The Commanding Officer exercising SCM powers is expected to do so judicially and with due regard to fairness and discipline alike.

In essence, the SCM functions as a military tribunal designed to dispense justice through a simplified procedure that is less elaborate than that followed by a District Court-Martial or a General Court-Martial. It occupies a middle ground between summary disposal by the Commanding Officer and the more formal procedures applicable to higher Courts-Martial.

The rationale underlying the SCM is that the Commanding Officer is personally acquainted with the accused, who serves under his command, and is therefore in a position to appreciate both the disciplinary requirements of the service and the circumstances of the offender. The procedure is accordingly intended to provide a quick and practical method of enforcing discipline while avoiding the complexity, delay, and expense associated with more formal military trials.

JURISDICTION

A Summary Court-Martial may try any person who is subject to the Army Act and is under the command of the Officer holding the trial, with the exception of Officers, Junior Commissioned Officers (JCOs), and Warrant Officers (WOs).[150]

150 Army Act 1950(AA 1950), § 120(3) & Regulations for the Army 1987 (RA 1987), ¶ 381.

Ordinarily, a Non-Commissioned Officer (NCO) or Sepoy is attached to his own unit for trial by SCM.[151] An exception exists in the case of deserters and absentees, who may be tried by the Commanding Officers of Regimental Centres, Training Centres, Schools, or other authorised establishments.

OFFENCES AND SENTENCES

A Summary Court-Martial may try any offence punishable under the Army Act.[152] However, the Commanding Officer should not ordinarily try offences falling under Sections 34,[153] 37,[154] and 69[155]of the Army Act, or offences committed against the Officer holding the trial, unless there exists a grave reason for immediate action and it would be detrimental to discipline to refer the matter to an Officer empowered to convene a District Court-Martial (DCM) or, during active service, a Summary General Court-Martial (SGCM).

In such cases, a certificate must be attached to the proceedings clearly setting out the reasons why the offence was tried summarily without reference to the superior authority competent to convene a higher Court-Martial.[156]

---

151 RA 1987, ¶381; *see also,* Mahipal Singh v. Union of India and Ors, 55 (1994) DLT 176, *available at* http://www.indiankanoon.org/doc/863242/ (Accessed on 02.04.2013).

152 AA 1950, §120(2).

153 AA 1950, § 34 (offences in relation to the enemy and punishable with death).

154 AA 1950, § 37 (mutiny).

155 AA 1950, 69 (civil offences like murder, culpable homicide not amounting to murder and rape)

156 AA 1950, § 120 & notes.

The SCM is empowered to award any sentence authorised under the Army Act, except a sentence of death or imprisonment exceeding one year. Where the Officer holding the SCM is below the rank of Lieutenant Colonel, the maximum sentence that may be awarded is three months' imprisonment, whether rigorous or simple.[157]

SUMMARY COURT- MARTIAL PROCEDURE

Summary proceedings are conducted like a civilian criminal trial. The accused is arraigned and is asked whether he pleads guilty or not guilty[158] and thereafter plea of the accused is recorded[159]. Before the plea the accused may offer plea to jurisdiction of Court.[160] While pleading guilty or not guilty, he may state in bar of trial that he has been previously convicted or acquitted or dealt with summarily or that the charge has been dismissed or condoned or that it is time barred.[161] The findings thereon shall not require confirmation vide Army Rule 114.

If the accused pleads guilty and the authority is satisfied that the effect and implication of the plea is understood, his signature is thereupon obtained and the accused is convicted.[162] In a case where the Court may pass a special finding when the Court itself or the accused offers a qualified plea as to a less severe offence than what he was originally charged with,[163] may record

157 AA 1950, § 120 (5).

158 *See* note 2 to AR 1954, r 111.

159 AR 1954, r 115(1).

160 AR 1954,. r 114.

161 AR 1954,. r 51 & 53 vide AR, r 114 (all such plea shall be treated in accordance to these sections).

162 AR 1954, r 115(2).

163 AA 1950, § 139 or AR 1954, r 121(3).

a finding accordingly.[164] The accused gets the opportunity to address the Court regarding his charge or for the purpose of mitigation of punishment as well as call witnesses who can vouch for his character.[165] If the statement provided by the accused or evidence brought out in writing in the Summary Of Evidence or otherwise, it seems that the accused did not fully understand what his plea may entail, the Court will alter his plea to 'Not Guilty' and proceed with the trial accordingly.[166] If the accused states anything which if proved would mitigate the offence the Court should permit him to call witness in proof thereof.[167]

If he pleads 'Not Guilty', the Commanding/ Presiding officer who is also a prosecutor takes evidence for the prosecution and at the close of the evidence for the prosecution the accused shall be asked if he has anything to say in his defense or if he wants to defer until he has called his own witness and no oath is administered to the accused[168].

The Court may in the interest of justice, call witnesses in reply to the defence.[169] If, after hearing the evidence, the summary authority forms the opinion that there is insufficient evidence to support any of the charge, the Court will acquit the accused of that charge.[170]

---

164 AR 1954, r 116(7) and in accordance with AR, r 115(2) &115(2A).

165 AR 1954, r 116(3); *see also,* Union of India v. Dinesh Prasad, Civil Appeal No 1961 of 2010.

166 AR 1954, r 116 (4).

167 AR 1954, r 116 (6).

168 AR 1954, r 118.

169 AR 1954, r 119.

170 AR 1954, r 121(2); *see also,* Newhouse, *supra* note 140.

If the finding regarding each of the charge is found not guilty, the accused shall be acquitted.[171] If the accused is found guilty, the authority then hears evidence relevant to sentencing like the accused record is consulted; his character evidence, gallantry or distinguished conduct and matters in mitigation are heard before imposing a sentence.[172]

The sentence awarded shall be promulgated and carried out as soon as is feasible.[173] But in an event when the officer holding the trial has less than five years of service, then except on active service, sentence given by such an officer cannot be carried out until approved by superior authority.[174]

The accused is also informed of his right to be put up a petition against the SCM award to the Central Government, Chief of Army Staff or any officer superior in command to the officer who held the trial, having powers not less than a Brigade Commander.[175] If the reviewing authority finds the award held in order it will countersign the proceedings or set aside the proceedings or reduce the sentence of the accused as it deems fit after due deliberation[176] and forward the proceedings to the Commanding Officer who will do the needful and who shall then forward the proceedings to the Record Officer concerned for preservation.[177]

---

171 AR 1954, r 122.

172 AR 1954, r 1954 & r 123.

173 AR 1954,. r 131.

174 AR 1954, r 132.

175 AA 1950, § 164(2).

176 AA 1950 § 162 & notes.

177 AR 1954, r 146.

ARE THE PROVISIONS OF SUMMARY COURT MARTIAL APPLIED IN LETTER AND SPIRIT?

Although the provisions of the Army Act and the associated rules for Summary Court-Martial appear to align with the principles of a fair trial on paper, outlining the responsibilities of Summary Authorities to administer justice impartially and without undue influence, the actual procedures raise significant concerns. In practice, there are issues that may undermine the fairness of the trial process and the protection of the accused's rights.

Justice Vikramjit Sen who was a judge of Delhi High Court in the year 2008, on 25th Jan, 2008 said in a case; 'It should also be noted that paragraph 448(c) of the defence Services Regulations, Regulations for the Army[178] prescribes valuable safeguards against abuse of SCMs, but the spirit of all these provisions is far too often ignored so much so that the vice has become the norm - SCMs invariably pass orders of dismissal from service.'[179]

---

178 RA 1987, ¶ 448 (it deals with Scale of Punishments Awardable by Summary Courts-martial.--The following general instructions are issued for the guidance of officers holding summary courts-martial in passing sentence, but nothing contained in them will be construed as limiting the discretion of the court to pass any legal sentence, whether in accordance with these instructions or not, if in its opinion, there is good reason for doing so:...(c) The award of imprisonment in a civil jail coupled with dismissal from the service must never be used merely as a mean of getting rid of a man from the service but should be imposed only when the offence by itself, or the offence and the man's previous record taken together, actually merits such a punishment. In other cases in which removal is considered desirable in the interest of the service, the discharge of the individual under the appropriate item of Army Rule 13 should be applied for by the CO and authorised by the brigade or superior commander).

179 Ex LN Vishav Priya Singh v. Union of India and others, 147 (2008) DLT 202 (DB).

He further opined that '..Summary Court- martial should be an exception and not a Rule, only to be applied where there is grave and compelling cause for taking immediate action. In such instances this immediate need for holding SCM has to be articulated and reasoned out in the writing in the order convening the SCM. Failure to do so would create good reasons to quash the SCM itself.'[180] It was further observed by the Court that '..routinely, and certainly far too frequently, the sentence passed by SCMs violates the spirit of Regulation 448(c) thereby taking away the sepoy's livelihood without affording them the normal procedural protections of law.'[181]

"The trials are often brief and superficial, prioritizing expediency over the procedural protections afforded to the accused."[182] While the accused has the right to question witnesses and present evidence, the commanding officer overseeing the trial frequently applies undue pressure, sometimes bypassing the examination or cross-examination of witnesses in an effort to expedite the process. Consequently, the military rules of evidence that apply in other courts-martial do not govern Summary Court-Martial. These rules are crucial for ensuring a fair trial and preventing wrongful convictions. The absence of such safeguards in the Summary Trial procedure significantly undermines the quality of justice delivered and heightens the risk of false convictions.

As previously mentioned, Summary Court-Martials are conducted by the accused's Commanding Officer or a delegate acting on their behalf, who alone constitutes the court. This individual takes on multiple roles, serving as the presiding officer,

---

180 *Id.*

181 *Id.*

182 *See* Bill C- 41, *supra* note 139.

judge, and decision-maker regarding the guilt or innocence of the accused, as well as determining the sentence. There is a potential for bias in the presiding officer's decisions, as their close relationship with the accused may lead to preconceived opinions prior to the trial. Additionally, Commanding Officers typically lack formal judicial training and experience, raising concerns about their ability to effectively apply legal concepts, such as assessing guilt beyond a reasonable doubt, and ensuring a fair trial. This unchecked discretionary power in the hands of the commanding officer can lead to arbitrariness or discrimination, which would contravene Article 14 of the Indian Constitution.

The proceedings throughout is attended by two other persons who shall be officers or Junior Commissioned Officers or one of either but who shall not as such be sworn or affirmed,[183] and who have no right to vote in determining either the findings or the sentence. The officer holding the trial may consult them if he so desires[184] but their opinion is not binding upon the Court. Thus their presence is merely a cosmetic procedural safeguard afforded to the accused.

In any SCM though an accused according to laid down criteria of Fair Trial, is allowed a person or a legal advisor to assist him in his trial but he shall neither address the Court nor cross- examine the witnesses.[185] It is also not obligatory for the Court to provide the accused with a 'Friend' but only that propriety demands that a person of his choice be provided to the accused. Also by not doing so there is no violation of Army Rule 129, vitiating

183 AA 1950, § 116.
184 MML, chapter IV, ¶ 105.
185 AR 1954, r129.

the whole trial.[186] It is this discretion in the hands of the CO of allowing a lawyer or a defending officer of one's choice, which is usually given a go by.

Summary proceeding with its seemingly fair provisions of allowing a fellow defence member to assist with the defense of the accused is not all that fair. Jean Crowder, New Democratic Party, Member of Parliament from Nanaimo, Cowichan, debating[187] on Bill C-15 and especially on Summary Trials, opposed it on the grounds that it reproduces the contents of the former Bill C-41 but the recommendations given therein were not found incorporated in Bill C-15. She put forth in her debate portions from Bill C-41 that 'assisting Officers are not required to have any legal training, or any previous experience with the summary trial process. They are generally other Officers in the accused unit, who only undertake this role sporadically in addition to their normal duties and are appointed for the role under the authority of the presiding officer at a summary trial, which in itself presents a conflict of interest'.[188] Many assisting Officers therefore lack sufficient training and experience to provide an accused with effective representation.

Another aspect is that a defendant and their defending officer or 'friend' may not present the story clearly, but a good lawyer with an eye for legal relevance will be able to turn a defendant's account into a case by asking the right questions, raising legal objections to evidence and making submissions on point of law, 'something

---

186 Union of India and others v. Ex Havildar Clerk Prithi Pal Singh, 1992 (2) SLJ 177.

187 *Availableat*http://openparliament.ca/politicians/jean-crowder/?page=5 (Accessed on 04.04.2013).

188 Newhouse, *supra* note 140; *See also* Bill C- 41, *supra* note 139.

that a layman might simply lack the knowledge to achieve.'[189] The mere fact that a lawyer is prohibited to represent the accused in SCM proceedings is by in itself an inherent injustice. Article 14(3) of the ICCPR sets out 'minimum guarantees' for an accused facing criminal charges which stipulates the provision to defend oneself in person or through legal assistance of own choosing.[190] India being signatory to ICCPR, Summary authorities hearing offences would therefore be required by international law to allow defendants legal representation.

Thus the SCM proceedings casts a doubt in the minds of reasonably informed people as to the accused being afforded a Fair Trial since although there exists all the procedural protections in the Indian Military Justice System, the same is not accorded

---

189 Newhouse, *supra* note 140.

190 ICCPR, *supra* note 2, cl. 3 (it states that "In the determination of any criminal charge against him, everyone shall be entitled to the following minimum guarantees, in full equality: (a) To be informed promptly and in detail in a language which he understands of the nature and cause of the charge against him;

(b) To have adequate time and facilities for the preparation of his defence and to communicate with counsel of his own choosing;

(c) To be tried without undue delay;

(d) To be tried in his presence, and to defend himself in person or through legal assistance of his own choosing; to be informed, if he does not have legal assistance, of this right; and to have legal assistance assigned to him, in any case where the interests of justice so require, and without payment by him in any such case if he does not have sufficient means to pay for it;

(e) To examine, or have examined, the witnesses against him and to obtain the attendance and examination of witnesses on his behalf under the same conditions as witnesses against him;

(f) To have the free assistance of an interpreter if he cannot understand or speak the language used in court;

(g) Not to be compelled to testify against himself or to confess guilt).

in actual practice. The fair assessment of the guilt of the accused cannot be judged by officers without any legal knowledge and with application of lesser evidentiary value there is increased likelihood that the accused individuals will be found guilty.

SUMMARY COURT-MARTIAL AND DUE PROCESS

'Institutional and procedural' fairness,[191] wherein tribunals and courts are independent and impartial and the rights of parties are respected in accordance with the principles of Natural Justice, forms the foundation upon which the proper administration of justice rests.[192] Although the Summary Court-Martial (SCM) procedure incorporates certain elements of due process, the degree of procedural protection afforded to the accused is significantly reduced, despite the fact that the consequences of conviction are often severe. It is therefore imperative that, if SCM is to continue as part of the Military Justice System, adequate procedural safeguards are incorporated to ensure its constitutional validity.

The concept of due process was succinctly explained by the eminent lawyer and orator Daniel Webster in 1819 during his argument in the Dartmouth College case, where he described due process as:

"the general law; a law, which hears before it condemns; which proceeds upon inquiry, and renders judgment only after trial, the meaning is that every citizen shall hold his life, liberty,

---

191 Icelandic Human Rights Centre, The Right to Due Process, *available at* http://www.humanrights.is/the-human-rightsproject/humanrights casesandmaterials/comparativeanalysis/therighttodueprocess/ process/ (accessed on 04.03. 2013).

192 *Id.*

property, and immunities, under the protection of the general rules which govern society….."[193]

The Army Act and the Rules framed thereunder outline the responsibilities of summary authorities and embody a limited procedural version of due process. For example, an accused person has the right to seek a review of the verdict and sentence. However, such reviews are conducted within the chain of command, where the reviewing authorities may not possess the degree of independence ordinarily associated with judicial review. Moreover, since one of the primary objectives of the system is the maintenance of discipline, concerns arise regarding the impartiality of such reviews.

A further difficulty lies in the fact that punishment ordinarily commences immediately after promulgation. Consequently, by the time a superior authority considers a petition seeking mitigation, remission, or setting aside of the sentence, the accused may already have undergone the entire punishment. Even where the sentence is subsequently modified, the consequences may be irreversible. The accused is not only deprived of personal liberty but may also suffer lasting damage to his service record, future employment prospects, and means of livelihood.

Due process is inseparable from the concept of a fair trial. Every person accused of an offence is entitled to procedural fairness, and it is the duty of every court or tribunal to ensure that due process permeates every stage of the proceedings. Experience

193 Trustees of Dartmouth College v. Woodward, 17 U.S. (4 Wheat.) 518, 4 L. Ed. 629 (1819), *available at* http://www.constitution.org/dwebster/dartmouth_oral.htm (Accessed on14.03.2012).

demonstrates that when individuals perceive that a justice system not only contains the safeguards of a fair trial but also applies them fairly and consistently, they are more willing to accept even adverse outcomes.

While an accused under the Army Act is entitled to cross-examine witnesses, it must be recognised that many soldiers come from educational and social backgrounds that may not equip them with the skills, confidence, or legal understanding necessary to conduct an effective cross-examination. It may therefore be argued that merely providing the opportunity to cross-examine satisfies the requirements of a fair trial. In substance, however, such a right may prove illusory if the accused lacks the ability to exercise it meaningfully.

The absence of legal representation assumes particular significance in this context. Effective cross-examination, identification of inconsistencies, objections to inadmissible evidence, and the presentation of legal arguments are functions that are ordinarily performed by trained legal practitioners. Denying legal representation in proceedings where both liberty and livelihood are at stake raises serious concerns regarding procedural fairness.

Similarly, an accused who wishes to contest the charge may, owing to lack of legal knowledge or misguided advice from a defending officer or a "friend of the accused," be induced to plead guilty or refrain from effectively challenging the prosecution case. In such circumstances, the apparent voluntariness of the plea may not truly reflect an informed and conscious decision.

Tom R. Tyler, in his work on procedural justice, observed that:

"People care about the decision-making process. They consider evidence about representation, neutrality, bias, honesty, quality of decision, and consistency."[194]

Tyler further established a strong connection between perceptions of procedural fairness and acceptance of legal outcomes. According to his findings, people generally believe that fair outcomes are produced by fair procedures, while "a procedure which consistently produces unfair outcomes will be viewed as unfair itself."[195]

Claire Newhouse similarly notes that:

"Tyler found that people who experience what they considered unfair procedures had a reduced view of the legitimacy of the authority involved."[196]

These observations assume particular significance in the military context. A justice system that is perceived as unfair does not merely affect individual litigants; it also undermines confidence in the authority administering that system. Where service personnel perceive that procedural protections exist only in theory and not in practice, faith in the legitimacy of the military justice system is inevitably diminished. The challenge, therefore, is not merely to provide procedural safeguards on paper but to ensure that they are meaningfully available and effectively applied in every case.

---

194 Tom R Tyler, *What is Procedural Justice?: Criteria Used By Citizens to Assess the Fairness of Legal Procedures*, 22, no 1, Law and Society Review, 103, 136 (1988); *also cited* in Newhouse, *supra* note 140.

195 *Id.*

196 Newhouse, *supra* note 140.

REASONS FOR REDUCTION OF DUE PROCESS IN SUMMARY COURT-MARTIAL

Claire Newhouse, in her Master's thesis, examined the application of Dr. Doreen McBarnet's theory to summary proceedings conducted under the Australian Defence Force Discipline Act, 1982, and questioned whether the reduced procedural protections afforded in such proceedings could be justified.[197]

Drawing upon McBarnet's work, Newhouse observed that the criminal justice system often operates through two distinct tiers of justice: an "ideology of justice" applicable to the higher courts and an "ideology of triviality" applicable to the lower courts. According to McBarnet, it is this perception of triviality that frequently justifies the reduced application of due process safeguards. She concluded that lower courts dealing with minor offences cannot realistically adhere to every procedural requirement associated with formal justice because their primary objective is the expeditious delivery of summary justice.[198]

The rationale underlying McBarnet's theory, however, becomes difficult to sustain when examined in the context of the Summary Court-Martial (SCM) system in India. Under the Army Act,

---

197 *Id.* (The process of summary justice is considered using the theoretical framework developed by socio-legal academic, Dr Doreen McBarnet in 1979. Her research, mainly involving observational study in Scotland's lower courts, resulted in seminal sociological study focused on the structure, substance and procedure of the law. In particular her ideology of triviality in the lower level of the legal system is applied to summary justice under the Australian Army. It is argued that summary proceedings are inherently unjust by comparison with the standards applied in higher courts in the way they are administered with a reduction of due process).

198 McBarnet, *supra* note 141.

almost every offence punishable under the Act, barring a few specified exceptions,[199] may be tried by an SCM. Moreover, an SCM is empowered to award any punishment authorised by law, except a sentence of death or imprisonment exceeding one year.

While certain offences tried by SCM, such as overstaying leave or conduct prejudicial to good order and military discipline, may appear minor at first glance, the consequences of conviction are far from trivial. A sentence of imprisonment involves deprivation of personal liberty and is frequently accompanied by adverse service consequences, including dismissal or discharge from service. Such punishment may leave a permanent blemish on the service record of the individual concerned, thereby adversely affecting future employment prospects and livelihood. In these circumstances, the application of robust due process protections becomes not merely desirable but essential.

The reduced application of due process safeguards in SCM proceedings, despite the protections ostensibly available under the Army Act and the Rules, may partly be attributed to the nature of the proceedings themselves. SCMs are conducted in closed forums without the participation of legally qualified adjudicators, and legal representation is generally unavailable. Proceedings and transcripts are not readily accessible for public scrutiny, thereby limiting transparency and accountability.[200]

Furthermore, service personnel adversely affected by SCM verdicts often lack the financial resources necessary to pursue prolonged litigation before constitutional courts. As a consequence, relatively few SCM decisions are subjected

---

199 AA 1950, §§34, 37 & 69 .

200 Newhouse, *supra* note 140.

to judicial scrutiny, limiting the development of precedents that could otherwise guide reform. Academic engagement with the subject has also remained limited, possibly due to the widespread perception that the offences and punishments involved are minor, that SCM proceedings do not raise complex legal questions, or that any procedural deficiencies are justified by the overriding requirement of maintaining discipline within the Army.

There can be little doubt that during war, active operations, or other exigent circumstances, the need for speedy trials assumes particular importance. In such situations, some relaxation of procedural safeguards may be justified in the interests of maintaining discipline and operational effectiveness. However, the justification becomes considerably weaker during peacetime, when ordinary conditions prevail and the practical difficulties associated with active operations are absent. In such circumstances, the procedural protections available to service personnel should approximate, as closely as possible, those available within the civilian criminal justice system.

An additional consideration arises from the fact that neither the Indian Navy nor the Indian Air Force provides for a system equivalent to the Summary Court-Martial. Despite the absence of such proceedings, both Services continue to maintain discipline and operational effectiveness. This raises a legitimate question as to why the Indian Army requires a mechanism that permits a greater degree of encroachment upon the liberty of its personnel than is considered necessary in the other two Services.

It may be argued that the vastly larger strength, wider deployment, and operational commitments of the Indian Army necessitate the retention of SCM proceedings. Even if that contention is accepted, it does not justify the uniform application of reduced procedural safeguards in all situations. A meaningful distinction ought to be drawn between exigent and non-exigent circumstances, with the degree of procedural protection varying accordingly. Such an approach would better reconcile the legitimate demands of military discipline with the constitutional commitment to fairness, liberty, and due process.

DISCIPLINE VERSUS DUE PROCESS: THE CONSTITUTIONAL DILEMMA OF SUMMARY COURT-MARTIAL

The constitutional validity of Summary Court-Martial (SCM) proceedings must be examined against the guarantees of equality and personal liberty embodied in Articles 14 and 21 of the Constitution of India. While military discipline undoubtedly constitutes a legitimate constitutional objective, the means adopted for its enforcement must satisfy the requirements of fairness, reasonableness, and non-arbitrariness that now form an integral part of Indian constitutional jurisprudence.

During the framing of the Constitution, the Constituent Assembly consciously omitted the expression "due process of law," largely to avoid judicial supremacy over legislative action. However, as Abhinav Chandrachud points out, by conferring upon Constitutional Courts the power of substantive review under Articles 14 and 19 and procedural review under Article 22, the Constitution effectively incorporated a doctrine closely resembling due process within Indian constitutional jurisprudence, notwithstanding the absence of the phrase itself.[201]

201 Abhinav Chandrachud, Due Process of Law, (Eastern Book Company, New Delhi, 2011).

Over the years, judicial interpretation of Article 21 has considerably expanded the protection of life and personal liberty. The Supreme Court has transformed the expression "procedure established by law" into a requirement that such procedure must be fair, just, and reasonable. In the foreword to Abhinav Chandrachud's work, former Supreme Court Judge Justice R. V. Raveendran observes that Indian constitutional jurisprudence has substantially bridged the gap between "procedure established by law" and "due process of law," thereby incorporating procedural fairness, the right to be heard before condemnation, adjudication only after a fair trial, and deprivation of life and liberty only in accordance with just, fair, and reasonable procedure.[202] The ambit of Article 21 has further expanded to include the right to legal representation, legal aid, privacy, and other protections commonly associated with substantive due process.

Article 14 complements these protections by guaranteeing equality before the law and equal protection of the laws. The legitimacy of any legal system depends upon the assurance that similarly situated persons are treated alike and that distinctions are based upon intelligible and rational criteria. This principle is also reflected in Article 14(1) of the International Covenant on Civil and Political Rights (ICCPR), which provides that "all persons shall be equal before the courts and tribunals."

When examined in the light of Articles 14 and 21, the Summary Court-Martial procedure appears difficult to reconcile with the constitutional commitment to equality and fairness. India, being a signatory to the ICCPR, is under an obligation to respect and promote the rights recognised therein. It may be argued that Article 33 of the Constitution empowers Parliament to restrict

202 *Id.*

or abrogate certain rights of Armed Forces personnel in the interests of discipline and operational effectiveness. However, Article 33 does not authorise discrimination amongst members of the Armed Forces themselves.

Yet this is precisely the anomaly created by the SCM system. Summary Court-Martial is applicable only to Non-Commissioned Officers and soldiers below that rank, and only within the Indian Army. Personnel of the Indian Navy and the Indian Air Force are not subjected to an equivalent procedure for the maintenance of discipline. Thus, even if members of the Armed Forces are regarded as a distinct class for constitutional purposes, a further classification is created within that class without any obvious rational basis.

The result is that Army personnel occupying the lowest rungs of the military hierarchy alone are exposed to a procedure characterised by reduced procedural safeguards, notwithstanding that the consequences may include deprivation of liberty, dismissal from service, and long-term damage to future employment prospects. Such a distinction raises serious concerns under Article 14 of the Constitution.

The Supreme Court itself has recognised the limits of military exceptionalism when it observed:

".......In the larger interest of national security and military discipline Parliament in its wisdom may restrict or abrogate such rights in their application to the Armed Forces but this process should not be carried so far as to create a class of citizens not entitled to the benefits of the liberal spirit of the Constitution. Persons subject to Army Act are citizens of this ancient land having a feeling of belonging to the civilised community governed by the liberty-oriented Constitution. Personal liberty makes for the worth of human being and is a cherished and prized right. Deprivation thereof must be preceded by an enquiry ensuring fair, just and reasonable procedure and trial by a judge of unquestioned integrity and wholly unbiased….."[203]

The constitutional concerns become even more pronounced when one considers the structure of the SCM itself. The Commanding Officer effectively combines the functions of investigator, prosecutor, judge, and sentencing authority. He determines whether charges are to be proceeded with, conducts the trial, records findings, and imposes sentence. The same officer may award punishments extending to confinement in military custody, imprisonment in a civil prison, and dismissal from service. Such concentration of authority in a single individual would be difficult to justify in any other system of criminal justice governed by constitutional norms.

The position is further aggravated by the absence of legal representation. The accused, whose liberty and livelihood may both be at stake, is ordinarily denied the assistance of a lawyer and must often rely upon a defending officer or a "friend of the accused," who may possess neither legal training nor experience in conducting trials. While the SCM procedure ostensibly affords an opportunity to cross-examine witnesses and present a defence, these rights may prove more theoretical than real when exercised by individuals lacking the legal knowledge necessary to effectively challenge the prosecution case.

Claire Newhouse, drawing upon McBarnet's work, notes that:

---

203 Lt. Col. P.P.S Bedi, *supra* note 73.

"according to McBarnet, the ideology of democratic justice required due process of law before permitting interferences with a person's liberty."[204]

The deprivation of liberty through a procedure that provides diminished procedural safeguards therefore raises fundamental constitutional concerns. The issue is not whether discipline should be maintained within the Armed Forces; rather, it is whether discipline can be enforced through a process that departs significantly from the standards of fairness ordinarily expected whenever the State seeks to interfere with an individual's liberty.

The significance of procedural fairness in SCM proceedings was also recognised by the Delhi High Court. In a recent judgment, Justice Vikramjit Sen observed:

"Mindful of the fact that Article 33 of the Constitution of India confers unbridled powers on Parliament to bring into place a situation which severely abridges the Fundamental Rights of a citizen it becomes the bounden duty of the Courts to ensure that the equality doctrine is not needlessly nullified. It also becomes essential that the Courts should interpret the law in a manner which will reduce to the minimum the inroads into the intangible rights contained in Chapter III of the Constitution."[205]

These observations underscore the central constitutional dilemma surrounding the Summary Court-Martial. While military discipline remains indispensable to operational effectiveness, constitutional guarantees cannot be rendered illusory merely because the individual concerned wears a

204 Newhouse, *supra* note 140.

205 Ex LN Vishav Priya Singh, *supra* note 88.

uniform. The challenge lies in striking an appropriate balance between the legitimate demands of discipline and the equally compelling requirements of equality, fairness, and personal liberty. Unless adequate procedural safeguards accompany the exercise of disciplinary power, the constitutional validity of the Summary Court-Martial procedure will continue to remain open to serious debate.

THE JUDICIARY IN RELATION TO SUMMARY COURT-MARTIAL

The provisions governing Summary Court-Martial proceedings contain a number of procedural safeguards intended to protect the rights of the accused. However, as discussed in the preceding sections, the implementation of these safeguards has often been found wanting. Prior to the enactment of the Armed Forces Tribunal Act, 2007, the findings and sentences of a Summary Court-Martial were, for all practical purposes, final. Even after the establishment of the Armed Forces Tribunal, no statutory right of appeal exists against the findings of an SCM unless the sentence awarded includes imprisonment exceeding three months.

Within the Indian Army, the Summary Court-Martial remains the most frequently employed mechanism for formally disciplining personnel. Its extensive use over the years has attracted considerable criticism from jurists, scholars, and courts alike. According to U. C. Jha, during the six-year period from 1999 to 2004, an average of 995 SCMs were conducted annually. Such extensive reliance upon a summary procedure has inevitably resulted in a large number of service personnel being deprived of their liberty, livelihood, pensionary benefits, and future career prospects through decisions rendered by their own commanding officers in the name of discipline.[206]

U. C. Jha further argues that:

"the unbridled discretionary power of a Commanding Officer to hold an SCM may degenerate into arbitrariness or discrimination and is, therefore, violative of Article 14."[207]

The constitutional concerns surrounding SCM proceedings have not escaped judicial scrutiny. The Supreme Court of India, various High Courts, and more recently the Armed Forces Tribunal, have repeatedly expressed reservations regarding the indiscriminate use of Summary Court-Martial proceedings, particularly against personnel belonging to the lower ranks of the Army.

Judicial pronouncements reveal a recurring concern that the procedure, though intended as an exceptional mechanism for dealing with urgent disciplinary situations, has often been employed as a matter of routine. Courts have observed that adequate safeguards against misuse are lacking and have, in numerous cases, interfered with SCM findings on grounds of procedural unfairness, bias, disproportionality of punishment, violation of principles of natural justice, and non-compliance with statutory requirements.

Several judgments have emphasised that Summary Court-Martial proceedings should be resorted to only in exceptional

206 U.C. Jha, *Summary Court Martial: A Colonial Legacy in Army*, The Hindu Open Page, Feb.17, 2008, *available at* http://www.hindu.com/op/2008/02/17/stories/2008021750011600.htm (Accessed on 11.03.2012).

207 *Id.*

circumstances where immediate disciplinary action is genuinely warranted. The judiciary has repeatedly cautioned that expediency cannot be permitted to override the fundamental requirements of fairness and justice, particularly when the consequences of conviction may include imprisonment, dismissal from service, loss of livelihood, and long-term social and economic hardship.

A survey of the important judicial decisions on the subject demonstrates the growing concern of constitutional courts regarding the manner in which Summary Court-Martial proceedings have been conducted and highlights the gradual evolution of judicial safeguards intended to protect the rights of service personnel. Some of the more significant decisions are discussed below.

VIOLATION OF MANDATORY PROCEDURAL REQUIREMENTS

Army Rule 115(2) of the Army Rules, 1954 is a mandatory provision. Before recording a plea of guilty, it is the duty of the Court to satisfy itself that the accused fully understands the nature of the charge, the implications of the plea, and the consequences likely to follow from such plea. The Rule further contemplates that where, upon consideration of the Summary of Evidence, it appears that the accused may not in fact be guilty of the offence charged, the Court should advise the accused to withdraw the plea of guilty and proceed with the trial in accordance with law.

Compliance with these safeguards is of particular importance because a plea of guilty dispenses with the necessity of a full trial and may result in serious consequences affecting the liberty, livelihood, and future prospects of the accused. Any departure from the prescribed procedure therefore strikes at the very foundation of a fair trial.

The mere fact that the plea of guilty was neither formally recorded nor signed by the accused in the original proceedings may itself indicate that the accused was not properly informed of the general effect of such plea. In such circumstances, findings based solely upon the alleged plea of guilty lose much of their legal significance.[208] The real issue is not whether the accused uttered the words "guilty," but whether the mandatory procedure prescribed by law was faithfully followed before such plea was accepted.

Similarly, Army Rule 125 of the Army Rules, 1954 mandates that:

"the Court shall put the date and sign the sentence and such signature shall authenticate the same."[209]

The requirement is not a mere formality. It is intended to ensure the authenticity and integrity of the proceedings and to provide a reliable record of the sentence awarded. Failure to comply with such mandatory provisions casts doubt upon the legality of the proceedings themselves.

A recurring criticism of Summary Court-Martial proceedings is the extraordinary haste with which they are often conducted. In many cases, the accused is served with the charge-sheet on the very day the trial commences, leaving little or no opportunity to

---

208 Ex. Havildar Clerk Prithipal Singh, *supra* note 208; *See also* Lachman (Ex Rect) v. Union of India and Others 2003 II AD (Delhi) 183.

209 Ex. Naik Mast Ram v. Union of India, T.A. 204 of 2010, W.P (C) No. 12289 of 2005 *available at* www.aftdelhi.nic.in/benches/...2/.../ Nayak%20Mast%Ram.pdf (Accessed on30.03.2012)

prepare an effective defence. Such practice appears inconsistent with the spirit, if not the letter, of Army Rules 34(1)[210] and 33(7),[211] which contemplate adequate notice and opportunity for preparation before trial.

Commenting upon such a practice, Justice Saran of the Allahabad High Court observed:

"Even otherwise, the Summary Court Martial, as the words suggest, is in fact a summary procedure of trial meant to be adopted in cases of extreme urgency, to meet out instant justice, which may be necessary for discipline and security in the Armed Force. In the present case, it is not understood as to what was the grave urgency after more than six months of the incident which is alleged to have taken place on 4.1.1992, that the entire

---

210 AR 1954, r 34 (1) (it states that the accused before he is arraigned shall be informed by an officer of every charge for which he is to be tried and also that on his giving the names of witnesses or whom he desires to call in his defence, reasonable steps will be taken for procuring their attendance, and those steps shall be taken accordingly. The internal between his being informed and his arrangement shall not be less than ninety six hours or where the accused in on active service less than twenty-four hours).

211 AR 1954, r 33 (7) (the Rule states that As soon as practicable after an accused has been remanded for trial by a General or District Court Martial, and in any case not less than ninety-six hours or an active service twenty-four hours before his trial, an officer shall be given to him free of charge a copy of the summary of evidence, an abstract of the evidence, and explain to him his rights under these Rules as to preparing his defense and being assisted or represented at the trial, and shall ask him to state in writing whether or not he wishes to have an officer assigned by the convening officer to represent him at the trial, if a suitable officer should be available. The convening officer shall be informed whether or not the accused so elects).

proceedings were to be initiated and concluded on the same date i.e., 6.7.1992."[212]

The above observation highlights a recurring concern in judicial scrutiny of Summary Court-Martial proceedings. A procedure designed as an exceptional mechanism to address situations of genuine urgency cannot be routinely invoked in circumstances where no immediate disciplinary necessity exists. Where considerable time has already elapsed between the alleged offence and the commencement of proceedings, the justification for dispensing with ordinary procedural safeguards becomes increasingly difficult to sustain. In such cases, haste may undermine fairness and raise legitimate doubts regarding the validity of the proceedings.

VIOLATION OF THE PRINCIPLES OF NATURAL JUSTICE

The Delhi High Court, in a judgment delivered by a Division Bench comprising Justices A. K. Sikri and J. M. Malik in the case of *LNK Gurdev Singh*,[213] came down heavily on the Army authorities while examining the validity of Summary Court-Martial proceedings and ultimately quashed the same.

The petitioner had been subjected to SCM proceedings on what were alleged to be false and concocted charges and was subsequently lodged in a civil jail. It was contended that the proceedings had been conducted without adherence to the prescribed procedure and in complete disregard of the principles

---

212 Ex Naik Natwarlal v. Union of India and Others (2004)1 UPLBEC 266.

213 LNK Gurdev Singh v. Union of India, W.P (C) 776 of 1995 dt 01.02.08 (Delhi H.C), *available at* http://www.indiankanoon.org/doc/1769443 (last visited on Mar.30, 2012)

of natural justice. The respondents sought to justify their actions by asserting that due process had been followed. However, their version stood contradicted by independent evidence, including certificates issued by the police authorities and medical records produced before the Court.

Upon examining the material on record, the High Court found the proceedings to be tainted by mala fides, procedural irregularities, and a complete absence of fair play. The Court held that the Summary Court-Martial proceedings were not only violative of the principles of natural justice but were also manifestly unjust and unsustainable in law.

The Court expressed serious displeasure regarding the conduct of the officer who had conducted the proceedings and observed that the circumstances of the case were such that it would have considered directing action against the concerned officer. However, since the services of the officer concerned, who was respondent No. 4 in the proceedings, had already been terminated, no such direction could effectively be issued.

The decision serves as a stark reminder that even within the military justice system, disciplinary considerations cannot override the fundamental requirements of fairness, impartiality, and adherence to the principles of natural justice.

FRIEND OF THE ACCUSED

In a typical Summary Court-Martial proceeding, the accused is ordinarily required to conduct his own defence, notwithstanding his limited knowledge of law and procedure. Unlike proceedings before ordinary criminal courts, the accused is not entitled to be represented by a legal practitioner or defending officer. He may, however, be assisted by a "Friend of the Accused," who may or may not be subject to the Army Act and may or may not possess any legal qualifications. The role of such a friend is severely restricted, as he may only advise the accused and is not permitted to address the Court or examine or cross-examine witnesses on the accused's behalf.

The importance of this safeguard was recognised in *Joga Singh's case*,[214] wherein it was held that a trial may stand vitiated if a proper friend is not made available to the accused. The Court further observed that, wherever possible, the friend should be a person of the accused's own choice and that the accused should be consulted before any individual is detailed for that purpose.

At the same time, the courts have adopted a somewhat limited approach towards this requirement. In *Ex. Havildar Prithi Pal Singh*,[215] it was held that the mere fact that the friend provided was not of the accused's choice would not, by itself, vitiate the entire trial.

However, where a particular individual is imposed upon the accused against his wishes, such action may amount to a denial of the right of assistance contemplated under Army Rule 129.[216] The object of the Rule is not merely the formal appointment of a friend but the provision of meaningful assistance to the accused during the trial process.

---

214 Joga Singh v. Union of India, 1996 Lab IC 677 (Delhi); *also cited* in Major JL Obheroi, *Military Law and Writs,* 346 (SAAR Printers, Chandigarh, 2007).

215 Ex. Havildar Clerk Prithipal Singh, *supra* note 208.

216 COAS v. Sep Dvr MZ H Khan, MIL LJ 2006 All 152 , *also cited* in Major JL Obheroi, *Military Law and Writs,* 346 (SAAR Printers, Chandigarh, 2007).

A different view emerged in *Havildar Akbar Singh's case*,[217] where the validity of the trial was upheld despite the absence of a Friend of the Accused. The Court reasoned that since the accused had pleaded guilty, there was no necessity for examination or cross-examination of witnesses and, consequently, the absence of a friend did not occasion any prejudice.

This reasoning has not escaped criticism. Commenting upon the decision, Major J. L. Oberoi observed:

"......the ruling in the case of Hav. Akbar Singh must not be regarded as a precedent. A friend, if provided to Hav. Akbar Singh, might have advised the accused to plead not guilty; also any points in mitigation of punishment including his antecedents, social and economic background, effect on family, could have been forcefully urged."[218]

The criticism appears well-founded. The value of a Friend of the Accused does not lie merely in assisting during the examination of witnesses. Equally important is the advice that such a person may provide before the plea is entered, particularly where the accused lacks legal knowledge and may not fully appreciate the consequences of pleading guilty. A competent friend may assist the accused in understanding the nature of the charge, evaluating available defences, and presenting mitigating circumstances relevant to sentence. The absence of such assistance therefore raises serious concerns regarding the fairness of SCM proceedings, especially when the accused faces consequences affecting both his liberty and livelihood.

---

217 Hav Akbar Singh v. Union of India, Mil LJ, 2005 All 102, *available at* http://indiankanoon.org/doc/941425/ (Accessed on 31.03.2012)

218 Major J.L.Obheroi, Military Law and Writs, 346 (SAAR Printers, Chandigarh, 2007).

BIAS AND THE RIGHT TO A FAIR TRIAL: JUDICIAL RESPONSES

One of the fundamental requirements of a fair trial is that justice must not only be done but must also be seen to be done. The concept of bias strikes at the very root of judicial fairness, for even the appearance of prejudice is capable of undermining public confidence in the administration of justice. This principle assumes particular significance in military justice, where the adjudicators often function within a command structure and are not institutionally insulated from the executive hierarchy.

In *Ranjit Thakur v. Union of India*,[219] the Supreme Court considered the question of bias in court-martial proceedings and quoted with approval the observations of Lord Denning in *Metropolitan Properties Co. (F.G.C.) Ltd. v. Lannon*:

"...in considering whether there was a real likelihood of bias, the court does not look at the mind of the justice himself or at the mind of the chairman of the tribunal, or whoever it may be, who sits in a judicial capacity. It does not look to see if there was a real likelihood that he would, or did, in fact favour one side at the expense of the other. The court looks at the impression which would be given to other people. Even if he was as impartial as could be, nevertheless if right-minded persons would think that in the circumstances there was a real likelihood of bias on his part, then he should not sit..."[220]

While adjudicating the issue, the Supreme Court further held:

219 Ranjit Thakur v Union of India, AIR 1987, SC 238.
220 [1969] 1 Q.B. 577, at 599 (cited in Ranjit Thakur's case).

"...the test of real likelihood of bias is whether a reasonable person, in possession of relevant information, would have thought that bias was likely and is whether respondent No. 4 was likely to be disposed to decide the matter only in a particular way. It is the essence of a judgment that it is made after due observance of the judicial process; that the Court or Tribunal passing it observes, at least the minimal requirements of natural justice, is composed of impartial persons acting fairly and without bias and in good faith. A judgment which is the result of bias or want of impartiality is a nullity and the trial 'coram non judice'. As to the tests of the likelihood of bias, what is relevant is the reasonableness of the apprehension in that regard in the mind of the party. The proper approach for the Judge is not to look at his own mind and ask himself, however honestly, 'Am I biased?' but to look at the mind of the party before him."[221]

The Court thus made it clear that the question is not whether actual bias can be proved, but whether a reasonable and informed person would apprehend a real likelihood of bias. The appearance of fairness is therefore as important as fairness itself. This principle is particularly relevant in Summary Court-Martial proceedings, where the Commanding Officer occupies multiple roles and exercises extensive authority over the proceedings.

The Supreme Court also addressed the issue of punishment and observed that although the choice and quantum of punishment ordinarily fall within the jurisdiction and discretion of the Court-Martial, such discretion is not unfettered. The Court held that:

"the sentence has to suit the offence and the offender. It should not be vindictive or unduly harsh. It should not be so

221 Ranjit Thakur, *supra* note 219.

disproportionate to the offence as to shock the conscience and amount in itself to conclusive evidence of bias."

The significance of *Ranjit Thakur* lies not merely in its recognition of bias as a ground for judicial intervention, but in its affirmation that military justice is subject to the same fundamental principles of natural justice that govern all judicial and quasi-judicial proceedings. The judgment underscores that a court-martial cannot be insulated from judicial review merely because it operates within the military sphere. Where there exists a reasonable apprehension of bias, lack of impartiality, or a punishment so disproportionate as to shock the judicial conscience, the courts are duty-bound to intervene.[222]

The decision therefore remains a landmark authority on judicial review of court-martial proceedings and serves as an important safeguard against arbitrary exercise of disciplinary power within the Armed Forces.

PUNISHMENT DISPROPORTIONATE TO THE OFFENCE: THE DOCTRINE OF PROPORTIONALITY

The doctrine of proportionality constitutes an important safeguard against arbitrary exercise of disciplinary and administrative power. While the Army Act, the Army Rules, and the Regulations for the Army prescribe various factors that should be taken into consideration while determining sentence, judicial experience has shown that these considerations are not always adequately applied in practice. The result is that punishments awarded in certain cases appear excessive when viewed in relation to the nature of the offence and the circumstances of the offender.

222 *Id*

Although dismissal from service occupies a comparatively lower position in the statutory scale of punishments,[223] its practical consequences may often be far more severe than a short term of imprisonment. Dismissal not only terminates a soldier's career but may also result in the loss of pensionary benefits, future employment opportunities, and social standing. Consequently, courts have increasingly scrutinised such punishments to ensure that they are proportionate to the misconduct alleged.

The importance of proportionality was recognised by the Himachal Pradesh High Court,[224] which, after examining the facts of the case before it, set aside the punishment of dismissal from service coupled with six months' rigorous imprisonment awarded through Summary Court-Martial proceedings. The accused had been charged with using criminal force against a superior officer while serving with the Indian Peace Keeping Force in Sri Lanka. The Court found the punishment imposed to be disproportionate to the offence and consequently interfered with the sentence awarded.

The doctrine received further judicial recognition in *Sardar Singh's case*,[225] wherein the Court referred to the celebrated observations of Lord Diplock in *Council of Civil Service Unions v. Minister for the Civil Service*:[226]

"Judicial review has I think developed to a stage today when, without reiterating any analysis of the steps by which the development has come about, one can conveniently classify under three heads the grounds on which administrative action

223 AA 1950, §71.

224 Chaudhry M.R Ex Sepoy v. Union of India, CWP No 563 of 1990.

225 Ex Naik Sardar Singh v Union of India, (1991) 3 SCC 213.

226 (1984) 3 All ER 935, 950.

is subject to control by judicial review. The first ground I would call 'Illegality', the second 'irrationality' and the third 'procedural impropriety'. This is not to say that further development on a case by case basis may not in course of time add further grounds. I have in mind particularly the possible adoption in the future of the principle of 'proportionality' which is recognised in the administrative law of several of our fellow members of the European Economic Community..."

The Court further observed that a similar approach had been adopted by the Supreme Court in *Ranjit Thakur v. Union of India*,[227] where the doctrine of proportionality was applied in the military justice context. In that case, the Supreme Court emphasised that while the choice and quantum of punishment ordinarily fall within the discretion of the Court-Martial, such discretion is not absolute and remains subject to judicial review where the punishment imposed is so excessive as to shock the conscience of the Court.

The principle emerging from these decisions is that every statutory power, however wide, carries within it legal limitations. Disciplinary authorities cannot exercise their powers arbitrarily or vindictively. As the courts have repeatedly emphasised:

"The wider the power, the greater the need for restraint in its exercise and correspondingly, more liberal the construction of the procedural safeguards envisaged by the statute."[228]

---

227 Ranjit Thakur *supra* note 219, Bhagat Ram v. State of Himachal Pradesh, A.I.R. 1983 SC, 454 (Court held: 'It is equally true that the penalty imposed must be commensurate with the gravity of the misconduct and that any penalty disproportionate to the gravity of the misconduct would be violative of Article 14 of the Constitution).'

228 *Id.*

The doctrine of proportionality therefore serves as an essential constitutional check upon military disciplinary powers. While discipline remains indispensable to the effectiveness of the Armed Forces, punishment must bear a reasonable relationship to both the offence committed and the circumstances of the offender. A sentence that is excessive, oppressive, or manifestly disproportionate not only undermines confidence in the military justice system but may itself become evidence of unfairness warranting judicial intervention.

SUMMARY COURT-MARTIAL SHOULD BE AN EXCEPTION, NOT THE RULE

A significant judicial restraint upon the indiscriminate use of Summary Court-Martial proceedings was articulated by the Delhi High Court in *Ex. Lance Naik Vishav Priya Singh v. Union of India*, decided on 25 January 2008.[229] The Division Bench emphatically held that the Summary Court-Martial procedure was intended to be an exceptional mechanism and not the normal mode of trial for service personnel.

The Court observed that an SCM should be resorted to only where there exists a grave and compelling necessity for immediate disciplinary action. In such circumstances, the urgency justifying the convening of an SCM must be expressly recorded and supported by reasons in writing. Failure to disclose the circumstances necessitating immediate action would itself constitute a valid ground for judicial interference and, where appropriate, for setting aside the proceedings.

229 Ex LN Vishav Priya Singh, *supra* note 88.

Examining the facts of the case, where the petitioners had not been tried by their own Commanding Officer, the Court laid down certain important principles governing the exercise of SCM jurisdiction.

First, the Court reiterated that, as a general rule, a soldier should be tried by his own Commanding Officer. Departure from this principle is permissible only in exceptional situations, particularly in cases involving deserters, and even then only when the Commanding Officer of the concerned unit is not readily available.

Secondly, the Court emphasised that the SCM is an extraordinary procedure designed to meet situations requiring urgent and immediate action. It cannot be employed as a matter of administrative convenience or routine disciplinary practice. The justification for invoking such a summary procedure must be based upon circumstances where delay would seriously prejudice military discipline or operational effectiveness. Consequently, where the alleged misconduct is purely individual in nature or primarily involves issues ordinarily falling within the realm of civil law, resort to an SCM would generally be inappropriate.

Thirdly, the Court held that the decision to convene an SCM must be supported by a reasoned order capable of withstanding judicial scrutiny. The recording of reasons is not an empty formality but an important safeguard against arbitrary exercise of power. It enables the courts to examine whether the exceptional procedure was genuinely warranted and whether the accused's right to a fair trial has been unnecessarily curtailed.

The Court expressed the view that if these safeguards are faithfully observed, the abridgement of procedural protections inherent in

SCM proceedings would remain confined to those rare situations where the demands of military discipline genuinely outweigh the minor civil rights affected by the procedure.[230]

The judgment in *Vishav Priya Singh* marks an important development in military jurisprudence. By insisting that Summary Court-Martial proceedings remain an exception rather than the norm, the Court sought to restore the balance between the legitimate requirements of military discipline and the constitutional obligation to ensure fairness, reasonableness, and due process. The decision serves as a reminder that the extraordinary nature of SCM proceedings must be matched by equally compelling circumstances justifying their use.

CONCLUSION

The institution of the Summary Court-Martial traces its origins to the aftermath of the Bengal Army Mutiny of 1857, when the British administration considered it necessary to equip Commanding Officers with extraordinary disciplinary powers to maintain order and suppress insubordination within the ranks. The system was conceived in an era when the protection of individual rights occupied a far less prominent position than the preservation of military discipline and imperial authority. More than a century and a half later, however, the legal and constitutional landscape has undergone a fundamental transformation. Across the world, and particularly in the United Kingdom from where much of India's military justice system derives its origin, military justice has increasingly evolved towards greater recognition of individual rights, procedural fairness, and judicial oversight.

---

230 *Id.*

The continued existence of Summary Court-Martial proceedings in their present form therefore raises important constitutional and policy questions. Under this procedure, soldiers may face imprisonment, dismissal from service, loss of pensionary benefits, and lifelong stigma, often without the benefit of legal representation and with only limited procedural safeguards. Moreover, where the sentence awarded is less than three months' imprisonment, there exists no statutory right of appeal before the Armed Forces Tribunal. Such consequences extend far beyond the sphere of military discipline and have a lasting impact upon the liberty, livelihood, and future prospects of the individual concerned.

The anomaly becomes more apparent when viewed in the context of the other branches of the Armed Forces. Neither the Indian Navy nor the Indian Air Force retains a comparable procedure, yet both continue to maintain discipline and operational effectiveness. This inevitably raises the question whether the exceptional powers embodied in the SCM remain necessary in their present form, or whether they require substantial modification to align with contemporary constitutional values.

A further concern arises from the structure of the proceedings themselves. The accused is tried by a Commanding Officer who may have had prior dealings with him and who ordinarily possesses no formal legal training. Although the Army Act and the Army Rules contain provisions intended to secure fairness, judicial decisions examined in this chapter demonstrate that these safeguards are not always observed in practice. The recurring concerns regarding bias, denial of adequate assistance, disproportionate punishment, procedural irregularities, and misuse of SCM proceedings have repeatedly invited judicial intervention.

This is not to suggest that the Commanding Officer should be divested of all disciplinary authority. The maintenance of discipline remains indispensable to the effectiveness of any armed force, and Commanding Officers must possess adequate powers to deal swiftly with minor misconduct and breaches of service discipline. However, where proceedings may result in serious penal consequences affecting personal liberty, livelihood, or reputation, a greater degree of procedural protection becomes both desirable and necessary. In such cases, consideration may be given to affording the accused a choice of forum or ensuring access to enhanced safeguards consistent with the principles of a fair trial.

There can be little doubt that Summary Court-Martial proceedings serve an operational purpose, particularly in exceptional circumstances requiring immediate disciplinary action. Nevertheless, the system suffers from concerns relating to structural independence, impartiality, and due process. The central question is therefore not whether discipline should be maintained, but whether the means employed to enforce discipline adequately respect the constitutional rights of the citizen-soldier.

Ultimately, a military justice system commands legitimacy not merely because it punishes misconduct swiftly, but because it does so fairly. A system that balances discipline with due process, authority with accountability, and operational necessity with constitutional values is more likely to inspire confidence among service personnel and strengthen, rather than weaken, military discipline. In the final analysis, respect for individual rights and the maintenance of discipline are not competing objectives; properly understood, they are complementary pillars of an effective and credible military justice system.

CHAPTER 06

Comparing the Pre-Trial, Trial, and Post-Trial Processes: Civilian Criminal Procedure vs. Military Law

INTRODUCTION

The administration of criminal justice in civilian society and within the Armed Forces is governed by distinct legal frameworks designed to achieve different objectives. While the civilian criminal justice system is primarily concerned with the maintenance of public order, protection of individual rights, and punishment of offences against society, the military justice system is directed towards the preservation of discipline, operational effectiveness, and command authority within the Armed Forces. These differing objectives have resulted in the evolution of separate procedural mechanisms governing the investigation, trial, and punishment of offenders.

Pre-Trial Process

The criminal process under the Criminal Procedure Code, 1973 (CrPC), now substantially replaced by the Bharatiya Nagarik Suraksha Sanhita, 2023 (BNSS), follows a structured sequence consisting of pre-trial, trial, and post-trial stages. The process ordinarily commences with the reporting of an offence and an investigation conducted by the police. The investigative stage includes the collection of evidence, examination of witnesses, arrest of suspects where necessary, and submission of a final report or charge sheet before the competent court. Judicial oversight forms an integral feature of this process, particularly in matters relating to arrest, detention, bail, and the framing of charges.

The civilian criminal justice system, however, continues to face several practical challenges. Delays in investigation, shortage of trained personnel, inadequate technological integration, procedural lapses, court congestion, and the growing backlog of cases often impede the timely administration of justice. Despite these difficulties, the system is structured around constitutional guarantees intended to safeguard the rights of the accused through judicial supervision and adherence to established procedural norms.

The military justice system operates within a significantly different institutional environment. Military offences are investigated and prosecuted under specialised statutory frameworks such as the Army Act, 1950, the Navy Act, 1957, and the Air Force Act, 1950. Unlike the civilian system, where responsibility for investigation, prosecution, adjudication, and appellate review is distributed among different authorities, military justice frequently concentrates several of these functions within the chain of command. The Commanding Officer occupies a central role in the disciplinary process and exercises substantial authority at various stages of the proceedings.

Where a service person is suspected of committing an offence, the matter may be investigated by military authorities, including the Military Police, Boards of Inquiry, Courts of Inquiry, or other designated investigating officers, depending upon the nature of the allegation. Military personnel may be placed in military custody, and decisions relating to further disciplinary action are often influenced by considerations unique to military service, including operational requirements, unit discipline, and command responsibility. Although procedural safeguards exist within the military justice system, their nature and extent differ considerably from those available under the civilian criminal process.

A comparison between the two systems reveals significant differences in the manner in which procedural rights are protected and exercised. The civilian criminal justice system is founded upon a separation of investigative, prosecutorial, and adjudicatory functions, whereas military justice places greater emphasis upon command responsibility and disciplinary control. These distinctions have generated continuing debate regarding the extent to which military procedures should conform to civilian standards of due process and fair trial, particularly where the liberty, livelihood, and reputation of service personnel are at stake.

For the sake of clarity and analytical coherence, the present chapter focuses primarily on the Army Act, 1950 and the procedures governing the Indian Army. Through a comparative examination of the pre-trial, trial, and post-trial stages under both civilian and military law, the chapter seeks to identify the distinctive features of military justice, evaluate the procedural safeguards available to service personnel, and examine whether the existing framework adequately balances the demands of military discipline with the requirements of fairness and due process.

COURT OF INQUIRY

A Court of Inquiry (COI) is a fact-finding body convened by a Commanding Officer (CO) to investigate a particular incident and submit a report enabling the competent military authority to determine the appropriate course of action in accordance with law. Comprising Officers, Junior Commissioned Officers (JCOs), and where necessary Non-Commissioned Officers (NCOs), the COI serves an investigative rather than adjudicatory function.[231, 232] Its primary purpose is the collection of evidence and the ascertainment of facts relating to matters referred to it by the convening authority.

In many respects, the role performed by a Court of Inquiry is comparable to the investigative process contemplated under Chapter XII of the Code of Criminal Procedure, 1973 and the corresponding provisions of the Bharatiya Nagarik Suraksha Sanhita, 2023. Both mechanisms are intended to gather relevant material, ascertain the circumstances surrounding an incident, and enable the competent authority to decide whether further proceedings should be initiated.

Army Rule 177 lays down the broad framework governing the constitution and functions of a Court of Inquiry. The Rule authorises the assembly of Officers, JCOs, Women Officers, or NCOs for the purpose of collecting evidence and reporting

231 Army Rules 1950 (AR 1950) Chapter VI , Rule (r) 177-186 (it provides the legal framework for the Court of Inquiry) (hereinafter COI)(the AR 1950, made under § 191 of the Act were subsequently replaced by the Army Rule 1954 (AR 1954)).

232 These provisions are supplemented by the Regulations for the Army 1987 (RA 1987), Chapter XII, ¶¶ 516 – 529, entitled as 'Courts of Inquiry, Boards, Etc.

upon any matter referred to them by an officer commanding a body of troops. Unlike the civilian criminal justice system, where an investigation may ordinarily be conducted by a single police officer of the rank of Sub-Inspector or above under the supervision of the Station House Officer or Magistrate having jurisdiction, military law generally contemplates an inquiry conducted by a panel consisting of two or more members. Thus, the Court of Inquiry functions as a collective investigative body rather than as an individual investigator.

One of the most distinctive features of military law is the protection afforded to a person whose character or military reputation is likely to be affected during the course of a Court of Inquiry. There is no direct equivalent to this safeguard within the civilian criminal justice system. Army Rule 180 requires that such a person be afforded a full opportunity to participate in the proceedings, including the right to be present throughout the inquiry, to cross-examine witnesses whose evidence may affect him, to make a statement in his defence, and to produce witnesses, including character witnesses, on his behalf.[233] This safeguard reflects the recognition that allegations affecting an individual's military reputation may have serious professional consequences and therefore warrant enhanced procedural protection even at the investigative stage.

Another important characteristic of the Court of Inquiry is that its proceedings are not admissible in evidence in subsequent legal proceedings.[234] This reinforces the conclusion that a COI is essentially an investigative mechanism rather than a judicial forum. Its purpose is to assist the Commanding Officer in

233 AR 1954, r 180.
234 *Id.* r 182.

determining whether an offence has been committed and whether disciplinary action should follow. In this respect, the Court of Inquiry performs a function broadly analogous to that of a police investigation in the civilian criminal justice system.

Where disciplinary proceedings are contemplated against an individual on the basis of material gathered during the inquiry, copies of relevant statements and documents are furnished to the accused.[235] This requirement bears similarity to Sections 207 and 208 of the Code of Criminal Procedure, 1973, and Sections 230 and 231 of the Bharatiya Nagarik Suraksha Sanhita, 2023, which require the supply of documents relied upon by the prosecution so as to enable the accused to prepare an effective defence.

The foregoing discussion makes it evident that a Court of Inquiry is not a court in the judicial sense of the term. It neither determines guilt nor imposes punishment. Its proceedings do not possess the evidentiary status of judicial proceedings, nor can they be treated as a substitute for trial. The COI is merely an investigative body established to ascertain facts and report its findings to the convening authority. Furthermore, it cannot exceed the scope of the reference entrusted to it and must confine itself strictly to the matters specified in the convening order.

The authority to convene a Court of Inquiry in disciplinary matters rests with an officer commanding an independent body of troops. This is consistent with the Commanding Officer's disciplinary responsibilities and his statutory obligation to maintain good order and military discipline within the command. The report of the Court of Inquiry is intended solely to assist the

235 *Id.* r 184.

Commanding Officer in determining the appropriate course of action and is not intended to operate as an adjudication of rights or liabilities.

Where a Commanding Officer proposes to initiate disciplinary proceedings on the basis of the findings of a Court of Inquiry, fairness demands that the person concerned be supplied with copies of those portions of the proceedings that relate to the allegations against him. Such disclosure must be made sufficiently in advance of the hearing of charge under Army Rule 22 so as to enable the accused to understand the case against him and prepare an effective response. This safeguard is of particular importance because the Court of Inquiry often forms the factual foundation upon which subsequent disciplinary proceedings are built.

HEARING OF CHARGE BY THE COMMANDING OFFICER

Taking of Cognizance

Whenever a person subject to the Army Act is alleged to have committed an offence, the matter is ordinarily dealt with by his Commanding Officer (CO) in accordance with the disciplinary framework established under military law. The hearing of charge under Army Rule 22 constitutes a crucial stage in the military justice process, as it is at this point that the Commanding Officer examines the allegations, considers the available evidence, and determines whether further disciplinary proceedings should be initiated.

Historically, the disciplinary procedures under the Army Act bear certain similarities to the criminal process that existed under the Code of Criminal Procedure, 1898, which governed civilian criminal courts prior to the enactment of the Indian Army Act, 1911. The procedural framework was originally developed during the colonial period and was intended to provide Commanding Officers with the authority necessary to maintain discipline within the Armed Forces.

A significant distinction, however, exists between the civilian and military systems. Under the civilian criminal justice system, the administration of justice is distributed among several authorities. The complainant initiates the process, the police investigate the offence, the Magistrate takes cognizance and, where necessary, commits the case for trial, the Judge conducts the trial and imposes sentence, and the prison authorities execute the punishment. This separation of functions serves as an important safeguard against the concentration of power within a single authority.

Military law adopts a different approach. Many of these functions are concentrated within the office of the Commanding Officer. Acting upon information received through a Court of Inquiry, military investigation, or other source, the Commanding Officer assesses the allegations, examines the evidence, determines whether disciplinary action should be initiated, and decides the appropriate course to be adopted. This concentration of authority reflects the military's emphasis upon command responsibility, efficiency, and the maintenance of discipline, which are regarded as essential to operational effectiveness.

Where the Commanding Officer is satisfied, on a prima facie assessment of the material placed before him, that an offence appears to have been committed by a person under his command, Army Rule 22 requires him to hear the charge personally. The Rule embodies an important procedural safeguard, ensuring that the accused is informed of the allegations against him and afforded an opportunity to respond before any further action is taken.

The hearing of charge is not a trial. Rather, it is a preliminary proceeding intended to enable the Commanding Officer to determine whether sufficient grounds exist for proceeding further. During this stage, the accused is furnished with a tentative charge sheet and afforded reasonable time to prepare his defence. He must then be directed to appear before the Commanding Officer at a specified time and place, of which due notice is given.

Army Rule 22 further requires that the evidence supporting the proposed charges be produced in the presence of the accused. Witnesses whose testimony forms the basis of the allegations must depose before the Commanding Officer, and their evidence is recorded. The accused is entitled to hear the evidence against him and must be informed of his right to cross-examine prosecution witnesses. Any questions put by the accused and the answers given by the witnesses are required to be recorded as part of the proceedings.

Upon completion of the prosecution evidence, the accused must be afforded an opportunity to make a statement in his defence and to produce witnesses on his behalf. Where defence evidence is led, the Commanding Officer is required to record, or cause to be recorded, the statement of the accused and the evidence of defence witnesses. This safeguard is intended to ensure that the accused is given a meaningful opportunity to explain his conduct and challenge the allegations before any decision is taken regarding the future course of the proceedings.

Upon completion of the hearing of charge, the Commanding Officer may adopt one of the following courses of action:

(a) **Dismiss the charge and discharge the accused** where, in his opinion, no offence is disclosed or where the charge ought not to be proceeded with;[236]

(b) **Dispose of the charge summarily** where the nature of the offence permits disposal under the summary disciplinary powers vested in the Commanding Officer;[237] or

(c) **Adjourn the case and order the evidence to be reduced to writing** where he is satisfied that the allegations warrant trial by Court Martial and that the evidence should be formally recorded for that purpose.[238]

These alternatives demonstrate the wide discretion vested in the Commanding Officer at the hearing of charge stage. The decision taken at this point determines whether the matter comes to an end, is dealt with summarily within the unit, or proceeds further within the military justice system through the preparation of Summary of Evidence and eventual trial by Court Martial.

The hearing of charge thus performs a function broadly comparable to the stage at which a Magistrate examines the available material and determines whether further proceedings should continue. Unlike the civilian system, however, the authority responsible for assessing the evidence, evaluating the allegations, and directing the future course of the proceedings is the Commanding Officer himself. This feature represents one of

---

236 *Id.* r 22(2).

237 AA 1950, § 80.

238 AR 1954, r 22(3) (c).

the most distinctive characteristics of the military justice system and highlights the central role occupied by command authority within the administration of military justice.

COMMITTAL PROCEEDINGS

It is important to appreciate that the proceedings conducted under Army Rule 22 are only at the stage where the Commanding Officer has taken cognizance of the alleged offence. At this stage, the Commanding Officer has not yet arrived at a final decision regarding the manner in which the case should be dealt with. He must still determine whether the offence is of such a nature that it may be disposed of summarily under his disciplinary powers or whether it warrants trial by a Court Martial of an appropriate description.[239]

In this respect, Army Rules 22 and 23 perform a function broadly analogous to the committal proceedings formerly contemplated under Section 207-A of the Code of Criminal Procedure, 1898.[240] Under that provision, the Magistrate was required to examine the material before him and determine whether:

239 Under the provisions of AA 1950, § 80.

240 This section was introduced to streamline the commitment process, outlining the Magistrate's responsibilities during the inquiry:

- Sub-section (4): Empowers the Magistrate to take witness testimonies.
- Sub-section (5): Grants the accused the right to cross-examine witnesses.
- Sub-section (6): Allows the Magistrate to discharge the accused if there's no prima facie case for trial.
- Sub-section (7): Mandates the framing of charges if a prima facie case exists.

(a) the case could be tried by him and adequately dealt with within the limits of his sentencing powers; or

(b) the matter ought to be committed to the Court of Session for trial.

Similarly, under military law, the Commanding Officer is required to assess the evidence collected during the hearing of charge before deciding whether the matter should be disposed of summarily or proceed towards trial by Court Martial.

Where the Commanding Officer concludes that the evidence should be formally reduced to writing, Army Rule 23 comes into operation.[241] This stage is known as the recording of the Summary of Evidence (SOE). The provisions relating to Summary of Evidence under Army Rule 23 come into operation when the Commanding Officer decides that the evidence should be reduced to writing following the hearing of charge and where the Commanding Officer is of the opinion that the allegations may require trial by Court Martial.

The recording of Summary of Evidence is not dependent upon the Commanding Officer personally reducing the evidence to writing. He may record it himself or direct another officer to do so. The evidence may be recorded manually, through a scribe, by typewritten means, or through any other recognised method

241 AR 1954, r 23(1) (it provides that the Evidence of the Witnesses who were present and gave evidence before the Commanding Officer (CO), whether against or for the accused; and of any other person, whose evidence appears to be relevant; shall be taken down in the presence and hearing of the accused, before the CO or Such Officer as he directs. Further AR 1954, r 23(2) provides right of the accused to cross-examine witnesses deposing at the Summary of Evidence (SOE)).

of recording proceedings. The essential requirement is that the evidence be properly recorded and authenticated in accordance with the provisions of the Army Rules.

The Summary of Evidence occupies a position of considerable importance within the military justice system. Although it is not itself a trial, it forms the evidentiary foundation upon which subsequent Court Martial proceedings are based. In this respect, it performs a role similar to that played by committal proceedings under the Code of Criminal Procedure and the present provisions governing commitment of cases for trial before a Court of Session. This is the procedure that is followed in trial before civil and criminal Courts also. It is also to be borne in mind that SOE proceedings are judicial in nature and these form the basis of trial by a Court-martial in the same manner as committal proceedings (under 1898 Cr. PC), Sec 209 Cr P.C, and Sec 232BNSS. of the Magistrate were made basis for committal of the case for trial at Sessions. Its purpose is to ensure that the evidence supporting the allegations is formally recorded and preserved before the matter proceeds further within the military justice system.

SUMMARY OF EVIDENCE

Once the Summary of Evidence has been recorded and placed before the Commanding Officer, Army Rule 24 provides him with several options. Upon consideration of the evidence, he may:

(a) re-hear the case and either dismiss the charge or dispose of it summarily;

(b) remand the accused for trial by a Court Martial which he is empowered to convene; or

(c) refer the matter to the appropriate superior military authority with a recommendation that a Court Martial of a description beyond his convening powers be assembled.

These alternatives demonstrate that the Summary of Evidence constitutes the principal evidentiary basis upon which the Commanding Officer determines the future course of the proceedings.

A significant issue arises at this stage concerning the practice commonly referred to as "Additional Summary of Evidence." Neither the Army Act nor the Army Rules expressly provide for the recording of an Additional Summary of Evidence once proceedings under Rule 23 have been completed. The statutory framework contemplates that the Commanding Officer should take his decision on the basis of the Summary of Evidence recorded pursuant to his directions. If the evidence fails to disclose an offence, the logical consequence is that the charge should be dismissed and the accused discharged.

Notwithstanding the absence of any express statutory provision, a practice has developed whereby witnesses who have already testified are recalled or fresh witnesses are examined under the rubric of an Additional Summary of Evidence. This practice raises important questions regarding its compatibility with the statutory scheme governing military disciplinary proceedings.

Army Rule's 23(1), 23(2) & 23(3) provide the manner in which the Evidence is to be reduced to writing on the orders of the CO.[242] Rule 23(3) first requires that the evidence of each witness be read over to the witness and signed by him or, where necessary,

242 AR 1954, r 22(3) (c).

attested by his mark as confirmation of its correctness. The Rule then proceeds to state:

"After all the evidence against the accused has been recorded, the accused will be asked: 'Do you wish to make any statement? You are not obliged to say anything unless you wish to do so, but whatever you say will be taken down in writing and may be given in evidence.'"

The language employed by the Rule is significant. The accused is invited to make a statement only after all the evidence against him has been recorded. This indicates that the prosecution case has been completed and that the proceedings have entered the defence stage.

It has been suggested that the practice of recording Additional Summary of Evidence derives support from Note 6 appended below Rule 23.[243] However, two objections arise.

First, executive notes and administrative instructions cannot override the express language of a statutory rule. Rule 23 clearly contemplates that the prosecution evidence must be completed before the accused is called upon to enter his defence. Any interpretation inconsistent with the Rule itself must necessarily yield to the statutory provision.

Secondly, permitting the prosecution to reopen its case after the defence stage has commenced appears inconsistent with fundamental principles of criminal jurisprudence. The

243 MML, vol II, r 23 (Note 6 reads as follows; "The formal caution provided for in sub-rule (3) must be given as soon as the evidence for the prosecution is closed. If it is necessary to take down additional summary, the accused must again be formally cautioned before he makes any further statement................")

disciplinary process under military law broadly consists of three stages: the hearing of charge before the Commanding Officer, the recording of Summary of Evidence, and finally the disposal of the matter either through summary action or trial by Court Martial. At each stage, the proceedings follow the familiar pattern of accusation, prosecution evidence, cross-examination, defence statement, and defence evidence.

Once the prosecution has concluded its evidence and the accused has been called upon to make his statement in defence, the control of proceedings effectively passes to the defence. The accused may choose to make a statement, produce defence witnesses, or remain silent. Permitting the prosecution thereafter to introduce additional evidence enables it to repair deficiencies exposed during cross-examination or defence preparation and places the accused at a procedural disadvantage. Any additional evidence in any manner would amount to jeopardizing the defence of the accused. That is what is known as Double Jeopardy and barred by the provisions of Article 20(2) of the Constitution of India as well as Army Act 1950, Section 121.

The concern is not merely technical. Allowing the prosecution a further opportunity to strengthen its case after the defence stage has commenced may result in surprise to the accused and undermine the fairness of the proceedings. It also permits the prosecution to fill gaps that have become apparent during the course of the proceedings, a practice that sits uneasily with established principles of criminal justice. Such a course raises serious questions regarding procedural fairness and the compatibility of the practice with the statutory framework governing military disciplinary proceedings.

MILITARY CUSTODY PRIOR TO TRIAL BY A COURT MARTIAL

Section 101 of the Army Act, 1950 authorises a person subject to military law to be taken into military custody upon being charged with an offence. The provision necessarily implies that the individual must be informed of the charge against him before such custody is imposed. The right to know the nature of the accusation is a fundamental safeguard, as a person cannot effectively challenge the legality of his detention without being apprised of the grounds upon which it is based.

Where a person is taken into military custody without being informed of the charge or where the statutory requirements governing such custody are not complied with, the detention may be rendered unlawful. In appropriate cases, the legality of such custody may be challenged before a High Court through a petition seeking a writ of *habeas corpus*, a remedy designed to protect personal liberty against unlawful detention.

It is important to note that military custody is not mandatory in every case where disciplinary proceedings are contemplated. The decision to place an accused in custody is discretionary and must be exercised judiciously by the Commanding Officer. The power is intended to serve specific disciplinary and administrative objectives rather than operate as an automatic consequence of every accusation.

Ordinarily, military custody may be justified where there exists a reasonable apprehension that:

(a) the accused may abscond or desert in order to evade disciplinary proceedings;

(b) the accused may cause harm to himself, other personnel, or witnesses connected with the case; or

(c) the accused may interfere with the investigation, influence witnesses, or tamper with evidence.

The exercise of this power must therefore be guided by necessity rather than convenience. The mere existence of an accusation does not, by itself, justify deprivation of liberty. As in civilian criminal jurisprudence, restrictions upon personal liberty should bear a rational relationship to the purpose sought to be achieved.

The Supreme Court's decision in *Bhuwneshwar Singh v. Union of India*[244] provides important guidance on the legality of military custody. The Court examined whether the appellant's detention was consistent with the requirements of Sections 101 to 103 of the Army Act and Rule 27 of the Army Rules. Upon examining the facts, the Court concluded that the detention had exceeded the period permitted by law and was therefore illegal.

Significantly, however, the Court distinguished between the illegality of the detention and the validity of the subsequent disciplinary proceedings. While holding the custody to be unlawful, the Court declined to invalidate the trial and conviction on that ground alone, observing that the procedural irregularity relating to detention had not vitiated the Court Martial proceedings themselves.

244 Bhuwneshwar Singh v. Union of India, Supreme Court of India, 1 September 1993, available at: https://www.casemine.com/commentary/in/compensation-for-illegal-pre-trial-detention-under-the-army-act:-analysis-of-bhuwneshwar-singh-v.-union-of-india/view (Accessed 9 November 2024).

The Court nevertheless recognised that unlawful deprivation of liberty required an effective remedy. Consequently, it enhanced the compensation awarded to the appellant from Rs. 1,000 to Rs. 30,000, emphasising that compensation must reflect the seriousness of the violation suffered. The decision is significant not only because it reinforces accountability within the military justice system, but also because it reaffirms the judiciary's role in safeguarding individual liberty while simultaneously recognising the legitimate requirements of military discipline.

The judgment thus illustrates an important principle underlying military justice: although the Armed Forces operate within a specialised disciplinary framework, the exercise of military authority remains subject to legal scrutiny. The maintenance of discipline cannot be divorced from the obligation to respect the statutory and constitutional safeguards designed to protect the rights of service personnel.

Table 6.1: Comparative Analysis of the Pre-Trial Process under BNSS and Military Law

Stage	BNSS 2023 (Civilian Criminal Justice System)	Military Justice System
Objective	Investigation of offences and collection of evidence	Maintenance of discipline and determination of disciplinary action
Investigating Authority	Police Officer	Military Police, Court of Inquiry, Investigating Officers
Fact-Finding Mechanism	Police Investigation	Court of Inquiry (Army Rule 177)

Protection of Reputation	No equivalent statutory protection	Army Rule 180 provides participation rights where reputation is affected
Supply of Documents	Sections 230–231 BNSS	Relevant COI proceedings and Summary of Evidence supplied to accused
Taking Cognizance	Magistrate/Court	Commanding Officer under Army Rule 22
Hearing of Allegations	Before Judicial Authority	Hearing of Charge by Commanding Officer
Custody Prior to Trial	Police/Judicial Custody subject to judicial scrutiny	Military Custody under Sections 101–103 Army Act
Committal Procedure	Section 232 BNSS	Summary of Evidence under Army Rule 23
Decision to Proceed	Judicial Authority	Commanding Officer

COMMENCEMENT OF TRIAL

Under the Code of Criminal Procedure, 1973 and the Bharatiya Nagarik Suraksha Sanhita, 2023, a criminal trial refers to the judicial process through which the guilt or innocence of an accused person is determined. For a trial to commence, the accused must first be informed of the charges against him. This occurs at the stage of framing of charge, when the court formally notifies the accused of the allegations he is required to answer. Consequently, a criminal trial does not begin when cognizance of an offence is taken; rather, it commences only after the charges have been framed by a competent court.

It is important to distinguish between the concepts of an inquiry and a trial. Since a trial begins only upon the framing of charges, all proceedings preceding that stage are generally regarded as inquiries. Inquiries conducted under Sections 200, 201, and 202 Cr.P.C./ sections 223, 224 & 225 BNSS, as well as Section 398 Cr.P.C./ 439 BNSS, are types of inquiries contemplated by Section 319 Cr.P.C/ 358 BNSS. Any materials gathered during these inquiries can be used to corroborate evidence presented during the trial.[245]

The distinction between inquiry and trial was considered by the Supreme Court in *Common Cause, A Registered Society through its Director v. Union of India and Others.*[246] The Court held that in trials before a Court of Session, the trial commences upon the framing of charges under Section 228 of the Code of Criminal Procedure, 1973. In warrant cases tried by a Magistrate on a police report, the trial begins when charges are framed under Section 240 of the Code. In warrant cases instituted otherwise than on a police report, the trial commences upon the framing of charges under Section 246 of the Code. The decision thus makes it clear that the commencement of trial is linked to the framing of charges rather than the earlier stages of investigation or inquiry.

The legal position may therefore be summarised by stating that an inquiry encompasses the proceedings undertaken prior to the framing of charges, whereas the trial begins only after the

245 Hardeep Singh vs State of Punjab & Ors, Supreme Court of India, 10 January 2014, available at: https://indiankanoon.org/docfragment/78958066/?formInput=commencement%20of%20trial%20in%20criminal%20%20doctypes%3A%20judgments (Accessed 9 November 2024).

246 AIR 1997 SC 1539, available at: https://indiankanoon.org/doc/1729519/ (Accessed 9 November 2024).

charges have been framed by a competent judicial authority. The purpose of the trial is to examine the allegations against the accused, assess the evidence presented by both sides, and determine whether the prosecution has established guilt beyond reasonable doubt. Every criminal trial must ultimately culminate in either an acquittal or a conviction.

The position under military law differs in certain respects. The first assembly of a Court Martial takes place in a closed session attended by the Presiding Officer, the Judge Advocate (where one is appointed), the Members of the Court, and any waiting Members. At this stage, the Court satisfies itself regarding a number of preliminary legal requirements, including the legality of its constitution, the validity of the convening order, the applicability of the Army Act to the accused, and the medical fitness of the accused to stand trial.[247]

In Court-martial proceedings, it is common practice for all proceedings to be recorded by the Judge Advocate General (JAG) using erasable pencil, and witnesses' statements are not always signed. This practice can lead to potential modifications of the statements. To avoid this issue, the accused should insist from the outset that all proceedings be recorded using a ballpoint or ink pen, and that witnesses personally sign their statements.

Unlike the civilian criminal justice system, where the framing of charges marks the commencement of trial, a Court Martial is generally regarded as having commenced once the Court assembles and undertakes the preliminary examination of the charges and its jurisdiction to proceed. The first assembly of the Court therefore performs a function similar to the stage at which

247 Union of India v Maj Gen ML Yadav, AIR 1996 SC 1340.

a civilian court satisfies itself that the matter is properly before it and is capable of proceeding to trial.

The distinction between the civilian and military systems is significant. While the civilian process draws a clear line between inquiry and trial through the formal framing of charges, military law treats the assembly of the Court Martial itself as the commencement of trial proceedings. This difference reflects the specialised nature of military justice and the procedural framework established under the Army Act and the Army Rules.

OBJECTIONS TO MEMBERS AND ALLEGATIONS OF BIAS

At the commencement of the Court Martial proceedings, the names of the Presiding Officer and the Members of the Court are read over to the accused.[248] This constitutes an important procedural safeguard, as it enables the accused to raise objections to any individual member whose participation may give rise to concerns regarding impartiality, disqualification, or bias.

The accused is not entitled to object to the Court Martial as a collective body. However, he may challenge the jurisdiction of the Court through an appropriate plea or object to the participation of particular Members on legally recognised grounds.[249] Such objections may include allegations that the Court has not been properly convened, that a Member suffers from a statutory disqualification, or that circumstances exist giving rise to a reasonable apprehension of bias.

---

248 AA 1950, § 130 (1) and AR 1954, r 44.

249 AR 1954, r 51.

Where an objection is raised against a Member, the issue is considered by the Court in closed session.[250] The Member against whom the objection is directed is required to withdraw during the deliberations concerning that objection. The remaining Members then determine whether the challenge should be sustained. In the event of equality of votes, the benefit of doubt operates in favour of the accused and the objection succeeds.[251]

The right to challenge Members of a Court Martial is of considerable importance because the legitimacy of any adjudicatory process depends upon both actual impartiality and the appearance of impartiality. Justice must not only be done but must also be seen to be done. This principle assumes particular significance in military justice, where Members of the Court may belong to the same service environment and chain of command as the accused.

The leading authority on the issue is the Supreme Court's decision in *Ranjit Thakur v. Union of India.*[252] In that case, the Court emphasised that the test of bias is not whether actual bias has been established but whether there exists a reasonable apprehension of bias in the mind of the accused. The Court observed that the relevant inquiry is whether a reasonable person, placed in the position of the accused, would entertain a genuine apprehension that he may not receive a fair and impartial hearing. Mere whimsical, capricious, or fanciful suspicions are insufficient; however, a reasonable apprehension founded upon objective circumstances is enough to vitiate the proceedings.

---

250 *Id.* r 44 (c); *see also,* Lt. Col. PPS Bedi v Union of India, AIR 1982 SC 1413.

251 AA 1950, § 132.

252 Ranjit Singh, *supra* note 61.

The significance of *Ranjit Thakur* lies in its recognition that military tribunals, no less than civilian courts, must satisfy the requirements of fairness and impartiality. The decision reaffirmed that confidence in the administration of justice depends not only upon the absence of actual prejudice but also upon the perception that the tribunal is free from improper influence or predisposition.

A different aspect of the law relating to objections was considered in *Lt. Col. J. S. Shekhon.*[253] The Court held that where no objection is raised at the trial under Section 130 of the Army Act, and where the Member concerned does not suffer from any statutory disqualification under Army Rule 39(1)(c), the issue of bias cannot ordinarily be raised subsequently through a writ petition. The decision underscores the importance of raising objections at the earliest available opportunity, thereby enabling the Court Martial itself to address and resolve such concerns before the trial proceeds further.

These principles reflect an attempt to balance two competing considerations. On the one hand is the requirement that military justice be administered fairly and by impartial decision-makers. On the other hand is the need for procedural finality, which requires that objections be raised at the appropriate stage rather than being reserved for challenge after an adverse verdict has been delivered. The law therefore recognises both the accused's right to an impartial tribunal and the obligation to assert that right in a timely manner.

The procedure permitting objections to Members thus serves an important constitutional and disciplinary function. It seeks to

253 Lt. Col. JS Shekhon v Union of India, 2002 Cri LJ 783.

preserve confidence in the fairness of Court Martial proceedings while ensuring that allegations of bias are addressed before the trial progresses to the evidentiary stage. In this manner, the military justice system incorporates safeguards intended to uphold the fundamental principle that no person should be judged by a tribunal whose impartiality may reasonably be called into question.

PROSECUTOR, DEFENDING OFFICER AND FRIEND OF THE ACCUSED

The fairness of any criminal trial depends not merely upon the impartiality of the tribunal but also upon the ability of the accused to present an effective defence. Recognising this principle, the military justice system incorporates provisions relating to prosecutors, defending officers, legal counsel, and friends of the accused. These safeguards are intended to ensure that the accused is not left without assistance while facing proceedings that may result in serious penal consequences.

A prosecutor appointed for a Court Martial must be a person subject to the Army Act who has no direct or indirect interest in the outcome of the case.[254] The requirement of impartiality is intended to ensure that the prosecution is conducted fairly and that the prosecutor does not possess any personal stake in securing a conviction.

Before the commencement of the trial, the accused is entitled to adequate notice of the proceedings. Where a legally qualified prosecutor or counsel is appointed, the accused is ordinarily

254 AR 1954, r 43 (a prosecution counsel may also be appointed under the provisions of RA 1987, ¶ 542 and Ministry of Defence letter no 43806/AG/DV-1/2278/DC (AG), dt. 21 May 1996).

required to be given seven days' notice before trial.[255] This safeguard enables the accused to prepare his defence and make appropriate arrangements regarding legal representation.

An important feature of military justice is the institution of the Defending Officer. Upon being warned for trial, the accused is furnished with a list of officers from which he may select a Defending Officer to assist him. Where the accused expresses a preference for an officer whose name does not appear on the list, reasonable efforts should be made to secure the services of that officer. If the officer selected by the accused is unavailable, the reasons for such unavailability should be explained to him and an opportunity afforded to nominate another officer.

Where the accused declines to select a Defending Officer or fails to make a choice despite being given an opportunity to do so, a legally qualified officer may be detailed to assist him. If the accused refuses such assistance or declines to nominate any officer, the fact is required to be recorded and certified for production before the Court Martial. The object of this procedure is to ensure that the accused is afforded every reasonable opportunity to obtain assistance in the preparation and presentation of his defence.

The significance of this safeguard was highlighted in *Maj. Gen. Inder Jit Kumar.*[256] The Court held that an accused who has repeatedly been afforded opportunities to engage a Defending Officer cannot subsequently complain of a violation of the principles of natural justice merely because he chose not to avail himself of those opportunities. The decision emphasises that procedural fairness requires that opportunities be provided; it does not compel an accused to utilise them.

---

255 *Id.* r's 96, 97 & 164.

256 Maj.Gen Inder Jit Kumar v Union of India, AIR 1997 SC 2085

The duties of a Defending Officer extend beyond mere formal representation. A Defending Officer is expected to assist the accused in understanding the charges, preparing the defence, examining witnesses, and presenting the case before the Court Martial. At the same time, the Defending Officer must respect the wishes of the accused and should not pursue a line of defence contrary to the instructions or interests of the person he represents.

In addition to the assistance of a Defending Officer, the accused is entitled to engage one or more legal practitioners at his own expense. The right to professional legal assistance constitutes an important safeguard, particularly in cases involving complex questions of law or serious penal consequences. Where the offence is punishable with death and the accused is unable to engage counsel at his own expense, legal representation is required to be provided at Government expense. Such counsel must be afforded a reasonable opportunity to communicate with the accused and must be competent to discharge the responsibilities of legal representation.[257] Failure to provide effective legal assistance in such circumstances may render the proceedings vulnerable to challenge.

However, the entitlement to State-funded counsel is generally confined to cases involving capital punishment.[258] In other cases, although the accused may engage counsel at his own expense, there is ordinarily no corresponding obligation upon the State to provide legal representation. Nevertheless, legal practitioners may appear before a General Court Martial, District Court Martial, or Summary General Court Martial

---

257 Ranjit Singh, *supra* note 61.

258 Union of India v Fl Lt. GS Bajwa, AIR 2004 SC 808.

unless the Convening Authority declares such appearance to be inexpedient in the interests of military service.[259]

Military law also recognises the institution of the "Friend of the Accused."[260] Unlike a Defending Officer or legal practitioner, a Friend of the Accused need not possess legal qualifications and may be either a civilian or a member of the Armed Forces of any rank. The Friend of the Accused may advise the accused on procedural and substantive matters and may suggest questions to be put to witnesses. However, he is not entitled to cross-examine witnesses himself, address the Court, or otherwise assume the role of legal counsel.

The institution of the Friend of the Accused is intended to provide moral and practical assistance to an accused who may be unfamiliar with legal proceedings. While the scope of assistance is necessarily limited, the provision reflects an acknowledgement that an accused facing disciplinary proceedings should not be left entirely unaided in presenting his case.

It is noteworthy that, unlike the accused, no corresponding right exists to object to the Prosecutor, the Judge Advocate, or an Officer under Instruction.[261] Once all objections to Members of the Court have been disposed of, the Members are required to take the prescribed oath or affirmation before the trial proceeds further.[262]

---

259 *Army Rule.* r's 96 & 164.

260 *Army Rule.* r's 96 & 164.

261 AA 1950, § 130 (Note 2) & AR 1954, r 46

262 AR 1954, r's 45 - 47 & Note 1 of AR, r 45 (appropriate Forms can be seen appended to these Rules).

Taken together, the provisions relating to prosecutors, defending officers, legal counsel, and friends of the accused represent an attempt to balance the demands of military discipline with the requirements of procedural fairness. Although the military justice system does not always provide the same level of legal assistance available in civilian criminal courts, these safeguards are intended to ensure that an accused person is afforded a reasonable opportunity to defend himself before a Court Martial.

ARRAIGNMENT

Following the administration of the prescribed oath or affirmation to the Members of the Court, the accused is arraigned. During arraignment, the accused is called upon by his number, rank, name, and description, and the charges are formally read out to him. He is then required to plead to each charge by stating whether he is "Guilty" or "Not Guilty." Where the accused pleads "Not Guilty," the Court proceeds to trial in accordance with the prescribed procedure.[263]

The arraignment constitutes a critical stage of the Court Martial process, as it is at this point that the accused is formally called upon to answer the charges against him. To ensure fairness, the accused must ordinarily have been warned for trial at least ninety-six hours prior to arraignment, or twenty-four hours in cases of active service. Where this requirement has not been complied with, the arraignment should be postponed and the Court adjourned to enable the accused to prepare his defence adequately.

---

263 Army Rule. r 48 and Note 2 thereto, read with AR1954, r 34(1).

Pleas Available to the Accused on Arraignment

Before recording a plea of "Guilty," the Court is under a duty to explain to the accused the nature of the charge, the general effect of a plea of guilty, and the procedural consequences that follow from such a plea. Compliance with Army Rule 52(2A) is mandatory,[264] and the prescribed endorsement confirming that the explanation has been given must be recorded. This safeguard is intended to ensure that a plea of guilty is made knowingly, voluntarily, and with full understanding of its consequences.

At the stage of arraignment, the accused may raise several objections or pleas before entering upon his defence.

(a) Objection to the Charge

The accused may object to a charge on the ground that it does not disclose an offence under the Army Act or that it has not been framed in accordance with the requirements of the Army Rules. Such objections go to the legal validity of the charge itself and must be considered before the trial proceeds further.[265]

(b) Objection to Jurisdiction

The accused may challenge the jurisdiction of the Court Martial. Such a challenge may relate to the authority of the Court to try the offence, the applicability of military law to the accused, or any other matter affecting the competence of the tribunal.[266] Unlike many other objections, a plea relating to jurisdiction may be raised at any stage of the proceedings.

---

264 Obheroi, *supra,* note 218,.

265 AR 1954, r 49.

266 *Id.* r 51.

(c) Plea in Bar of Trial

The accused may raise a plea in bar of trial.[267] Such a plea is founded upon the contention that the accused cannot lawfully be tried because the matter has already been disposed of or because some legal impediment exists to further proceedings.[268]

A plea in bar may arise where the accused has previously been convicted or acquitted of the same offence by a criminal court or a Court Martial, has already been dealt with summarily, has received a reproof, or where the charge has previously been dismissed by the competent authority.[269] Once a Commanding Officer has dismissed a charge, a Court Martial cannot ordinarily be convened in respect of the same matter.[270]

A plea in bar may also arise where the offence has been pardoned or condoned by the competent military authority or where the proceedings are barred by limitation.[271] Questions relating to the applicability of such bars are required to be determined by the Court Martial itself.

(d) Plea of Embarrassment in Defence

Where the charge sheet contains multiple charges, the accused may contend that being tried on all charges together would embarrass or prejudice his defence. In such circumstances, he may seek separate trials in respect of individual charges.[272]

267 *Id.* r 53.

268 *Id.* r 22(1) vide AA 1950, § 121, AR, r53 (1) (a) and Notes 1 and 2 thereto, MML, vol 1, ¶ 20 and RA, 1987, ¶ 327.

269 AR 1954, r 53 (b).

270 Union of India v Maj. VJ Kharod, Guj HC LPA 224/ 85 in SCA 497/81.

271 AA 1950, § 122 vide AR 1954, r 53 (1) (c) and Note 1 thereto.

272 AR 1954, r 79 (5).

(e) Plea of Guilty

The accused may plead "Guilty" to a charge.[273] He may also offer a qualified plea of guilty,[274] admitting certain elements of the charge while disputing others. A valid plea of guilty enables the Court to record a finding of guilt and proceed directly to the question of sentence without requiring the prosecution to prove the charge through evidence.[275]

PROCEDURE FOLLOWING A PLEA OF GUILTY

Before accepting a plea of guilty, the Presiding Officer or the Judge Advocate must satisfy himself that the accused fully understands the nature of the charge, the effect of the plea, and the procedural consequences that follow from it. This requirement is particularly important because a plea of guilty amounts to an admission of the allegations and dispenses with the necessity of a full trial.

A plea of guilty is not accepted in cases where conviction may result in the death penalty.[276] Furthermore, where the Summary of Evidence or other material before the Court indicates that the accused may have a valid defence, the Court is under a duty to advise the accused to withdraw his plea of guilty and enter a plea of not guilty instead.[277]

Where a combination of pleas has been entered, the Court must first proceed to try, up to and including findings, those charges to which the accused has pleaded "Not Guilty."

273 *Id.* r 52(1).
274 *Id.* r 62 (9).
275 MML, vol 1, ¶ 68 (It covers all errors and omissions in the evidence).
276 AR 1954, r 52 (4).
277 *Id.* r 's 52 (2) &52 (2) (a).

If alternative charges have been framed and the accused pleads guilty to the more serious charge, the remaining alternative charges may be withdrawn. Conversely, where the accused pleads guilty only to a lesser offence, the Court may proceed as though he had pleaded "Not Guilty" and require the prosecution to prove the allegations through evidence.[278]

Once the plea of guilty has been accepted, any statement made by the accused in relation to the charge may be recorded and considered by the Court.[279] The Summary of Evidence is then examined and attached to the proceedings as an exhibit. Where the material available is insufficient to enable the Court to determine an appropriate sentence, additional evidence may be recorded for that limited purpose.[280]

The accused is also entitled to make a statement in mitigation of punishment.[281] He may call witnesses regarding his character and place before the Court any circumstances that may properly be taken into consideration while determining sentence.[282]

Where the Summary of Evidence or the statement of the accused reveals that he did not fully understand the effect of his plea of guilty, the Court is required to alter the plea to one of "Not Guilty" and proceed accordingly.[283] The relevant test is whether the facts asserted by the accused, if accepted as true, would constitute a valid defence to the charge.[284]

---

278 *Id.* r's 52(3) & 54(2).

279 *Id.* r 54 (3).

280 *Id.* r 54 (3).

281 *Id.* r 54 (4).

282 *Id.* r's 54 (4) & (7).

283 *Id.* r 54 (6) and Note 5 to 9 thereto.

284 Obheroi, *supra*, note 218, **at p 158.**

Similarly, where the accused alleges provocation or raises facts that may substantially affect criminal responsibility or punishment, the Court should ordinarily record a plea of "Not Guilty" and permit the matter to be determined upon evidence.[285] This ensures that all relevant facts are properly examined and that the accused is not deprived of a potentially valid defence or mitigating circumstance.

PROCEDURE TO BE FOLLOWED WHERE THE ACCUSED PLEADS NOT GUILTY

Where the accused pleads "Not Guilty" to the charges framed against him, the Court records the plea and proceeds with the trial. Before the evidentiary stage commences, the Court ordinarily satisfies itself that the accused has had sufficient time to prepare his defence and that the procedural requirements prescribed under the Army Act and the Army Rules have been complied with. The accused is specifically asked whether he has any grievance regarding compliance with procedural safeguards or whether he requires additional time for the preparation of his defence. Where the Court finds merit in any such contention, it may grant an adjournment in the interests of justice.[286]

Following the recording of the plea, the Prosecutor may, and if directed by the Court shall, make an opening address.[287] The purpose of the opening address is to place before the Court an outline of the prosecution case and indicate the evidence upon which reliance is proposed to be placed. The address is ordinarily based upon the material contained in the Summary of

285 AR 1954, r 52, Note 6 & r 54, Note 9.

286 *Id.* r 56 (1).

287 *Id.* r 56 (3).

Evidence and is intended to provide the Court with a coherent understanding of the allegations against the accused.

The accused, either through his legal counsel or Defending Officer, is entitled to respond to the prosecution's opening address. In doing so, the defence may challenge the allegations, dispute the reliability of the evidence relied upon by the prosecution, and place before the Court its broad theory of the case. This stage enables the accused to identify the principal issues in dispute and ensures that the trial proceeds in an orderly and structured manner.

Once the opening addresses have been concluded, the prosecution proceeds to lead its evidence. Witnesses who have previously deposed during the Court of Inquiry, the hearing of charge before the Commanding Officer, or the recording of Summary of Evidence are called one by one before the Court.[288] After being duly sworn or affirmed,[289] they are examined and their testimony is recorded by the Judge Advocate or, where no Judge Advocate is present, in accordance with the prescribed procedure.

It is important to note that the Prosecutor is not bound to call every witness whose evidence appears in the Summary of Evidence.[290] However, where the prosecution proposes to examine a witness whose evidence has not previously been recorded during any earlier stage of the proceedings, the accused must be afforded adequate notice of such evidence. The accused is entitled to receive an abstract of the proposed testimony and be given reasonable time to prepare his defence. Where such

288 *Id.* r 56 (4)

289 AA 1950, § 131 (2) & AR 1954, r 140.

290 AR 1954, r 134.

notice has not been provided, the accused is entitled to seek an adjournment, and it is the duty of the Court to inform him of this right.[291]

After examination-in-chief by the prosecution, each witness is subject to cross-examination by the accused through his legal counsel or Defending Officer.[292] Following cross-examination, the witness may be re-examined on matters arising out of the cross-examination. This process serves the important purpose of testing the credibility, reliability, and accuracy of the evidence presented against the accused.

Once the prosecution has concluded its case, the defence is called upon to present its evidence. Defence witnesses are examined, cross-examined, and re-examined in the same manner as prosecution witnesses. This procedural parity reflects the fundamental principle that both parties should be afforded a fair opportunity to present their respective cases before the Court.

The Court and the Judge Advocate are not passive observers during the trial. Both may put questions to witnesses whenever clarification is considered necessary. Where such questions are asked, the Prosecutor and the accused, acting through his counsel or Defending Officer, may seek permission to put further questions arising out of the answers given.[293] This ensures that ambiguities are resolved while preserving fairness to both sides.

---

291 AR 1954, r 134.

292 Capt. Virendra Sharma v Union of India, Rajasthan HC, Civil WP No 88 of 1985 (it was held that the accused is entitled to be defended by defending officer of his choice).

293 AR 1954, r 142.

As a general rule, evidence is recorded in narrative form by the Judge Advocate or, in his absence, by the Presiding Officer.[294] The purpose of recording evidence in this manner is to create an accurate and comprehensive record of the proceedings for future reference, review, or appellate scrutiny.

After the prosecution evidence has been closed, the Court or the Judge Advocate may, without prior warning, question the accused regarding any circumstances appearing in the evidence against him. The object of such questioning is to afford the accused an opportunity personally to explain any incriminating facts or circumstances that may have emerged during the trial. No oath or affirmation is administered to the accused during this stage, and his responses are not treated as sworn testimony.

An additional safeguard exists where the Prosecutor elects not to call a witness whose evidence appears in the Summary of Evidence. Similarly, where the prosecution has notified the accused that a particular witness will not be examined at trial, the accused may nevertheless require that witness to be produced for cross-examination.[295] This provision ensures that potentially relevant evidence is not withheld from the scrutiny of the defence merely because the prosecution chooses not to rely upon it.

Finally, the accused retains the right at any stage of the proceedings to alter his plea and plead "Guilty."[296] In such circumstances, the Court may proceed in accordance with the rules governing pleas of guilty and determine the matter accordingly.

---

294 *Id.* r 92.

295 *Id.* r 134.

296 *Id.* r's 52(2), (2A), (3), (4) subject to compliance) & 55.

The procedure followed where an accused pleads "Not Guilty" reflects the adversarial character of Court Martial proceedings. Through examination, cross-examination, re-examination, and the presentation of defence evidence, the Court is provided with the material necessary to determine the truth of the allegations. These safeguards are intended to ensure that findings of guilt are based upon evidence tested in the presence of the accused and evaluated in accordance with the principles of fairness and military justice.

QUESTIONING OF THE ACCUSED, DEFENCE, CLOSING ADDRESSES, AND SUMMING UP BY THE JUDGE ADVOCATE

After the prosecution has concluded its case, the Court proceeds to the next stage of the trial, which includes consideration of whether a prima facie case has been established, questioning of the accused, presentation of the defence, closing addresses, and the summing up by the Judge Advocate. These stages constitute important procedural safeguards designed to ensure that the accused is afforded a full and fair opportunity to answer the allegations before findings are recorded.

Submission of No Case to Answer

At the close of the prosecution case, the defence may contend that the evidence led by the prosecution is insufficient to establish a prima facie case against the accused. Accordingly, a submission of "No Case to Answer" may be made in respect of one or more charges.

Upon hearing the submissions of both parties, the Court may determine that the prosecution has failed to establish a case requiring an answer from the accused. Where the Court is satisfied that no reasonable tribunal could convict on the evidence adduced, and that no special finding is open on the evidence, it shall record a finding of "Not Guilty" on the relevant charge or charges, accompanied by brief reasons. In cases of doubt, the matter may be referred to the Convening Authority. The Court may also raise the issue on its own motion after hearing the Prosecutor. Any such finding remains subject to confirmation in accordance with the provisions of military law.[297]

Questioning of the Accused

Following the close of the prosecution case, the Court or the Judge Advocate is required to question the accused for the limited purpose of enabling him personally to explain any circumstances appearing in the evidence against him. This safeguard is mandatory and serves a function comparable to the examination of an accused under civilian criminal procedure.[298]

No oath or affirmation is administered to the accused during this process.[299] The accused is not obliged to answer any question and may refuse to do so. Any answers given are not treated as sworn testimony, and the accused cannot be punished for declining to answer or for giving inaccurate responses.

297 *Army Rule.* r 57 (Notes thereto).

298 Keshavamurthy v State, 2002 Cri LJ 103 Karnataka HC (It was held that on charge of causing death by negligent driving, witness who examined the vehicle states that the accident was not due to any technical defect in the vehicle, Court is duty bound to question the accused on this).

299 AR 1954, r58.

Defence of the Accused

The accused is then called upon to enter upon his defence. He is asked whether he wishes to make an unsworn statement and whether he intends to adduce evidence in his defence.

An unsworn statement may be made orally, in which case it is recorded verbatim, or it may be submitted in writing.[300] Since such a statement is not made on oath, the accused cannot be cross-examined upon it. This enables the accused to place his version of events before the Court without exposing himself to questioning by the prosecution.

If, however, the accused elects to give evidence on oath as a witness, he assumes the position of a witness in the proceedings and becomes liable to cross-examination by the Prosecutor as well as questioning by the Court. Where the accused chooses to testify, he is ordinarily examined before any other defence witness is called.

The accused is also asked whether he wishes to call witnesses regarding his character or to produce witnesses capable of supporting his defence. Importantly, no adverse inference may be drawn from the accused's decision not to testify or not to call evidence. The exercise of the right to remain silent cannot be treated as evidence of guilt.

Military law traditionally affords considerable latitude to the accused in presenting his defence. In the course of his statement or defence, the accused may challenge the credibility of witnesses, question the conduct of the investigation, raise objections to evidence, suggest alternative explanations of events, or

300 *Id.* r 58.

draw attention to matters which he believes are relevant to his defence.[301] This latitude reflects the principle that a person facing serious disciplinary consequences should be afforded every reasonable opportunity to answer the allegations against him.

Where, in the course of his defence, the accused refers to a Government official in relation to a charge involving absence or another matter requiring official verification, the Court may make a reference to the concerned authority and admit the response in evidence if it is considered relevant to the determination of the issues before it.[302]

Defence Witnesses

Where the accused intends to call witnesses on matters of fact, other than himself, he may make an opening address outlining the nature of the defence case. Defence witnesses, including those called solely to speak to the accused's character, are then examined by the accused's counsel or Defending Officer.[303]

As with prosecution witnesses, defence witnesses are subject to cross-examination and re-examination. Where a defence witness gives evidence that directly challenges the prosecution case, the Prosecutor is expected to cross-examine that witness. Failure to challenge material aspects of such testimony may result in the evidence being treated as uncontroverted, thereby enhancing its evidentiary weight.

301 *Id.* r 77 (3) & Notes 5 and 6 thereto.
302 AA1950, § 143 &Vol 1, ¶ 3.
303 AR 1954, r 58 (3).

Closing Addresses

After the defence evidence has concluded, the Prosecutor is entitled to make a closing address summarising the evidence and urging the Court to accept the prosecution's case. The defence is then afforded an opportunity to reply and present its final submissions in support of acquittal or other appropriate relief.[304]

Where the defence raises questions of law during its closing address, the Prosecutor may, with the permission of the Court, make further submissions confined to those legal issues. Neither side is permitted to refer to matters of fact that have not been admitted in evidence during the trial.[305] The purpose of closing addresses is to assist the Court in evaluating the evidence and the legal issues arising from it rather than to introduce new material.

Summing Up by the Judge Advocate

Following the closing addresses, the Judge Advocate delivers a summing up. This constitutes one of the most important stages of the Court Martial process. The Judge Advocate explains the charges, the relevant principles of law, the issues that arise for determination, and the evidence bearing upon those issues.

In performing this function, the Judge Advocate must remain impartial. His role is to assist the Court in understanding the legal and evidentiary issues and to ensure that the Members apply the correct legal principles. While recapitulating the evidence, he should not indicate his personal opinion regarding the guilt or innocence of the accused.[306]

---

304 *Id.* r 59.

305 *Id.* r 58 & Notes 13 and 14.

306 *Id.* r 60.

Recall of Witnesses and Incidental Questions

Before the prosecution and defence cases are formally closed, witnesses may, where necessary, be recalled. The prosecution may be permitted to call a new witness to rebut material evidence introduced by the defence, to address a new issue that could not reasonably have been anticipated, or to challenge evidence relating to the accused's good character by proving previous convictions where admissible.

In exceptional circumstances, the Court itself may call and examine a witness before recording its findings. Such witnesses are examined through the Court, and both parties are afforded an opportunity to question them. The Judge Advocate may also put questions with the permission of the Court.[307]

During the course of the proceedings, either party may raise incidental questions relating to law, evidence, or procedure. Such matters are ordinarily determined by the Court sitting in closed session.[308] Where a party remains aggrieved by a ruling of the Court, a complaint may subsequently be made to the Confirming Authority in accordance with the provisions governing military justice.[309]

The procedures governing the defence stage, closing addresses, and summing up are designed to ensure that the accused receives a meaningful opportunity to answer the prosecution case before findings are recorded. Together, these safeguards reinforce the principles of fairness, procedural justice, and due process that lie at the heart of a legitimate system of military justice.

---

307 *Id.* r 105 (7).
308 *Id.* r 58.
309 AA 1950, §164 (1).

Table 6.2: Comparative Analysis of the Trial Process under BNSS and Military Law

Stage	BNSS 2023	Military Justice System
Commencement of Trial	Framing of Charge	Assembly of Court-Martial
Trial Forum	Criminal Courts	Court-Martial
Judicial Independence	Independent Judiciary	Military Officers sitting as Members
Legal Representation	Constitutional and statutory right	Defending Officer, Legal Practitioner, Friend of the Accused
Challenge to Adjudicator	Recusal and bias principles	Objections under Section 130 Army Act
Plea of Accused	Guilty / Not Guilty	Guilty, Not Guilty, Plea in Bar, Jurisdictional Objections
Evidence	Led before Court	Based upon Summary of Evidence and oral testimony
Cross Examination	Full right	Full right
No Case to Answer	Available	Available
Questioning of Accused	Under BNSS provisions	By Court/Judge Advocate
Standard of Proof	Beyond Reasonable Doubt	Beyond Reasonable Doubt
Finding of Guilt	Judicial Determination	Finding by Court-Martial Members

FINDINGS OF THE COURT

The findings of a Court Martial represent its determination on the guilt or innocence of the accused in respect of each charge. However, unlike the verdict of a civilian criminal court, the findings of a Court Martial do not attain finality immediately upon their pronouncement. They remain subject to confirmation by the competent confirming authority and are therefore in the nature of recommendations pending such confirmation.

The determination of findings takes place in a closed court attended only by the Members of the Court, the Judge Advocate,[310] and any officers under instruction who are authorised to be present.[311] The confidentiality of these deliberations is intended to ensure free and uninhibited discussion amongst the Members while preserving the integrity of the decision-making process.

In arriving at its findings, the Court is required to confine itself strictly to the evidence and material properly before it. Findings must be based solely upon the testimony of witnesses, documentary evidence, admissible exhibits, and such observations as may legitimately arise from matters personally observed by the Court, including the demeanour of witnesses or observations made during any authorised viewing of the scene of occurrence. Extraneous considerations, personal opinions, or matters not introduced into evidence cannot lawfully form the basis of a finding.

As in civilian criminal jurisprudence, the burden of proving the charge rests upon the prosecution. The prosecution must

310 AR 1954, r 61 (1).
311 *Id.* r 80 (2).

establish the guilt of the accused beyond reasonable doubt. The accused is not required to prove his innocence. However, where the defence seeks to rely upon an exception, proviso, or special defence recognised under the Indian Penal Code, the burden of establishing the factual basis for such a defence lies upon the accused.[312] In considering such pleas, the Court is entitled to evaluate all evidence placed before it and may, where necessary, call or recall witnesses before recording its findings. The Judge Advocate may similarly require additional clarification through the Court where the interests of justice so demand.[313]

The opinion of each Member of the Court is taken separately on every charge upon which the accused has been arraigned. Voting takes place orally, and each charge is considered independently.[314] Where there is an equality of votes, the benefit of doubt operates in favour of the accused,[315] and the issue is determined accordingly.

A separate finding must be recorded in respect of each charge. In recording its conclusions, the Court is required to provide brief reasons supporting its findings. These reasons form an important safeguard against arbitrariness and demonstrate that the Court has considered the evidence and rival contentions placed before it. The reasons are recorded and signed by the Judge Advocate or, in his absence, by the Presiding Officer.[316]

---

312 Vide Indian Evidence Act, § 105.

313 AR 1954, r143 (4), MML, vol 1, ¶¶ 71 - 73 & Notes 4 & 5 to AR 1954, r's 61, 105 (7).

314 AR 1954, r 61 (2).

315 AA 1950, 132 (1) & MML, Vol 1 ¶ 77; *see also*, Army Head Quarter letter no 35418/AG/DV-1 dt. 01 March 1994 (for guidelines).

316 AR 1954, r 62 (1).

It should be apparent from the proceedings that the Court has fairly considered both the prosecution case and the defence advanced by the accused.[317]

Where two or more charges have been framed in the alternative, the Court cannot record findings of guilt on more than one of such alternative charges.[318] The purpose of alternative charges is to address uncertainty regarding the precise legal characterisation of the conduct alleged and not to permit multiple convictions arising from the same factual foundation.

Once the findings have been determined, they are announced in open court, subject to confirmation.[319] Where the accused is found "Not Guilty" on all charges, the proceedings are signed by the Presiding Officer and the Judge Advocate and forwarded to the confirming authority in accordance with the prescribed procedure.[320]

Where a finding of "Guilty" is recorded, the Court proceeds to the sentencing stage. At this stage, evidence relating to the accused's general character, age, rank, service record, decorations, distinguished conduct, and other relevant circumstances may be produced before the Court. Such material is not directed towards establishing guilt but assists the Court in determining an appropriate sentence.

The accused is also afforded an opportunity to address the Court in mitigation of punishment.[321] Through such a statement, he may

---

317 Union of India v Sunil Tiwari, Mil LJ 2001 SC 159.
318 AR 1954, r 62 (7).
319 *Id.* r 62 (10).
320 *Id.* r 63.
321 *Id.* r 64.

draw attention to circumstances that justify leniency, including previous good service, personal hardships, provocation, remorse, or any other factor relevant to the determination of sentence. This stage reflects the principle that punishment should be individualised and proportionate, taking into account not only the offence but also the circumstances of the offender.

The recording of findings therefore represents the culmination of the adjudicatory phase of the Court Martial process. By requiring deliberation in closed court, adherence to the standard of proof beyond reasonable doubt, reasoned findings, and consideration of both prosecution and defence evidence, military law seeks to ensure that conclusions regarding guilt are reached through a process that is fair, rational, and consistent with the principles of justice.

SENTENCE BY THE COURT

Upon recording a finding of guilt, the Court Martial proceeds to determine the appropriate sentence. As a general rule, the Court awards a single sentence in respect of all offences of which the accused has been convicted.[322] The sentencing powers of a Court Martial are confined to those punishments specifically authorised under Section 71 of the Army Act, 1950. No punishment outside the statutory framework may be imposed.

The determination of sentence is a collective responsibility of the Members of the Court. Each Member is required to participate in the decision-making process and vote upon the quantum of punishment to be awarded.[323] Where the Court considers

322 *Id.* r 65.

323 Jha, *supra note* at p77

that mercy or clemency should be recommended, the reasons supporting such recommendation must be recorded.[324] Once determined, the sentence is announced in open court, subject to confirmation by the competent confirming authority.[325]

In deciding upon the appropriate punishment, the Court is required to consider a variety of factors relevant to both the offence and the offender. These include the necessity of maintaining discipline within the Armed Forces, the degree of criminality involved, the presence or absence of premeditation, the existence of provocation, the influence of unusual or unaccustomed surroundings, and the circumstances in which the offence was committed. The Court may further take into account the service record of the accused, whether he is a first-time offender or a habitual offender, his previous conduct, and the particular demands of the service in which he is employed.[326] In cases involving offences against a superior officer, the rank and position of the person affected may also be relevant considerations. Certain forms of military service may involve exceptional responsibilities, and the Court is entitled to consider such circumstances when assessing the appropriate punishment.

The punishment awarded may be the punishment specifically prescribed for the offence or any lesser punishment authorised under Section 72 of the Army Act. Where the conviction relates to a civil offence triable under military law, the Court Martial may award the punishment prescribed under the corresponding civil law or such punishment as is authorised by the Army Act,

---

324 AR 1954, r 66.

325 *Id.* r 67.

326 *Id.* r 64 (Vide Note 6).

including rigorous imprisonment for a term extending up to seven years.[327] However, where civil law prescribes a mandatory punishment for a particular offence, the Court is ordinarily required to impose that punishment.

Military law also permits the award of more than one punishment in combination where such combination is authorised by statute and considered appropriate in the circumstances of the case.[328] The exercise of this power, however, remains subject to the fundamental requirement that punishment must be lawful, proportionate, and just.

The principle of proportionality occupies an important place in military sentencing. The punishment imposed must bear a reasonable relationship to the gravity of the offence and the circumstances of the offender. A sentence that is excessively severe, vindictive, arbitrary, or disproportionately harsh may undermine confidence in the administration of military justice and, in exceptional cases, may itself constitute evidence of unfairness or bias in the decision-making process.[329]

The requirement of proportionality is particularly significant in military justice because the consequences of conviction frequently extend beyond the immediate punishment imposed. In addition to penal sanctions, a conviction may adversely affect the service career, reputation, future employment prospects, and livelihood of the accused. The sentencing process must therefore balance the legitimate demands of military discipline with the

327 AA 1950, § 69.

328 *Id.* § 73.

329 Ranjit Thakur v Union of India, AIR 1987, SC 238. ; Ex Naik Sardar Singh v Union of India, (1991) 3 SCC 213.

equally important requirement of fairness to the individual service member.

Once sentence has been awarded, the proceedings are forwarded to the appropriate confirming authority for consideration and confirmation in accordance with the statutory scheme governing Court Martial proceedings.[330] Until such confirmation is granted, the sentence does not attain finality.

CONFIRMATION AND REVISION

One of the most distinctive features of the military justice system is the requirement that the findings and sentence of a Court Martial do not attain legal validity until confirmed by the competent confirming authority. Unlike judgments delivered by civilian criminal courts, the findings and sentence of a General Court Martial (GCM), District Court Martial (DCM), and Summary General Court Martial (SGCM) remain in the nature of recommendations until confirmation is granted in accordance with the provisions of the Army Act.[331] Consequently, a challenge to such findings prior to confirmation is ordinarily regarded as premature, since no enforceable determination has yet come into existence.[332]

The competent confirming authority varies according to the nature of the Court Martial concerned. In the case of a General Court Martial, confirmation may be granted by the Central Government or by an officer empowered through an A-2 or

330 Jha, *supra* note 62 at p. 78.

331 AA 1950, §153.

332 Capt. Ashok Kumar Rana v Union of India, 1982 Cri LJ NOC 120 (Delhi).

A-3 warrant issued by the Central Government.[333] In the case of a District Court Martial, the competent authority is an officer empowered to convene a General Court Martial or an officer authorised under a B-1 warrant.[334] In respect of a Summary General Court Martial, confirmation ordinarily rests with the Convening Authority, although the matter may be referred to a superior authority where so directed.[335]

Special provisions apply in certain categories of cases. A sentence of death requires confirmation by the Central Government.[336] Similarly, where the Court Martial records a finding of "Not Guilty" in respect of an offence punishable with death or where the accused holds, or held at the relevant time, the rank of Brigadier, the power to confirm or withhold confirmation is vested in the Chief of the Army Staff. In all other cases involving acquittal, the power of confirmation or non-confirmation ordinarily rests with the General Officer Commanding-in-Chief.[337]

The confirmation process serves as an additional layer of scrutiny within the military justice system. The confirming authority is required to examine the legality, propriety, and correctness of the proceedings before deciding whether the findings and sentence should be confirmed. However, unlike the appellate process in civilian courts, confirmation is primarily an administrative review conducted within the military chain of command.

---

333 AA 1950, §154.
334 *Id.* § 155.
335 *Id.* § 157.
336 RA 1987, ¶ 472 (a).
337 *Id.* ¶ 472 (d).

Where the confirming authority is dissatisfied with the findings or sentence, it may direct that the proceedings be revised. In appropriate cases, the authority may also require the Court Martial to receive additional evidence before reconsidering the matter. Revision is conducted by the same Court Martial composed, so far as practicable, of the same Members who participated in the original proceedings.[338]

For the purpose of revision, the Court reassembles in open court and receives any additional evidence directed to be taken. Thereafter, the Members deliberate in closed court and reconsider the issues referred for revision. Following such reconsideration, the Court records fresh findings or sentence, as the case may be, and the earlier determination stands superseded.[339] The revised proceedings are then forwarded once again to the confirming authority through the Judge Advocate for further consideration.[340]

Where only the sentence has been referred for revision, the Court is not entitled to reconsider or alter its findings. Equally important is the principle that the power of revision may be exercised only once. If, after revision, the Court adheres to its original view, the confirming authority is ordinarily bound to confirm the proceedings.[341] The process therefore seeks to balance supervisory control with a degree of finality in judicial decision-making.

The principle against double jeopardy also applies within the military justice system. Whether the accused has been convicted

---

338 AA 1950, 160.

339 AR 1954, r 68.

340 RA 1987, ¶ 471.

341 Jha, *supra* note 62 at 79.

or acquitted, he cannot ordinarily be tried a second time for the same offence.[342] This safeguard protects the accused against repeated prosecutions and reinforces the finality of Court Martial proceedings once they have passed through the statutory process of confirmation.

Although the confirming authority possesses extensive supervisory powers, those powers are not unlimited. The authority cannot substitute its own findings for those of the Court Martial, nor can it enhance the sentence imposed by the Court.[343] It may, however, mitigate, remit, or commute the punishment awarded.[344] These powers are intended to operate as safeguards against excessive punishment and to permit consideration of factors that may justify leniency.

A significant criticism of the confirmation and revision process is that the accused is not ordinarily afforded an opportunity of being heard before the confirming authority decides whether to confirm the proceedings or direct revision. The decision is taken administratively, without any formal hearing, and the statutory framework provides limited opportunity for the accused to challenge the process at that stage.

This aspect of military justice has attracted considerable criticism. Where revision is directed, the practical consequence is often that the Court Martial is expected to reconsider its earlier decision in light of the concerns expressed by a superior authority. Given the hierarchical nature of military command, concerns have occasionally been raised that the views of the confirming

---

342 AA 1950, § 121.

343 *Id.* §153 (Vide Note 5).

344 *Id.* § 158.

authority may exert considerable influence upon the Members of the Court Martial. Since the confirming authority occupies a position of superior command and exercises administrative control over the careers of subordinate officers, questions have arisen regarding the extent to which the revision process may affect the independence of military adjudication.

These concerns have frequently been the subject of challenge before civilian courts and form part of the broader debate regarding the compatibility of the military justice system with contemporary principles of judicial independence and procedural fairness.[345] While confirmation and revision were historically intended as safeguards against error, their continued operation raises important questions regarding the balance between command control and adjudicatory independence within the military justice system.

PROMULGATION

Following confirmation or non-confirmation of the proceedings, the charge, findings, sentence, recommendation for mercy (if any), and the order of confirmation or non-confirmation are formally promulgated to the accused. Until promulgation takes place, the findings and sentence do not attain legal validity.[346] At this stage, the accused is also informed of his right to submit a statutory petition against the findings or sentence.[347]

The fact of promulgation is recorded in the proceedings in the prescribed form. In cases resulting in complete acquittal, or where all findings of guilt have not been confirmed, the relevant

345 Jha, *supra*, note 62 at 79

346 AR 1954, R 71.

347 RA 1987, ¶365 (m).

modifications are made in the record. Promulgation is ordinarily carried out by the appropriate military authority depending upon the rank and status of the accused.

The Confirming Authority in the case of a General Court Martial, District Court Martial, or Summary General Court Martial, and the Commanding Officer in the case of a Summary Court Martial, may direct promulgation to take place at a parade. If accused absents himself before promulgation, after he has been declared as such by a COI held under Army Act Section 106, promulgation can be effected by publication of necessary information in unit orders (Part I in case of Officers and Part II in case of others).[348] Promulgation constitutes the final stage in the confirmation process, and confirmation remains incomplete until it has been duly carried out.[349] Significantly, even where a convicted person ceases to be subject to the Army Act after promulgation, the statutory right to submit a petition against the findings or sentence continues to remain available under the Army Act.[350]

APPEAL OF COURT MARTIAL DECISIONS

Prior to the establishment of the Armed Forces Tribunal (AFT), the Army Act, Navy Act, and Air Force Act did not provide a statutory right of appeal against the findings and sentences of Courts Martial. Consequently, Courts Martial functioned as the first and final forums of adjudication in military criminal

348 AR 1954, r 71 and RA 1987, ¶ 473

349 AR 1954, r 70 vide Note 4; *see also* Maj Parvesh Chander Suri v. Union of India, (1987) 5 SLR 648.

350 AA 1950, § 164 (2) ; *see also* SN Mukherjee v. Union of India, (1990) 4 SCC 594.

matters. The principal judicial remedy available to service personnel was through the writ jurisdiction of the High Courts and the Supreme Court. However, such review was limited to examining issues of legality, procedural irregularity, jurisdictional error, or violation of the principles of natural justice, and did not ordinarily extend to re-appreciation of evidence or reconsideration of the quantum of punishment.[351]

The position changed with the establishment of the Armed Forces Tribunal in 2009. The AFT was vested with jurisdiction to hear appeals against the findings, orders, and sentences of Courts Martial, together with matters connected therewith. The Act further provides for an appeal to the Supreme Court against decisions of the Tribunal in specified circumstances.[352] The creation of the AFT thus introduced, for the first time, a dedicated appellate mechanism within the military justice system.

The only remedy that the accused had, before the sentence was confirmed[353] and after the finding and sentence has been finally confirmed, was to submit a petition to the confirming authority against the finding and sentence of the Court-martial.[354]

Under the Navy Act, 1957, an additional safeguard exists in the form of judicial review of Court Martial proceedings by the Judge Advocate General, though such review is recommendatory

351 Col Harjeet Singh, *Armed Forces Tribunal: An Appraisal*, 26.2, April-June 2011, *available at* http://www.indiandefencereview.com/news/armed-forces-tribunals-an-appraisal/2/ (Accessed on 12.07.22).

352 Lt. Col. Prithi Pal Singh Bedi *supra* note 73.
(held: the absence of even one appeal with the power to review the findings and punishment is a glaring lacuna in Military law in India).

353 Also known as Pre-confirmation Petition under AA 1950,§ 164 (1).

354 *Id.* § 164 (2).

in nature.[355] In cases involving capital punishment or where directed by the President, the matter is referred by the Chief of the Naval Staff to the Central Government with appropriate recommendations.[356] However, an acquittal recorded by a Court Martial cannot ordinarily be set aside by the Judge Advocate General, the Chief of the Naval Staff, or the Central Government.[357]

PARDONS AND REMISSIONS UNDER SECTION 179 OF THE ARMY ACT

Section 179 of the Army Act empowers the Central Government, the Chief of the Army Staff, and prescribed independent commanders to grant remission, commutation, pardon, or release on parole to persons sentenced by a Court Martial. In accordance with the Regulations for the Army, such powers cannot ordinarily be exercised by an authority subordinate to the Confirming Authority or by an authority that has already passed an order under Section 179.[358]

Remissions cannot be granted by State Governments unless authorised by the President or a competent authority under the Army Act. While pardon, remission, and release on parole may be made subject to conditions accepted by the convicted person, mitigation and commutation cannot be conditional in nature.[359]

In addition to the statutory powers under the Army Act, the President of India possesses the constitutional power under

355 Jha, *supra* note 62 at 82; *See also*, Navy Act 1957, § 160.
356 NA 1957, § 161(1).
357 *Id.* § 161(2).
358 Kashmir Singh v. Union of India, 1990 Cri L J 1417.
359 AA 1950, § 180 and Note 5 (a) to AA § 179.

Article 72 to grant pardons, reprieves, respites, suspensions, remissions, or commutations in appropriate cases. Although this power is wide in scope, its exercise remains subject to judicial review on recognised constitutional grounds.

The Central Government, the Chief of the Army Staff, and other prescribed authorities may also suspend a sentence of imprisonment either before or after the convicted person has been committed to prison or military custody.[360] After the sentence is suspended the accused is released from custody.[361] The power of suspension is distinct from, and in addition to, the powers of remission, mitigation, commutation, and pardon available under military law.

Table 6.3: Comparative Analysis of the Post-Trial Process under BNSS and Military Law

Stage	BNSS 2023	Military Justice System
Sentencing Authority	Judge	Court-Martial
Effect of Judgment	Effective upon Pronouncement	Requires Confirmation
Confirmation Process	Not Applicable	Mandatory
Revision	Revisional Courts	Confirming Authority may order Revision
Promulgation	Not Applicable	Essential for finality
Appeal	Multi-tier Judicial Appeals	Armed Forces Tribunal and Supreme Court

360 *Id.* § 182 (1).
361 *Id.* § 184.

Review Mechanism	Judicial Review	Statutory Petitions, AFT, Judicial Review
Pardon / Clemency	Articles 72 and 161 Constitution	Section 179 Army Act and Article 72
Final Objective	Justice and Public Order	Discipline and Justice

CONCLUSION

The comparison between the civilian criminal justice system and the military justice system reveals significant structural and procedural differences. In most organised services, disciplinary authorities are empowered only to investigate and adjudicate service-related misconduct. The consequences of such proceedings are generally administrative in nature and may include censure, suspension, stoppage of increments, loss of seniority, recovery of damages, or dismissal from service. Although these penalties may have serious professional consequences, they do not ordinarily involve criminal sanctions affecting an individual's liberty.

The position in the Armed Forces is fundamentally different. Military authorities are empowered not only to deal with service offences but also, in appropriate cases, to try civil offences through the mechanism of a Court Martial. The jurisdiction exercised by military courts is therefore considerably broader than that exercised by disciplinary tribunals in other services. A Court Martial may impose punishments ranging from minor disciplinary sanctions to imprisonment and, in exceptional cases, even the death penalty. The consequences of conviction thus extend far beyond service matters and may directly affect an individual's liberty, reputation, and future livelihood.

Another distinguishing feature of the military justice system is that the adjudicatory function is ordinarily performed by serving military officers selected in accordance with the provisions of the Army Act and the Army Rules. While such officers possess considerable experience in matters of command, discipline, and military administration, they are not necessarily trained legal professionals. The system therefore relies upon the assistance of the Judge Advocate and the procedural safeguards incorporated within military law to ensure that legal principles are correctly applied and that justice is administered fairly.

The study of the pre-trial, trial, and post-trial stages of Court Martial proceedings demonstrates that military law contains an elaborate procedural framework intended to protect the rights of the accused. At the same time, the chapter has highlighted certain structural features that distinguish military justice from its civilian counterpart, including the concentration of multiple functions within the chain of command, the process of confirmation and revision, and the limited role historically accorded to appellate review. These characteristics have been the subject of continuing debate regarding their compatibility with contemporary notions of judicial independence, due process, and fair trial rights.

The maintenance of discipline remains an indispensable requirement for the operational effectiveness of the Armed Forces. However, the greater the powers exercised by a justice system and the more serious the consequences it may impose, the greater is the need for procedural safeguards and institutional fairness. A military justice system that successfully balances the demands of discipline with the requirements of fairness not only strengthens public confidence in its legitimacy but also reinforces the trust of service personnel who are subject to its jurisdiction.

The Court Martial system therefore occupies a unique position within the legal framework of the nation. It serves an essential disciplinary function while simultaneously exercising powers that may profoundly affect the life and liberty of members of the Armed Forces. The continued evolution of military justice must therefore strive to ensure that the imperatives of discipline are harmonised with the constitutional commitment to fairness, due process, and the rule of law.

CHAPTER 07

Unlawful Command Influence and Institutional Corruption[362]

INTRODUCTION

Unlawful Command Influence (UCI) has often been described as the greatest threat to the integrity of a military justice system. It arises when an authority, in a position of command and influence, exerts pressure—whether direct or indirect—upon Court Members, the Judge Advocate, witnesses, or any other individual connected with Court-Martial proceedings. In the context of the present study, the focus is upon the role of the Convening Authority and the extent to which the powers vested in that office may create opportunities for the exercise, or perception, of undue influence.

The exercise of such influence strikes at the very foundation of military justice. It not only compromises the fairness and impartiality of judicial proceedings but also affects the confidence of service personnel in the legitimacy of the system itself. A noteworthy aspect of the Indian Military Justice System is that neither the Army Act nor the allied statutes

362 This chapter has joint inputs by Dr. Jyoti Puri and Colonel Chandra Nath (retd.), an independent researcher in Information Security, Privacy and Law, residing in Los Angeles, California, USA.

governing the Armed Forces expressly define the concept of Unlawful Command Influence. Nor do they contain a specific prohibition against the exercise of such influence or coercion. Consequently, although service personnel may be affected by its operation, they possess limited statutory means of objecting to its application.

The concept of corruption is ordinarily associated with financial impropriety, bribery, or abuse of public office for personal gain. However, contemporary scholarship recognises that corruption may assume broader institutional forms. References are commonly made to police corruption, judicial corruption, political corruption, and academic corruption.[363] The present chapter is concerned with corruption within a self-contained military justice system and, more specifically, with the manner in which institutional structures may create conditions conducive to the abuse of authority.

As has been observed:

"When a person in authority motivated by sadistic pleasure abuses his/her power by meting out cruel and unjust treatment to those subject to his/her authority, [he or she] is not engaging in an economic crime motivated by economic considerations but surely motivated by a desire to exercise power for its own sake rather than by a desire for financial reward."[364]

---

363 Justice Olubunmi Oyewole, High Court of Lagos, Lecture at the National Convention of Charleans in Diaspora at Irwing Convention Plaza, Texas: Corruption: Challenge to Good Governance and Development in Nigeria (Aug. 7, 2010), *available at* http://www.anticorruptionleague.org/articles/corruption-challenge-to-good-governance-and-development-in-nigeria.php (Accessed on 05.04. 2013).

364 Miller, Seumas, "Corruption", *The Stanford Encyclopedia of Philosophy (Spring 2011 Edition)*, Edward N. Zalta (ed.), available at:

Such conduct may not involve financial gain, yet it raises serious concerns regarding the abuse of institutional power. In this sense, corruption need not be confined to pecuniary misconduct; it may also manifest itself through the misuse of authority in a manner that undermines fairness, accountability, and justice. It is this form of institutional corruption, operating within the framework of military justice, that forms the central focus of the present chapter. Indeed, it may be argued that Unlawful Command Influence provides fertile ground upon which such corruption can flourish.

A similar understanding emerges from judicial pronouncements referred to by R. Kannan,[365] wherein the Supreme Court observed:[366]

"The word 'corruption' does not necessarily include an element of bribe taking. It is used in a much larger sense as denoting conduct which is normally unsound or debased. The word is not synonymous with the words dishonestly or fraudulently but is much wider. It even includes conduct which is neither fraudulent nor dishonest, if it is otherwise blameworthy or improper."[367]

This broader conception of corruption is particularly relevant in the context of military justice. The concern is not merely whether an official derives a personal benefit, but whether institutional

---

http://plato.stanford.edu/entries/corruption/ (Accessed on 25.08. 2011).

365 R.Kannan, *Corruption the Malicious Virus that Haunts our Society*, Integrity in Public Life and Service Personal Website (Feb. 7, 2011), *available at* http://kannanpersonal.com/projects/corruption-misconduct/corruption.html (Accessed on 04.02. 2012).

366 Union of India vs. Dr. S. Dutt, AIR 1966, S.C. 523.

367 *Id. also cited* in Kannan, *supra* note 365.

processes are distorted in a manner that compromises fairness, impartiality, and public confidence in the administration of justice.

In order to understand the nature and implications of Unlawful Command Influence, it is first necessary to examine the office capable of exercising such influence and the mechanisms through which it may operate. This requires an examination of the role of the Convening Authority—a central figure in the military justice system who possesses extensive powers at multiple stages of Court-Martial proceedings. The concentration of such authority, while historically justified on grounds of discipline and command responsibility, inevitably raises questions regarding institutional independence, accountability, and the potential for abuse. It is within this framework that the relationship between Unlawful Command Influence and institutional corruption must be examined.

DISPENSER OF FAVOUR AND FORTUNE: THE ALL-POWERFUL CONVENING AUTHORITY – RISK OF CORRUPTION

The concentration of extensive powers in a single authority inevitably raises concerns regarding accountability, arbitrariness, and the potential misuse of power. It is often observed that when wide discretionary powers are vested in one individual without corresponding institutional safeguards, the risk of abuse increases. For this reason, any examination of military justice must begin with the office of the Convening Authority, for military justice, in many respects, both begins and ends with this authority.

The Convening Authority occupies a central position within the military justice system. Empowered by the requisite warrant under the Army Act, he bears responsibility for initiating and supervising Court-Martial proceedings. His involvement commences at the earliest stages of the disciplinary process. He may order a Court of Inquiry, appoint the officers who conduct it, and determine whether its findings warrant further action. Decisions regarding the preferring of charges and the type of Court-Martial to be convened also fall within his jurisdiction.

The Convening Authority further determines the venue, date, and time of the trial and appoints the Presiding Officer and Members of the Court. He requests the appointment of a Judge Advocate through the Judge Advocate General's Department and, in certain circumstances, may himself arrange for such appointment. The Prosecuting Officer and Defending Officer are similarly appointed, either directly or through subordinate commanders acting under his directions. Thus, the Convening Authority exercises influence at virtually every stage of the military justice process.[368]

Informal accounts from officers who have participated in Court-Martial proceedings as Presiding Officers or Judge Advocates suggest that, on occasion, Convening Authorities may communicate their expectations regarding the outcome of particular proceedings. While such accounts remain anecdotal and cannot be independently verified due to the anonymity of the individuals concerned, they nevertheless raise important questions regarding the perception of independence within

368 Charles W. Schiesser & Daniel H. Benson, *A Proposal to Make Court-Martial Courts: The Removal of Commanders from Military Justice*, 7, Texas Tech Law Review, 561 (1975-76), *available at* http://repository.law.ttu.edu/bitstream/handle/10601/1558/7TexTechLRev559.pdf?sequence=1 (Accessed on 24.09. 2012).

the military justice system. Even the appearance of external influence may affect confidence in the fairness and impartiality of the process.

The responsibilities of the Convening Authority extend beyond the constitution of the Court. He is required to ensure the attendance of prosecution witnesses, facilitate the preparation of the defence, and secure the attendance of defence witnesses reasonably requested by the accused. In this respect, he performs functions that significantly affect both the prosecution and defence aspects of the proceedings.

The Convening Authority also possesses the power to dissolve a Court-Martial before or during trial where such action is considered necessary in the interests of justice. Additionally, in cases requiring confirmation, he may comment upon the proceedings before taking a decision regarding their validity and effectiveness.

Historically, the role of the Convening Authority has attracted particular attention because the same authority often exercises both convening and confirming functions. Court-Martial findings and sentences do not ordinarily become operative until confirmation has been granted. Although legal advice may be sought from the Judge Advocate General's Department, the Convening Authority is not bound to follow such advice. He may postpone confirmation, remit or mitigate punishment, or otherwise exercise powers vested in him by law. Furthermore, where advice is received from the Judge Advocate General's Department during the review process, neither the fact that such advice has been obtained nor its contents are necessarily disclosed to the accused.

As Schiesser & Benson, observed:

"When performing within prescribed statutory limits, a Convening Authority is exercising his command duties and responsibilities, and in so doing, he is exerting what may be called 'lawful' command influence upon the administration of military justice under his command."[369]

This observation highlights the distinction between lawful command responsibility and unlawful command influence. The exercise of command authority is an indispensable feature of military administration. Nevertheless, concerns arise where the concentration of powers creates circumstances in which personal prejudices, preconceptions, or institutional pressures may affect decision-making.

The possibility of such influence is particularly significant because the Convening Authority may possess knowledge of facts, evidence, or circumstances unknown to the accused. In situations where substantial discretionary powers are concentrated in one office, the fairness of the system depends largely upon the good faith, objectivity, and integrity of the individual exercising those powers. The administration of military justice must therefore be guided not by a desire to secure convictions but by the broader objective of ensuring that justice is done.

From an institutional perspective, corruption may arise when extensive powers are vested in public officials without adequate mechanisms of accountability. As has been observed:

"This means the more activities public officials control or regulate the more opportunities exist for corruption. Furthermore, lower

369 *Id.* at p 559-618.

the probability of detection and punishment, the greater the risk that corruption will take place."[370]

The relevance of this observation to military justice lies not in suggesting that corruption necessarily exists, but in recognising that institutional structures may create opportunities for its emergence if adequate safeguards are absent.

A similar concern is reflected in the views expressed by Glenda Ewing, a representative of an advocacy group for military families in the United States, who stated:

"The court-martial is not an instrument of justice and impartiality; it is a tool used to destroy those targeted by corrupt men who would manipulate the system for their own devious ends. For in the military, there are different rules, two distinct sets of laws. You're either in a category 'above it', or mercilessly beneath its crushing weight. And what does that do to the families of our service men? It causes deep bitterness within the soul of humanity. It carelessly and with impunity destroys the very roots of the Constitution on which this nation was founded."[371]

While such remarks undoubtedly reflect a deeply personal perspective, they nevertheless illustrate the intensity of

---

370 Center for Democracy and Governance, Handbook on Fighting Corruption (Feb 1999), *available at* www.usai.gov/our_work/democracy_and_governance/publications/pdfs/pnac070.pdf (Accessed on 28.09.2011).

371 Major Glenn MacDonald, *Marine Mom Takes on Military "Justice" System- Glenda Ewing, Courageous Fighter For Reform, Testifies Before the Cox Commission in Washington D.C*, Military Corruption. Com, *available at* http://www.militarycorruption.com/marinejustice.htm (Accessed on 28.09.2011).

concern that may arise whenever a justice system is perceived as lacking independence or impartiality. Whether justified or not, such perceptions have the potential to erode confidence in the legitimacy of military justice. It is therefore essential that military institutions not only ensure fairness in practice but also maintain structures that inspire confidence in the fairness of their processes.

WHAT CONSTITUTES UNLAWFUL COMMAND INFLUENCE?

Military justice systems recognise a distinction between lawful command influence and unlawful command influence. The former is an inevitable and legitimate aspect of military command and discipline,[372] whereas the latter constitutes an impermissible interference with the administration of justice. While commanders are entitled to exercise authority in matters of discipline and military administration, they are not permitted to influence judicial outcomes or interfere with the independent functioning of Court-Martial proceedings.

Unlawful Command Influence (UCI) may manifest itself in several forms, including actual, apparent, and perceived influence.[373] Actual UCI exists where, having regard to the totality of circumstances, the evidence would lead a reasonable person to conclude that command influence affected the disposition

372 United States v. Wallace 39 MJ 284(CMA 1994) (The Commanders suggestion that company commander reconsider the decision to dispose of offences by non-judicial punishment was not considered as unlawful command influence).

373 David A Schlueter, Military Criminal Justice: Practice and Procedure, (LexisNexis, USA 2004); *See also* United States v. Allen 31 MJ 572 (NMCMR 1990).

of the case and prejudiced those responsible for adjudicating it. Apparent or perceived UCI may arise even where no actual interference has occurred, if the circumstances are such as to create a reasonable perception that the independence of the proceedings has been compromised. Both forms are significant because military justice depends not only upon fairness in fact but also upon public confidence in its fairness.

The concerns associated with command influence were recognised by the Supreme Court of India, which observed:

"Courts-martial are typically ad hoc bodies appointed by a military officer from among his subordinates. They have always been subject to varying degrees of 'command influence'. In essence, these tribunals are simply executive tribunals whose personnel are in the executive chain of command. Frequently, the members of the court-martial must look to the appointing officer for promotions, advantageous assignments and efficiency ratings—in short, for their future progress in the service. Conceding to military personnel that high degree of honesty and sense of justice which nearly all of them undoubtedly have, the members of a Court-martial, in the nature of things, do not and cannot have the independence of jurors drawn from the general public or of civilian judges."[374]

The concern that command influence may undermine judicial independence is not unique to India. In the United States, the celebrated Vanderbilt Report examined the dangers arising from excessive command control over military justice and recommended measures to insulate Courts-Martial from improper influence. The Report observed:

---

374 Lt. Col. Prithi Pal Singh Bedi *supra note* 73,; Reid v Covert, 354 U.S. 1(1956) at 1174.

"Undoubtedly there was in many instances an honest conviction that since the appointing authority was responsible for the welfare and lives of his men, he also had the power to punish them, and consequently the courts appointed by him should carry out his will. We think that this attitude is completely wrong and subversive of morale; and that it is necessary to take definite steps to guard against the breakdown of the system at this point by making such action contrary to the Articles of War or regulations and by protecting the courts from the influence of the officers who authorize and conduct the prosecution."[375]

The significance of these observations lies in the recognition that military discipline and judicial independence are not mutually exclusive concepts. On the contrary, confidence in military justice is strengthened when adjudicatory bodies are protected from external pressures and are perceived to decide cases solely on the basis of evidence and law.

Viewed from this perspective, concerns arise where a single authority exercises substantial influence over multiple stages of the military justice process, including the initiation of proceedings, constitution of the Court, appointment of key participants, and post-trial review. The issue is not whether such powers are invariably misused, but whether the concentration of authority creates circumstances in which the possibility, perception, or appearance of influence may arise. In modern systems of justice, institutional safeguards are generally designed to minimise precisely such risks.

---

375 Arthur T. Vanderbilt, *Advisory Committee on Military Justice*, 7 (Dec. 13, 1946), *available at* http://www.loc.gov/rr/frd/Military_Law/pdf/report-war-dept-advisory-committee.pdf,1 (Accessed on 02.10.2012).

A useful illustration may be drawn by comparing military justice with an equivalent civilian model. If a civilian system were established in which an executive authority determined when courts would sit, selected the adjudicators, appointed both prosecution and defence representatives, controlled the review of decisions, and retained the power to approve the outcome before it became effective, serious questions would inevitably arise regarding the independence of that system. Such comparisons help illuminate why concerns regarding command influence continue to occupy a central place in discussions of military justice.

Comparable concerns have also emerged in constitutional jurisprudence outside India. Analysis of decisions of the High Court of Australia[376] demonstrates the longstanding tension between military tribunals and the constitutional requirement of judicial independence. Although Courts-Martial are created by statute, they have often been criticised on the ground that they remain part of the executive structure rather than the judicial branch. The absence of security of tenure, institutional independence, and final decision-making authority has frequently been cited as raising constitutional concerns. These observations acquire particular relevance in the Indian context, where Court-Martial findings remain subject to executive confirmation and military tribunals continue to operate within the chain of command.

The United States has sought to address these concerns legislatively. Article 37 of the Uniform Code of Military

376 Lane v Morrison (2009) HCA 29, 26 August 2009, C3/2008, *available at* http://www.clrg.info/2011/02/lane-v-morrison-2009-hca-29-26-august-2009/ (Accessed on 26.09.2012).

Justice expressly identifies and prohibits conduct amounting to unlawful command influence.[377] The provision reflects a recognition that confidence in military justice requires not merely an assumption of fairness but statutory safeguards against improper interference. The absence of an equivalent and express prohibition in Indian military legislation raises important questions regarding whether greater statutory clarity may be desirable.

The distinction between actual and apparent UCI is significant. Actual UCI directly affects the fairness of a particular proceeding, whereas apparent UCI affects public confidence in the legitimacy of the military justice system.[378] Even where a proceeding is technically fair, a perception that decisions are influenced by command considerations may undermine confidence in the administration of justice.

---

377 Unified Code of Military Justice (UCMJ), art. 37 (it states in part: No authority convening a general, special, or summary court martial, nor any other commanding officer, may censure, reprimand, or admonish the court or any member, military judge, or counsel thereof, with respect to the findings or sentence adjudged by the court, or with respect to any other exercise of its or his functions in the conduct of the proceeding. No person subject to this chapter may attempt to coerce or, by any unauthorized means, influence the action of a court-martial or any other military tribunal or any member thereof, in reaching the findings or sentence in any case, or the action of any convening, approving, or reviewing authority with respect to his judicial acts).
available at http://www.afjag.af.mil/shared/media/document/AFD-120531-050.pdf (Accessed on 01.10.12).

378 United States v. Rodriguez 16 MJ 740 (AFCMR 1983).

The consequences of such influence were highlighted in proceedings before the Delhi High Court, where the Court observed:[379]

"Law reigns supreme and that is the constitutional mandate in this country. The Military Intelligence Directorate cannot, under the parameters fixed under the Constitution and under the provisions of the Army Act and Army Rules, assume the role of a prosecutor and a judge of its own cause. To give an air of verisimilitude the respondents (military authorities) had held the Court-martial proceedings which are wholly void."[380]

At its core, the debate surrounding unlawful command influence concerns a principle common to all systems of justice: every individual is entitled to be presumed innocent until proven guilty by an independent and impartial tribunal. Military service does not diminish the importance of that principle. On the contrary, where liberty, career, reputation, and in some cases life itself are at stake, the need for impartial adjudication becomes even more compelling.

The challenge for any military justice system is therefore to ensure that the legitimate demands of command and discipline do not encroach upon the independence of the adjudicatory process. It is in this context that Lord Acton's enduring observation remains relevant:

"Power tends to corrupt and absolute power corrupts absolutely."[381]

---

379 Jha, *supra* note 62, at 194.

380 Ex Major NR Ajwani v Union of India,95 (2002) DLT 770.

381 John Emerich Edward Dalberg Acton, first Baron Acton (1834–1902). The historian and moralist, who was otherwise known simply as Lord

The significance of the aphorism lies not in suggesting that power will invariably be abused, but in emphasising the need for institutional safeguards that prevent the concentration of authority from undermining fairness, accountability, and public confidence in the administration of justice.

BIRD'S-EYE VIEW OF THE ROLE OF THE CONVENING AUTHORITY AND THE POTENTIAL FOR UNLAWFUL COMMAND INFLUENCE

For a clearer understanding of how institutional influence may operate within the military justice system, the role of the Convening Authority may be viewed across the following stages:

I. Court of Inquiry Stage

The Convening Authority initiates the Court of Inquiry, appoints its members, and retains the power to accept or reject its findings. Given the hierarchical nature of military command, concerns may arise regarding the extent to which subordinate officers remain insulated from command expectations.

II. Review of Preliminary Findings

Where the findings of a Court of Inquiry are considered unsatisfactory, a fresh inquiry may be directed. This power, though lawful, has occasionally been criticised on the ground that repeated inquiries may create a perception that a particular outcome is being sought.

Acton, expressed this opinion in a letter to Bishop Mandell Creighton in 1887.

III. Constitution of the Court-Martial

The Convening Authority determines the type of Court-Martial to be assembled and appoints its President and Members. Consequently, the authority responsible for initiating proceedings also plays a significant role in constituting the adjudicatory body.

IV. Defence Representation

Although Defending Officers are expected to discharge their duties fearlessly and independently, concerns have occasionally been expressed regarding whether officers serving within the same command structure may feel constrained when defending an accused against the interests of the command.

V. Confirmation and Revision

Court-Martial findings do not ordinarily become effective until confirmed by the competent authority. The power to confirm, remit, mitigate, or direct revision of proceedings has been cited as one of the principal areas in which concerns regarding institutional independence arise.

VI. Role of the Judge Advocate

The Judge Advocate serves as the principal legal adviser to the Court-Martial and plays an important role in guiding the Members on questions of law and procedure. However, because the Judge Advocate functions within the broader military framework, questions are sometimes raised regarding whether the office enjoys the same degree of institutional independence that characterises civilian judicial systems.

INSTITUTIONAL CORRUPTION AND ITS EFFECT ON THE RIGHTS OF CITIZEN-SERVICEMEN

The theory of Institutional Corruption, as discussed in the *Stanford Encyclopaedia of Philosophy*,[382] provides a useful framework for examining the operation of military justice systems and the potential impact of Unlawful Command Influence upon them. The principal elements of the theory may be summarised as follows:

1. The Personal Character of Corruption

Individuals play a central role in all forms of corruption, including institutional corruption. Institutional processes are ultimately shaped by the actions and decisions of those who occupy positions of authority within them.

2. The Causal Character of Corruption

An act may be regarded as institutionally corrupt where it undermines a legitimate institutional process, frustrates an institutional purpose, or compromises the integrity of those performing institutional roles. In the context of military justice, Unlawful Command Influence may be viewed as an example of conduct capable of undermining the independence and legitimacy of the adjudicatory process.

3. The Moral Responsibility of Corruptors

Institutional corruption presupposes a degree of moral responsibility. An individual who intentionally causes harm to

---

382 Miller, Seumas, Corruption, *The Stanford Encyclopedia of Philosophy*, (Edward N. Zalta ed., Spring 2011 ed.), *available at* http://plato.stanford.edu/archives/spr2011/entries/corruption/ (Accessed on 29.09.2011).

institutional processes, foresees such harm, or reasonably ought to have foreseen it, bears responsibility for the consequences of that conduct.

4. The Asymmetry Between Corruptors and the Corrupted

Institutional corruption frequently operates through unequal power relationships. Within military justice, such asymmetry may arise between the Convening Authority, Court Members, Judge Advocates, witnesses, and the accused, each of whom occupies a markedly different position within the military hierarchy.

5. Institutional Actors and Institutional Processes

Institutional corruption involves actors whose conduct undermines legitimate institutional objectives. The concern is not confined to individual wrongdoing but extends to systemic practices that may impair the fairness, integrity, or effectiveness of institutional processes.

Viewed through this framework, it becomes evident that personal gain is not always the primary motivation behind corruption. In military institutions, corruption may arise not only from individual misconduct but also from outdated structures, flawed procedures, or institutional arrangements that permit undue influence to operate unchecked. The concern is therefore broader than financial impropriety; it encompasses any practice that compromises the integrity of the justice system.

From this perspective, the prevention of undue pressure upon adjudicators, legal advisers, witnesses, and other participants becomes essential to maintaining confidence in military justice. A system perceived to be vulnerable to improper influence risks eroding not only the trust of service personnel but also public confidence in the Armed Forces as institutions governed by law. Failure to recognise and address such vulnerabilities may ultimately weaken the legitimacy of the military justice system itself.

Particular concern arises where command expectations, whether explicit or implicit, are capable of influencing the decision-making process. For example, where adjudicators perceive that severe punishment is expected in order to convey a disciplinary message, questions may arise as to whether sentencing decisions are being made solely on the basis of evidence and law. 'With this mantle of command authority the adjudicators of the accused toe the line of action, as implicitly given by the Convening Authority and the accused is left without any hope of a feasibly Fair Trial.'[383] In such circumstances, the appearance of independence may be as important as independence itself.

As one can observe in journals speaking on UCI-

"The general concern regarding Unlawful Command Influence is that the Commander has the ability to influence judicial proceedings and participants in such a way as to deprive the accused of his right to a Fair Trial."[384]

---

383 United States v Stombaugh 40 MJ 2008 (C.M.A 1994). (The language actually predates *Stombaugh*, but it effectively became part of the test for command influence in Stombaugh).

384 Jack L. Rives & Steven J. Ehlenbeck, *Civilian Versus Military Justice in the United States: A Comparative Analysis*, 52 Air Force Law Review, 213, 232, at 226, (2002), *available at* http://www.afjag.af.mil/shared/media/document/AFD-081204-027.pdf (Accessed on 05.10.2012); Lindsy Nicole Alleman, *Who is in Charge and Who Should Be? The Disciplinary Role of the Commander*

'There is no provision in the statues governing Military Law which can hold the Convening Authority responsible and accountable for the use of such implicit or explicit opinions and perceptions which potentially effects the rights of the service personnel. 'The rights of the servicemen cannot be abridged completely either by the constitution nor by the statutes beyond what is the minimum need for the proper functioning of the land, sea and air forces in a war like situation.'[385]

A notable feature of the Indian military justice system is the absence of any express statutory provision specifically addressing or prohibiting Unlawful Command Influence. Consequently, questions of accountability become difficult to address where influence is exercised indirectly through perceptions, expectations, or institutional pressures rather than through overt instructions.

The importance of protecting the rights of service personnel has been repeatedly recognised in constitutional jurisprudence. The rights of members of the Armed Forces may be restricted to the extent necessary for the effective functioning of the military, but such restrictions cannot extend beyond what is reasonably required for that purpose. Military necessity cannot become a justification for the complete erosion of fundamental principles of fairness and justice.

---

in Military Justice Systems, 16, Duke Journal of Comparative and International Law 169,191 (2006), *available at* http://scholarship.law.duke.edu/cgi/viewcontent.cgi?article=1110&context=djcil (Accessed on 04.10.2012).

385 Evolving Military Justice (Eugene. R. Fidel & Dwight Hall Sullivan eds., Navel Institute Press, 2002), *available at* http://books.google.co.in/books?id=G3tYljWV_zEC&printsec=frontcover&source=gbs_ge_summary_r&cad=0#v=onepage&q&f=false (Accessed on 01.03.2012).

The Supreme Court of India has emphasised the importance of limiting discretionary power by observing:

"Our Constitution envisages a society governed by Rule of Law. Absolute discretion uncontrolled by guidelines which may permit denial of equality before law is the antithesis of rule of law. Equality before law and the absolute discretion to grant or deny benefit of law are diametrically opposed to each other and cannot co-exist."[386]

The relationship between authority and influence was similarly examined in *Youngblood*, where the Court observed:[387]

"....military subordinates take seriously what their superiors say. When those superiors make strong statements about military justice, it is unreasonable to expect that those subordinate commanders can block out those opinions and perceptions and make decisions wholly unaffected by their superiors' statements. Moreover, it is unreasonable to expect non-lawyers to put command pressure in neat boxes... Under the circumstances, we hold that it was 'asking too much' of [the officers] to expect them to impartially adjudge an appropriate sentence without regard for its potential impact on their careers."

The observations in *Youngblood* reflect a broader concern regarding the relationship between hierarchy and adjudicatory independence. Military commanders necessarily exercise extensive authority, and such authority is indispensable to discipline and operational effectiveness. Nevertheless, where disciplinary authority intersects with judicial functions, heightened scrutiny becomes necessary to ensure that justice is

386 Sudhir Chandra v. Tata Iron and Steel Co. Ltd, A.I.R 1984, S.C 064

387 United States v Youngblood 47 M.J 338 at p 342 (1997).

both done and seen to be done. The military Commander's role is wide and powerful and with this comes the problem of him using it in an arbitrary manner. 'Because of this, the words of commanders warrant the greatest scrutiny.'[388]

As Lindsey Nicole Alleman observed:

"By establishing such a dominant role for the Convening Authority, the Military Justice System presents the potential problem of a commander using his power and influence in such a way as to thwart the fairness, impartiality, and integrity of disciplinary proceedings."[389]

Ultimately, the issue is not whether senior officers may offer guidance or advice to their subordinates. Rather, the concern is whether the structure of the system provides sufficient safeguards to ensure that adjudicators remain free to accept or reject such views without fear of adverse professional consequences. A reasonably informed observer may question the independence of proceedings where authority over appointments, promotions, postings, and disciplinary processes is concentrated in the same hierarchy responsible for the administration of military justice. It is this perception, as much as actual interference, that lies at the heart of concerns regarding Unlawful Command Influence and institutional corruption.

---

388 Lieutenant Colonel Lawrence J. Morris, *This Better Be Good: The Courts Continue to Tighten the Burden in Unlawful Command Influence Cases*, DA-PAM- 27-50-306, The Army Lawyer, 49,67,(1998), *available at* https://www.jagcnet.army.mil/DOCLIBS/.../Article%204.pdf (Accessed on 03.10.2012).

389 Lindsy Nicole Alleman, *Who Is in Charge, and Who Should Be? The Disciplinary Role of the Commander in Military Justice Systems*, p 171, 16 Duke J. Comp. & Int'l L. 169 (2006).'

CONCLUSION

The present study demonstrates that corruption within a military justice system need not be confined to bribery or personal enrichment. It may also manifest through institutional structures that permit, encourage, or create the perception of undue influence over judicial decision-making. In the Indian Military Justice System, the concentration of extensive powers in the office of the Convening Authority creates a risk of Unlawful Command Influence and raises legitimate concerns regarding fairness, independence, and accountability.

A comparative examination of military justice systems in other democratic jurisdictions reveals a clear trend towards limiting the role of convening authorities and strengthening institutional safeguards designed to protect the independence of military courts. Such reforms have been undertaken not to weaken discipline but to enhance confidence in the legitimacy of military justice.

The continued vesting of investigative, administrative, adjudicatory, and review-related powers within the same command structure creates an environment in which actual or perceived influence may arise. Even where no improper influence is intended, the perception that career advancement, postings, or professional assessments may be affected by judicial decisions has the potential to undermine confidence in the impartiality of proceedings.

Military judges must be insulated from the non-legal chain of command. Full-time trial and defense functions should be outside the influence of military commanders. Removing the Judge Advocate General (JAG) from the chain of command and placing it under the Ministry of Defence would help ensure fair trials, free from the undue influence of the Convening Authority. An independent JAG should be present during Court-Martial trials and should have the authority to make legal decisions, rather than simply advising the Court on legal matters. This is crucial because the Court Members are typically officers with little legal expertise. Additionally, the JAG should have input on the quantum of punishment, ensuring that it aligns with principles of penology and jurisprudence, thus helping to prevent unjust or disproportionate sentencing.

To effectively eliminate corruption within the Military Justice System, it is essential that the Appellate Tribunal be empowered to punish those responsible for miscarriages of justice and to award compensation to those wronged by the system. This will ensure that authorities act more judiciously and are held accountable for their decisions.

Meaningful reform therefore requires the creation of stronger institutional safeguards. The powers of confirmation and revision should be reconsidered, military judges and Judge Advocates should enjoy greater independence from the non-legal chain of command, and prosecutorial, administrative, and adjudicatory functions should be more clearly separated. Equally important is the establishment of effective mechanisms of accountability and judicial review capable of addressing instances of improper influence and compensating those adversely affected by miscarriages of justice.

Ultimately, the objective is not to diminish military discipline but to strengthen it through a justice system that commands the confidence of both service personnel and the public. A military justice system that is independent, transparent, and fair is not inconsistent with discipline; rather, it is essential to its legitimacy. The establishment of a dedicated task force to examine and implement reforms would constitute a constructive step towards achieving a system that effectively balances operational necessity with the constitutional values of fairness, due process, and the rule of law.

CHAPTER 08

Through the Prism of Independence and Impartiality

Military Justice Reforms in the United Kingdom, United States, and India

INTRODUCTION

This chapter examines the evolution of military justice systems in the United Kingdom, the United States, and India through the lens of judicial independence and impartiality. The British Military Justice System assumes particular significance because it served as the foundation upon which the Indian Military Justice System was originally constructed. Despite subsequent legislative developments, many of the structural features of the Indian system continue to reflect their British origins. Similarly, the American Military Justice System traces its roots to the British Articles of War of 1774, although it has since undergone extensive reform in response to constitutional, legislative, and judicial developments.

Over the past century, both the United Kingdom and the United States have undertaken significant reforms aimed at strengthening the independence, impartiality, and legitimacy of military courts. These reforms form part of a broader international movement towards aligning military justice systems with contemporary standards of due process and fair trial rights. The gradual reduction of command influence, the creation of independent prosecutorial mechanisms, the establishment of standing courts, the expansion of appellate review, and the strengthening of the rights of accused service personnel are among the notable developments that have shaped modern military justice in these jurisdictions.[390]

A comparative study of these reforms provides a useful framework for evaluating the Indian Military Justice System and identifying areas where further institutional development may be warranted. The experiences of the United Kingdom and the United States demonstrate that the maintenance of military discipline is not incompatible with judicial independence. Rather, confidence in military justice is enhanced when disciplinary objectives are balanced with procedural fairness and effective safeguards against arbitrariness.

The contemporary understanding of the right to a fair trial has been significantly influenced by international human rights instruments and the jurisprudence developed under them. Among the most influential are the European Convention on Human Rights (ECHR), the American Convention on Human Rights, and the International Covenant on Civil and Political Rights (ICCPR). The standards articulated by these instruments, particularly in relation to independent and impartial tribunals,

390 Arne Willy Dahl, Presentation at the Global Military Appellate Seminar at Yale Law School: International trends in Military Justice (Apr. 1&2, 2011), *available at:* http://www.law.yale.edu/2011-04_International_trends.pdf (Accessed on 20.12.2012).

have played an important role in shaping reforms within military justice systems across democratic jurisdictions.

Against this backdrop, the present chapter analyses the major reforms undertaken in the United Kingdom and the United States, before examining corresponding developments within India. The objective is not merely to trace legislative changes, but to assess the extent to which these reforms have strengthened the independence, impartiality, and fairness of military justice institutions while preserving the essential requirements of military discipline and operational effectiveness.

CHANGES IN THE BRITISH MILITARY JUSTICE SYSTEM – A BRIEF INTRODUCTION

The origins of the Court-Martial system in England may be traced to around 1296, when Military Courts accompanied the English Army in Scotland.[391] The enactment of the Mutiny Act of 1689 formally recognised military courts and conferred parliamentary sanction upon the exercise of their jurisdiction. Until 1805, however, Court-Martial proceedings were not formally recorded, and neither witnesses nor members of the Court were required to take an oath.[392]

391 James Stuart-Smith, *Without Partiality, Favour or Affection,* Il-2, The Military Law and Law of War Review (1963), *available at* http://heinonline.org/HOL/LandingPage?collection=journals&handle=hein.journals/mllwr2&div=18&id=&page=/ (Accessed on 04.12. 2012).

392 Stephen Stratford, *British Military and Criminal History in the Period of 1900-1999, available at* http://www.stephen-stratford.co.uk/history_cm.htm, (Accessed on 20.09. 2012).

By the late eighteenth century, the Military Court had begun to acquire characteristics of a modern judicial institution. One notable deficiency, however, was the dual role of the Judge Advocate, who functioned both as legal adviser and prosecutor. This position was rectified by amendments to the Articles of War in 1860, which confined the Judge Advocate's role to that of a legal adviser. The Royal Air Force, established on 1 April 1918, adopted a similar system, which was subsequently reformed following the Lewis Committee Report and incorporated into the Air Force Act, 1955.[393]

Military discipline and criminal justice in the United Kingdom were traditionally governed by three principal enactments: the Army Act 1955, the Air Force Act 1955, and the Naval Discipline Act 1957, collectively known as the Service Discipline Acts.[394] Under these statutes, three forms of Court-Martial existed: the General Court-Martial (GCM), the District Court-Martial (DCM), and the Field General Court-Martial (FGCM).[395] While the FGCM was primarily intended for active service conditions, the GCM and DCM functioned during peacetime. The DCM

393 James Stuart-Smith, *Military Law: Its History, Administration and Practice,* 85 Law Quarterly Review, 478 (1969); *also cited* in Jha, *supra* note 319 at 86.

394 Armed Forces Bill Team, Ministry of Defence, An Overview of the Service Justice System and the Armed Forces Act, *available at* http://www.mod.uk/NR/rdonlyres/0D289346-3BAA-4446-9164-4600458D1CE9/0/AnOverviewoftheServiceJusticeSystemandtheArmedForcesAct.pdf (Accessed on 15.09. 2012).

395 *Serving Those Who Serve,* Court Martial UK- Forces Law (Jun. 2, 2012, 21:39:26), *available at* http://www.forceslaw .com/services/courts_martial.htm (Accessed on 12.09. 2012).

possessed limited sentencing powers, whereas the GCM could award any punishment authorised by law.[396]

Officers were ordinarily tried by a General Court-Martial, while Warrant Officers could be tried by a District Court-Martial. A DCM generally consisted of not fewer than three officers, whereas a GCM comprised at least five members together with a Judge Advocate appointed through the Judge Advocate General's Branch. Unlike the permanent Crown Courts, Courts-Martial were constituted on an ad hoc basis for individual cases. Prosecutions were conducted by service prosecutors, while the accused was entitled to legal representation of his choice.[397]

STEPPING FORWARD: THE UNITED KINGDOM MILITARY JUSTICE SYSTEM

The question of providing service personnel with a meaningful right of appeal emerged as a significant issue in the development of British military justice. The Darling Committee Report (1919), constituted to examine the law and procedure governing Courts-Martial, and the Oliver Committee Report (1938), which considered the feasibility of appeals from Courts-Martial to civilian courts, generally concluded that the existing system of review provided adequate safeguards for the administration of justice.[398]

A decisive shift occurred with the Lewis Committee Report (1946), which recommended that members of the Armed Forces should be granted a right of appeal to an independent judicial

---

396 *Id.*

397 *Id.*

398 Jha, *supra* note 62 at p 258.

forum. The Committee further proposed that this appellate mechanism should replace the existing system of confirmation and review by the Judge Advocate General. It recommended that appeals should be confined to questions of law and should be directed against findings rather than sentences.[399]

These recommendations formed the foundation of the Court-Martial (Appeals) Act, 1951, which established the Court-Martial Appeal Court (CMAC).[400] The new appellate structure provided service personnel with an independent avenue for challenging Court-Martial convictions and introduced an additional safeguard against miscarriages of justice beyond the traditional military review process.[401]

Further reforms followed in the human rights era. Although the death penalty for murder had been abolished earlier, it remained available for certain military offences such as mutiny, failure to suppress or report mutiny, and treason. These provisions were ultimately abolished by the Human Rights Act, under Section 21(5) of the Act 1998.[402]

A major turning point in British military justice came with the decision of the European Court of Human Rights in *Findlay*

---

399 Court Martial (Appeals) Bill, HC Deb, vol. 483, 595- 674 (Order of Second Reading, Read, Jan. 25, 1951), *available at* http://hansard.millbanksystems.com/commons/1951/jan/29/courts-martial-appeals-bill (Accessed on 05.11. 2012).

400 The appeal to Court-Martial Appeal Court(CMAC), is against conviction involving death, unreasonable punishment to supported by evidence or any kind of miscarriage of justice or faulty decisions involving points of law. Decisions of CMAC are final and appeals from CMAC lies with the House of Lords only with its leave.

401 Court Martial (Appeals) Bill *supra* note 395.

402 Stratford, *supra* note 388.

v. United Kingdom.[403] The judgment raised serious concerns regarding the independence and impartiality of the Court-Martial system and accelerated the process of reform that culminated in the Armed Forces Acts of 1996 and 2006. The Court emphasised that public confidence in military justice depended not only upon actual fairness but also upon the appearance of fairness.[404]

This principle echoed the celebrated observation of Lord Chief Justice Hewart that:

"It is not merely of some importance, but is of fundamental importance that justice should not only be done, but should manifestly and undoubtedly be seen to be done."[405].

---

403 *Findlay supra note* 124. (The Court conscious of the conflicting role of the Convening authority as a key Prosecutor as well as selector of member under his chain of command for the Court-martial, thereby raising the question of their independence and impartial nature, held that Court-martial was not structured in a way that guaranteed independence and impartiality as required by Article 6 of ECHR. The Court was further concerned about the Convening authority's power to dissolve Court-martial before or during the Trial and acting as Confirming Officer after the Trial so that Court-martial conviction and sentence were not effective until confirmed by the Convening authority. This vesting of power of convening as well as confirming on a single authority undermined the judicial nature of the Court-martial. the Court also pointed out that the Judge Advocates role was very limited and only that of being advisory in nature).

404 Wing Commander Simon P. Rowlinson, *The British System of Military Justice*, 52 Air Force Law Review, 17, 51 (2002), *available at* http://www.afjag.af.mil/shared/media/document/AFD-081204-027.pdf (Accessed on 01.05. 2012).

405 Rex, *supra* note 9; *see also* Re: Sussex Justices (1924) 1 KB at 256.

THE ARMED FORCES ACT, 1996

The Armed Forces Act, 1996[406] amended the three Service Discipline Acts—the Army Act 1955, the Air Force Act 1955, and the Naval Discipline Act 1957—with the objective of bringing the military justice system into closer conformity with the requirements of the European Convention on Human Rights. A central feature of the reforms was the reduction of the Convening Authority's influence by distributing its functions among separate authorities within the military justice framework.[407]

Under the new system, decisions regarding the disposal of cases were entrusted to a higher authority, which determined whether a matter should be dealt with summarily or referred for trial. Prosecutorial functions were assigned to an independent Prosecuting Authority, while Court Administration Officers, independent of both the prosecuting and higher authorities, became responsible for selecting Court-Martial members.

The Act introduced several significant structural and procedural reforms:

1. **Separation of Functions:** The authority responsible for deciding the mode of trial no longer selected Court-Martial members, thereby reducing the possibility of command influence over the composition of the Court.
2. **Enhanced Role of the Judge Advocate:** The Judge Advocate became an integral participant in Court-Martial proceedings. His rulings on questions of law

406 Armed Forces Act 1996, *available at* http://www.legislation.gov.uk/ukpga/1996/46/contents, also *available at* http://ukinnepal.fco.gov.uk/en/news/?view=Speech&id=23132445 (Accessed on 10.09. 2012).

407 Rowlinson, *supra* note 400 at p. 20.

became binding upon the Court, and he participated in sentencing, though not in determining guilt or innocence. Reasons for sentence were required to be announced in open Court.

3. **Abolition of Confirmation:** The traditional requirement of confirmation of findings and sentences was abolished, although the system of review was retained.
4. **Expanded Appellate Rights:** In addition to appeals against conviction, service personnel were granted a right of appeal against sentence.[408]
5. **Police and Evidentiary Reforms:** The powers of the Service Police and rules relating to evidence were substantially revised to strengthen procedural fairness.[409]
6. **Unified Redressal Mechanism:** A common system for the redress of complaints was introduced for personnel of all ranks.

These reforms marked a significant step towards enhancing the independence, transparency, and fairness of the British Military Justice System while preserving its disciplinary function.

THE ARMED FORCES DISCIPLINE ACT, 2000

The Human Rights Act, 1998, which came into force on 2 October 2000, necessitated a review of several provisions contained in the Service Discipline Acts to ensure compliance

408 Armed Forces Act 1996, *available at* http://www.legislation.gov.uk/ukpga/1996/46/crossheading/review-and-appeal (Accessed on 10.09.2012).

409 *Id.*

with the European Convention on Human Rights. The most significant reform introduced by the Armed Forces Discipline Act, 2000 was the establishment of the Summary Appeal Court, providing service personnel with a right of appeal against findings and punishments awarded during summary proceedings. The Act also strengthened safeguards relating to custody and expanded the right of an accused to elect trial by Court-Martial.[410]

Another important reform concerned sentencing powers. The General Court-Martial became the sole military court empowered to award life imprisonment, while the death penalty was abolished. The Act further brought arrest and custody procedures within all three Services

into conformity with Article 5 of the European Convention on Human Rights.[411]

---

410 Armed Forces Discipline Act 2000, *available at* http://www.legislation.gov.uk/ukpga/2000/4/contents (Accessed on 16.09.2012)

411 The European Convention for the Protection of Human Rights and Fundamental Freedoms, art. 5, cl., 1950 (it states that 'everyone has the right to liberty and security of the person. No one shall be deprived of his liberty save in the following cases and in accordance with a procedure prescribed by law:
(a) the lawful detention of a person after conviction by a competent court;
(b) the lawful arrest or detention of a person for non-compliance with the lawful order of a court or in order to secure the fulfilment of any obligation prescribed by law;
(c) the lawful arrest or detention of a person effected for the purpose of bringing him before the competent legal authority on reasonable suspicion of having committed an offence or when it is reasonably considered necessary to prevent his committing an offence or fleeing after having done so; ... ').

THE ARMED FORCES ACT, 2006

The Armed Forces Act, 2006,[412] which came fully into force on 31 October 2009, replaced the separate service systems with a unified code of service law applicable to all branches of the United Kingdom Armed Forces.[413] The Act sought to simplify military justice administration while preserving the link between command and discipline.[414]

Among its significant reforms was the establishment of a Standing Court-Martial, replacing the earlier ad hoc model. Service personnel retained the right to elect trial by Court-Martial instead of summary disposal, while convictions arising from summary proceedings became appealable before the Summary Appeal Court. Convictions by Court-Martial remained subject to appeal before the Court-Martial Appeal Court (CMAC).[415]

The Act further strengthened prosecutorial independence through the creation of the Service Prosecuting Authority (SPA), an organisation independent of the chain of command and responsible for decisions relating to prosecution and the conduct of Court-Martial proceedings. Serious offences were required to

412 Armed Forces Act 2006, *available at* http://www.legislation.gov.uk/ukpga/2006/52/contents (Accessed on 11.09.2012).

413 HE John A Tucknott, HMA Speech on ICJ/NJA Event, Guaranteeing Fair Trial Rights in Military Court (Nov. 1, 2010), *available at* http://ukinnepal.fco.gov.uk/en/news/?view=Speech&id=23132445 (Accessed on 10.09.2012).

414 Armed Forces Act 2006, *available at* http://www.legislation.gov.uk/ukpga/2006/52/part/14/crossheading/redress-of-individual-grievances (Accessed on 16.09.2012).

415 *Ibid,*

be referred to the Service Police and thereafter considered by the Director of Service Prosecutions.[416, 417]

The complaints system was also modernised. An independent Service Complaints Commissioner was established to oversee the effectiveness, fairness, and efficiency of the complaints process and to report annually to Parliament. These reforms significantly enhanced the independence, accountability, and transparency of the British Military Justice System.[418]

THE ARMED FORCES ACT, 2021

The Armed Forces Act, 2021[419] represents the latest stage in the evolution of the United Kingdom's military framework. Its principal objective was to strengthen the Armed Forces Covenant by placing a legal duty upon specified public authorities to give "due regard" to its principles when exercising relevant functions. The Act recognises the unique obligations and sacrifices associated with military service and seeks to ensure that serving personnel, veterans, and their families are not disadvantaged in accessing public services.

The Act also introduced measures aimed at improving the Service Justice System and further enhancing confidence in its fairness and effectiveness. In addition, amendments were made to the Reserve Forces Act 1996 by replacing the traditional

416 Tucknott, *supra* note 413.

417 Armed Forces Act 2006, *available at* http://www.legislation.gov.uk/ukpga/2006/52/part/14/crossheading/redress-of-individual-grievances (Accessed on 16.09.2012).

418 *Id.*

419 Available at, https://www.legislation.gov.uk/ukpga/2021/35/contents (Accessed on 14.11.2024).

full-time service commitment with a more flexible continuous service commitment, thereby allowing reservists to serve on either a full-time or part-time basis.

A significant provision of the Act is Clause 8, which amends the Armed Forces Act 2006 by requiring authorities to have due regard to the principles of the Armed Forces Covenant. These include recognising the unique demands of military service, removing disadvantages suffered by service personnel and veterans, and permitting special measures where justified by the circumstances of service.

The Armed Forces Act, 2021 therefore reflects a continuing commitment to the welfare of service personnel, veterans, and their families, while simultaneously strengthening the institutional framework of the Service Justice System.

CHANGES IN THE AMERICAN MILITARY JUSTICE SYSTEM

The American Military Justice System has undergone a series of significant reforms, particularly in 1916, 1920, 1950, 1968, 1983, 2016, and 2021. These reforms reflect a gradual movement away from the command-centric model inherited from the British Articles of War towards a system that affords greater procedural safeguards to service personnel. Nevertheless, debates continue regarding the extent to which military justice should remain under command control while meeting contemporary standards of due process and fairness.

Historically, the system lacked many of the safeguards associated with modern criminal justice. Commanders exercised extensive control over the preferring of charges, constitution of courts, and post-trial review. There were no standing courts, military judges, organised defence services, or comprehensive appellate mechanisms. The rights available to accused service personnel were therefore considerably more limited than those recognised today.

BRIEF HISTORY

American military law traces its origins to the British Articles of War of 1774 and predates both the United States Constitution and the Declaration of Independence. Early military justice was characterised by a small standing army and a disciplinary framework heavily influenced by British practice.

An important catalyst for reform arose in 1786 when Major John Wyllys ordered the execution of deserters without trial. The incident prompted congressional scrutiny and led to procedural safeguards requiring review of Court-Martial sentences before execution.[420] Similarly, the controversial actions of Captain Alexander Mackenzie in 1843, involving the execution of sailors following proceedings conducted without basic procedural protections, exposed serious deficiencies in the military justice system and strengthened demands for appellate review and judicial safeguards. The need for some form of appellate procedure was championed and in 1949-1950 the Court of Military Appeals came into being.[421]

---

420 Fay Jones, Book Review (reviewing Jonathan Lurie, *Military Justice in America: The U.S. Court of Appeals for the Armed Forces, 1775-1980,* (Jul. 2001)), *available at* http://www.bsos.umd.edu/gvpt/lpbr/subpages/reviews/Lurie01t.htm. (Accessed on 20 .10.2012).

421 *Id.* (Captain Alexander Mackenzie of the U. S. Navy in 1843 held a Court-martial at sea wherein he executed three members of the

Thus Unification of the Armed Forces in matters of Military Justice System came about in 1947. The then first Secretary of Defence, Secretary Forrestal, brought some major changes which changed the face of the United States Military Justice System. His greatest contribution was the proposal of unified code to be applied to all branches of the Armed forces and thus began the stage for a new uniform system of discipline.[422]

A major turning point occurred following the unification of the Armed Forces in 1947. Under the leadership of Secretary of defence James Forrestal, efforts were initiated to establish a uniform system of military justice applicable to all branches of the Armed Forces. These reforms ultimately culminated in the adoption of the Uniform Code of Military Justice (UCMJ) and The Manual for Courts-Martial (MCM), which today constitute the foundation of American military law.

Under the UCMJ, military justice is administered through three forms of Court-Martial: the Summary Court-Martial, the Special Court-Martial, and the General Court-Martial. Accused

---

crew, one of whom, Philip Spencer, was the son of the secretary of war. This incident brought about Mackenzie's Court-martial where he was acquitted of improper conduct. When this matter came up for review it came to light that the trial of those three crew member was held secretly and the accused were given no opportunity to cross examine any witnesses or justify any of their actions. Moreover it was further found that Mackenzie had exerted his influence of that of the Commander over the Members of the Court-martial which brought about the conviction and execution of the accused sailors. In fact Mackenzie had acted as accuser, judge, jury and executioner all in one.)

422 Military Justice Fact Sheets, *available at* http://www.hqmc.marines.mil/Portals/135/MJFACTSHTS[1].html (Accessed on 20 .10.2012).

personnel are afforded substantial procedural protections, including the right to legal representation, the right to present evidence, the right to cross-examine witnesses, and the right to appellate review. The UCMJ also recognises the importance of mental capacity in criminal responsibility, providing safeguards where an accused is unable to understand proceedings or assist in his defence due to mental disease or defect.[423]

IMPORTANT CHANGES PRIOR TO THE UNIFORM CODE OF MILITARY JUSTICE

Before the enactment of the Uniform Code of Military Justice (UCMJ),[424] American military justice was governed by the Articles of War of 1916, 1920, and 1948, together with the Manual for Courts-Martial promulgated by Presidential authority. These enactments progressively transformed military justice from a purely command-driven system into one incorporating greater procedural safeguards and judicial oversight.

ARTICLES OF WAR, 1916

The Articles of War, 1916 introduced several important reforms. The jurisdiction of General Courts-Martial was expanded, procedural rules relating to depositions and limitation periods were modernised, and reviewing authorities were empowered to approve lesser included offences. Voting requirements for the imposition of the death penalty were also strengthened.

---

423 R. Chuck Mason, Congressional Research Service, Military Justice: Court Martial, An Overview (Mar. 31, 2011), *available at* http://www.fas.org/sgp/crs/natsec/R41739.pdf, (Accessed on 12 .09 .2012).
Judge Advocate Generals School, US Army, The Background of Uniform Code of Military Justice (1970),

424 *Ibid.*

A significant debate emerged during this period between Brigadier General Samuel T. Ansell and Major General Enoch H. Crowder regarding the scope of review by the Judge Advocate General's office. Ansell advocated a stronger system of legal review independent of command influence, while Crowder viewed such review as advisory to commanders. This debate raised fundamental questions regarding the compatibility of military discipline with the rule of law and laid the groundwork for future reforms.[425]

ARTICLES OF WAR, 1920

Following extensive study of British, French, and Belgian military justice systems, the Articles of War, 1920 introduced substantial procedural safeguards. Enlisted personnel were granted rights comparable to officers in preferring charges, and accused persons received expanded rights of cross-examination during preliminary proceedings.

The Convening Authority was required to obtain pre-trial and post-trial advice from the Staff Judge Advocate, while the appointment of defence counsel became mandatory. Provision was also made for Law Members, rehearings, suspension of sentences, and mandatory appellate review of all General Courts-Martial.

The reforms further strengthened voting requirements for convictions and capital punishment, prohibited reconsideration

---

425 Walter T. Cox III, *The Army, The Courts, and The Constitution: The Evolution Of Military Justice*, 118 Military Law Review, 10 (1987), *available at* http://www.loc.gov/rr/frd/Military_Law/Military_Law_Review/pdf-files/277C61~1.pdf (Accessed on 28 .10.2012).

of acquittals, and restricted the imposition of harsher sentences upon revision. These measures significantly enhanced fairness and reduced the risk of arbitrary decision-making.

The experience of the two World Wars exposed deficiencies in military justice, particularly the limited procedural protections available to accused personnel. Growing criticism from professional organisations, including the American Bar Association and various military legal associations, generated momentum for comprehensive reform, culminating in the Elston Bill and subsequent legislative changes.[426]

ARTICLES OF WAR, 1948

The Articles of War, 1948, enacted following the recommendations embodied in the Elston Bill, marked a major advance in military justice. Warrant Officers and enlisted personnel became eligible to serve as Court-Martial members, while Trial Judges and Defence Counsel were required to be legally qualified members of the Judge Advocate General's Corps.

The reforms strengthened protections against self-incrimination, expanded the powers of Law Members, enhanced the accused's ability to secure witnesses and documents, and authorised re-hearings in specified circumstances. For the first time, appellate bodies such as the Boards of Review and the Judicial Council were empowered to review questions of fact, assess witness credibility, and evaluate the sufficiency of evidence.

Perhaps most significantly, Convening Authorities and Commanding Officers were expressly prohibited from censuring

426 Military Justice Fact Sheets, *supra* note 422.

or influencing Courts-Martial or their members in relation to findings, sentences, or judicial functions. These provisions represented an early statutory attempt to curb command influence and strengthen the independence of military adjudication.

THE UNIFORM CODE OF MILITARY JUSTICE (UCMJ)

The Uniform Code of Military Justice (UCMJ), which came into force on 31 May 1951, was the product of the extensive study undertaken by the Forrestal Committee. It marked a decisive shift in American military justice by strengthening procedural safeguards, expanding the rights of accused service personnel, and reducing the influence traditionally exercised by commanders over Court-Martial proceedings.[427] The UCMJ also established a uniform system of military justice applicable to all branches of the Armed Forces and created an independent appellate structure through the Court of Military Appeals.

For fostering the essence of uniformity, under this Code offences made punishable are identical for all the Armed forces. There is

---

427 Beth Hillman, Review (Reform), *Chains of Command*, Legal Affairs, (May- June 2002), *available at* http://legalaffairs.org/issues/May-June-2002/review_hillman_mayjun2002.msp (Accessed on 24.07.2012); *See also*, *Noyd v. Bond*, 395 U.S, 683, at 694, (1969), (wherein the court stated specifically: "When, after the Second World War, Congress became convinced of the need to assure direct civilian review over military justice, it deliberately chose to confide this power to a specialized Court of Military Appeals so that disinterested civilian judges could gain, over time, a fully developed understanding of the distinctive problems and legal traditions of the Armed Forces"), *available at* http://supreme.justia.com/cases/federal/us/395/683/case.html (Accessed on 27.10.2012).

one system of Court with same jurisdiction limitation. All the procedure followed are similar from inception to culmination as are the qualifications of the Members and legal officers. The Court of Military Appeals which finally decides questions of law, is the Court of last resort for each of the Armed Forces and also acts with the Judge Advocates General as an advisory body with a view to securing uniformity in policy and in sentences and in discovering and remedying defects in the system and its administration.[428]

The Code sought to balance the competing demands of military discipline and legal accountability. While preserving the commander's role in the disciplinary process, it introduced significant protections designed to promote fairness and limit arbitrary decision-making. Among its important features[429] were:

1. The right to legal counsel at the pre-trial stage.
2. Prohibition of charges unsupported by sufficient evidence or failing to disclose an offence.
3. Mandatory appointment of legally qualified counsel for both prosecution and defence.
4. Protection against compulsory self-incrimination.
5. Equal opportunity for the prosecution and defence to obtain witnesses and evidence.
6. Trial by a panel including peers of the accused, with enlisted personnel entitled to representation by enlisted members.
7. Secret-ballot voting on findings and sentence.

---

428 Judge Advocate Generals School, *supra* note 423.
429 *Id.*

8. Written legal instructions on matters such as the presumption of innocence, burden of proof, and elements of offences.
9. Automatic appellate review of specified cases by Boards of Review, with legal representation for the accused.
10. Prohibition on accepting guilty pleas in capital cases.
11. Further review of questions of law by the Court of Military Appeals.

Despite these reforms, substantial authority remained vested in the Convening Authority. Military judges, as understood today, were not originally contemplated under the UCMJ, and Law Officers continued to function within a system influenced by command structures. Summary Courts-Martial did not provide legal counsel as of right, although an accused could elect trial by a higher Court-Martial where legal representation was available.[430]

The expansion of procedural safeguards continued through judicial intervention. In 1966, the United States Supreme Court[431] recognised the right of an accused to be informed of the right to counsel during custodial interrogation, a protection later reflected in military practice. Article 31 of the UCMJ

430 Fedric. L. Lederer & Barbara Hundley Zeliff, *Needed an Independent Military Judiciary: A Proposal to Amend the Uniform Code Of Military Justice, in* Evolving Military Justice 27 (Eugene. R. Fidel & Dwight Hall Sullivan eds., Navel Institute Press, 2002) p 629,(This article in chapter three originally appeared in the Wake Forest Law Review), *available at* http://books.google.co.in/books?id=G3tYljWV_zEC&printsec=frontcover&source=gbs_ge_summary_r&cad=0#v=onepage&q&f=false (Accessed on 02.03.2012).

431 Miranda v. Arizona, 384 U.S, 436 (1966)

further strengthened safeguards by requiring that a suspect be informed of the nature of the offence under investigation before questioning. Under Article 31 of the Code of UCMJ, an accused is advised of the offense or offenses of which he is suspected of, which allows him to answer questions more intelligently. The Uniform Code clearly provides that the duties of counsel do not end with the trial. [432]

'In a series of well-known decisions in the 1950s and '60s, the Court refused to extend Court-martial jurisdiction to include non-service members, frustrating commanders who sought control over civilians accompanying military personnel overseas.'[433]

The Supreme Court also played an important role in limiting military jurisdiction. In *Reid v. Covert* (1957),[434] it held that civilians accompanying the Armed Forces overseas could not be subjected to military criminal jurisdiction where doing so would deny them the constitutional protections available in civilian courts.[435] The decision reinforced the principle that military necessity cannot justify the complete displacement of fundamental legal rights.

---

432 UCMJ, art. 38 (c) (it provides for: ' in every court-martial proceeding, the defense counsel may, in the event of conviction, forward for attachment to the record of proceedings a brief of such matters as he feels should be considered in behalf of an accused on review, including any objection to the contents of the record which he considers appropriate').

433 Hillman, *supra* note 427.

434 Reid V. Covert, 354, U.S 1, (1957), *available at* http://www.law.cornell.edu/supct/html/historics/USSC_CR_0354_0001_ZO.html (Accessed on 25.10.2012).

435 Hillman, *supra* note 423.

THE MILITARY JUSTICE ACT, 1968

The Military Justice Act, 1968 represented a major step towards the judicialisation of the American Military Justice System. Its principal objective was to strengthen judicial independence by creating the office of the Military Judge,[436] with legally qualified officers appointed through the Judge Advocate General's Corps. Unlike earlier arrangements, Military Judges were not directly responsible to commanders, thereby reducing command influence over Court-Martial proceedings.

The Act further permitted trial by a Military Judge sitting alone at the request of the accused[437] and provided for legally trained defence counsel in Special Courts-Martial empowered to award a bad-conduct discharge. These reforms significantly enhanced procedural fairness and brought military trials closer to civilian judicial standards.

Judicial scrutiny of military jurisdiction continued during this period. In *O'Callahan v. Parker* (1969),[438] the United States Supreme Court restricted Court-Martial jurisdiction to offences that were "service-connected."[439] The Court held that offences committed off military installations and unrelated to military duties should ordinarily be tried in civilian courts. The decision reflected judicial concern regarding the adequacy of safeguards available in military proceedings and the need to protect

---

436 United States v. Mitchell, 37 M.J. 903, 903 (N.M.C.M.R. 1993).

437 Cox, *supra* note 425 at 19.

438 O' Callahan v. Parker, *supra* note 97 (the Supreme Court declared (p-265)that: court-martial is not yet an independent instrument of justice but remains, to a significant degree, a specialized part of the overall mechanism by which military discipline is preserved).

439 Hillman, *supra* note 427.

constitutional rights through civilian judicial processes and that courts-martial lacked the safeguards present in Article III courts.[440]

THE MILITARY JUSTICE ACT, 1983

The Military Justice Act, 1983[441] represented another important stage in the evolution of American military justice. The Act directed the Secretary of Defense to establish a commission to examine the military justice system and make recommendations for further reform. Among the proposals considered was the reconstitution of the Court of Military Appeals as an Article III court in order to enhance its independence from the military establishment.[442]

A significant objective of the Act was to streamline pre-trial and post-trial procedures while preserving the fundamental rights of service personnel. One of its most important reforms was the introduction of a mechanism permitting direct review by the Supreme Court of the United States through writs of certiorari in specified cases, thereby strengthening civilian judicial oversight of military justice.[443]

The Act also reduced the burden on commanders in matters involving legal assessment. In General Courts-Martial, the Staff Judge Advocate assumed a greater role in advising on the referral of charges and post-trial review. At the same time, the accused

440 Lederer & Hundley, *supra* note 430 at 629.

441 H.R. REP. NO. 98-549 (Nov. 15, 1983) (Military Justice Act of 1983), *available at* http://www.loc.gov/rr/frd/Military_Law/pdf/HR-98-549.pdf (Accessed on 26.10.12).

442 Cox, *supra* note 425 at 27.

443 Military Justice Act of 1983, *supra* note 441.

was afforded the right to respond to the Staff Judge Advocate's recommendations and to submit matters in mitigation, clemency, or rebuttal through counsel.

Further reforms included the right of an accused to waive or withdraw an appeal before the Court of Military Review, while preserving automatic appellate review in cases involving death sentences, punitive discharge, or confinement exceeding one year. Cases not subject to appeal continued to undergo review by the Judge Advocate General.

The Act also expanded access to the Supreme Court through discretionary review, although such access remained limited. Concerns regarding the scope of appellate review led to proposals such as the *Equal Justice for Our Military Act, 2011*, which sought to provide broader access to the Supreme Court for service personnel convicted by Court-Martial.

Notwithstanding these reforms, debate continued regarding the independence of military judges. Critics argued that the absence of fixed tenure and the continued influence of the Judge Advocate General over assignments, evaluations, and promotions could affect judicial independence. However, in *Weiss v. United States* (1994),[444] the Supreme Court upheld the

444 Weiss v. United States, *supra* note 135 (Justice Scalia, concurring, observed: With respect to the Due Process Clause challenge, I think it neither necessary nor appropriate for this Court to pronounce whether 'Congress has achieved an acceptable balance between independence and accountability .. As today's opinion explains, a fixed term of office for a military judge "never has been a part of the military justice tradition .... Courts-martial ... have been conducted in this country for over 200 years without the presence of a tenured judge. . . .' Thus, in the Military Justice Act of 1968 the people's elected representatives achieved a balance between independence and accountability which,

constitutionality of the system, observing that Congress had achieved an acceptable balance between judicial independence and military accountability.[445] Nevertheless, concerns regarding the perceived independence of military judges continued to be raised within military appellate jurisprudence.

MILITARY JUSTICE REFORMS (2019)

The military justice reforms that came into effect in 2019[446] represented a further effort to modernise the Uniform Code of Military Justice and adapt it to contemporary challenges. The reforms strengthened protections for victims, expanded judicial authority, addressed emerging forms of misconduct, and streamlined court-martial procedures.

---

whether or not acceptable to five Justices of this Court, gave members of the military at least as much procedural protection, in the respects at issue here, as they enjoyed when the Fifth Amendment was adopted and have enjoyed ever since. That is enough, and to suggest otherwise arrogates to this Court a power it does not possess).

445 United States v. Mitchell 37 MJ 903 (N.M.C.M.R 1993), (The Court complained that, 'For these reasons, although we find nothing actually inimical to our independence in this arrangement, arguably a reasonable observer may conclude that it is inappropriate for an officer whose duties do not include supervising the Court's judges, but whose professional responsibilities are so directly and closely affected by the Court's decisions, to participate in the evaluation of the appellate judges').

446 Sheftick, G. (2019) '2019 brings changes to military justice system', *Army News Service*, 3 January. Available at: https://www.army.mil/article/215594/2019_brings_changes_to_military_justice_system#:~:text=FORT%20MEADE%2C%20Md., crime%20laws%2C%20and%20much%20more (Accessed: 15.11. 2024).

1. Adultery Redefined

The offence of adultery was replaced with the broader offence of extramarital sexual conduct, thereby extending its application irrespective of gender. Legal separation was also recognised as an affirmative defence in appropriate cases.

2. Protection of Junior Service Personnel

Article 93a introduced enhanced penalties for recruiters, drill instructors, and other persons in positions of authority who abuse their power over recruits or trainees. The reforms also strengthened protections against retaliation, with Article 132 criminalising reprisals against victims and whistle-blowers.

3. Cyber and Computer-Related Offences

Recognising the growing importance of cyber security, the reforms strengthened offences relating to unauthorised access to government computer systems, cyberstalking, and fraudulent use of electronic access devices.

4. Reforms to Courts-Martial

The reforms expanded the availability of judge-alone trials in certain categories of cases, standardised court-martial panel composition, and revised voting requirements for conviction. These measures were intended to improve consistency and efficiency in military trials.

5. Expanded Judicial Powers

Military judges were granted broader authority in relation to investigative subpoenas and pre-trial proceedings. Article 32 hearings were also strengthened, ensuring greater procedural protection for both accused persons and victims.

6. Changes to Punitive Offences

Amendments were made to several substantive offences, including burglary and the unauthorised wearing of military decorations and medals, with corresponding revisions to punishment provisions.

7. Procedural Modernisation

Additional reforms streamlined trial, post-trial, and appellate procedures, thereby improving the efficiency of military justice administration. The amendments were made prospective in operation and applied only to cases referred after their commencement. New rules ensure that these changes are not retroactive, but will apply to cases referred after January 1, 2020.

THE NATIONAL DEFENSE AUTHORIZATION ACT, 2022

The National Defense Authorization Act for Fiscal Year 2022 (NDAA 2022),[447] signed into law on 27 December 2021, introduced some of the most significant reforms to the American Military Justice System since the enactment of the Uniform Code of Military Justice. The reforms were primarily aimed at enhancing fairness, strengthening victim protection, and

447 Lewis, M. (2022) 'Major Changes in the Uniform Code of Military Justice', *National Conference of Specialized Court Judges*, 7 October. Available at: https://www.americanbar.org/groups/judicial/publications/judicial_division_record_home/2022/vol26-1/major-changes-in-uniform-code-of-military-justice/ (Accessed on 15.11.2024). *see also,* Schlueter, D.A. and Schenck, L. (2023) 'Transforming Military Justice: The 2022 and 2023 National Defense Authorization Acts', *Military Law Review*, 231, Available at https://commons.stmarytx.edu/facarticles/736/ (Accessed on 11.11.2024).

reducing the role of commanders in the prosecution of certain serious offences.

1. Establishment of Special Trial Counsel

The most significant reform was the transfer of prosecutorial authority over specified victim-centric offences, including sexual assault, from commanders to independent and specially trained military lawyers known as Special Trial Counsel (STC). These counsel were granted exclusive authority to determine whether such offences should be prosecuted.

2. Judicial Sentencing

The Act introduced a system under which military judges, rather than Court-Martial panels, determine sentences in most cases. This reform was intended to promote greater consistency, objectivity, and predictability in sentencing.

3. Sentencing Guidelines

The NDAA 2022 provided for the formulation of sentencing guidelines applicable across the military justice system. While judges may depart from these guidelines, reasons for such departures must be recorded.

4. Military Sentencing Parameters and Criteria Board

To support the new sentencing framework, the Act established a **Military Sentencing Parameters and Criteria Board**, responsible for developing and reviewing sentencing guidance.

5. Military Justice Review Panel

The Act also created a Military Justice Review Panel to assess the effectiveness of the Uniform Code of Military Justice and recommend further reforms where necessary.

6. Continuing Role of Commanders

Although the authority to prosecute specified serious offences was transferred to Special Trial Counsel (STC) , commanders retained responsibility for disciplinary matters and offences falling outside the jurisdiction of the STC system, thereby preserving their role in maintaining military discipline.

The NDAA 2022 marks a significant shift away from the traditional command-centric model of military justice and reflects a continuing effort to enhance independence, accountability, and public confidence in the administration of military justice.

PERCEPTION OF AN INDEPENDENT AND IMPARTIAL MILITARY JUSTICE SYSTEM

Despite the substantial reforms introduced over the years, concerns continue to be expressed regarding the independence and impartiality of the American Military Justice System. The Cox Commission, an independent body convened in 2001 by the National Institute of Military Justice to examine the military criminal justice system, recommended a significant reduction in the role of Commanding Officers in Court-Martial proceedings. The Commission proposed that a commander who initiates charges against a service member should no longer participate in the selection of Court-Martial members. It further recommended strengthening the authority and independence of military judges by providing them with secure terms of office, thereby protecting them from potential adverse consequences arising from unpopular decisions. However, these recommendations were not fully implemented.[448]

---

448 Hillman, *supra* note 427.

Consequently, the debate surrounding the role of commanders and the potential for unlawful command influence continues to occupy an important place in discussions on military justice. In particular, the power of the Convening Authority to select Court-Martial members and the absence of fixed tenure for military judges have often been cited as factors that may affect, or appear to affect, judicial independence and impartiality.

As observed by Fidell and Young,[449] the Military Justice Act of 2016 and the National Defense Authorization Acts for Fiscal Years 2022 and 2023 introduced important reforms to the military justice system. Nevertheless, these reforms largely preserved the fundamental structure of the existing system. While the changes undoubtedly represented progress, they stopped short of a comprehensive restructuring of military justice.

The reforms introduced through the FY 2022–23 NDAAs have, in effect, created two parallel systems of military justice: one in which charging decisions continue to be influenced by commanders, and another in which such decisions are made by legally trained professionals operating outside the chain of command. Although these developments have reduced the scope for command influence in certain categories of offences, they have not entirely eliminated the concerns associated with the traditional command-centric model.

Thus, notwithstanding the considerable advances made in strengthening due process, judicial oversight, and prosecutorial

449 Fidell, E. and Young, J.A., 2022. *Military Justice and Modernity.* (online) Available at: https://ssrn.com/abstract=4301436 or http://dx.doi.org/10.2139/ssrn.4301436 (Accessed 14.11.2024).

independence, the question of whether the American Military Justice System has achieved complete institutional independence from command influence remains a matter of continuing debate.

CHANGES IN THE INDIAN MILITARY JUSTICE SYSTEM

Unlike the military justice systems of the United Kingdom and the United States, which underwent gradual reforms throughout the twentieth century, the Indian Military Justice System remained largely unchanged until the establishment of the Armed Forces Tribunal (AFT) in 2007. For decades, it was believed by both the Government and the military hierarchy that the existing system contained adequate safeguards and did not require substantial reform. Consequently, service personnel remained without a statutory right of appeal against Court-Martial convictions and sentences.

The question of providing an appellate remedy was raised during the enactment of the Army Act, 1950 and the Air Force Act, 1950, but the proposal was rejected. Similarly, although the Navy Act, 1957 drew inspiration from the recommendations of the Lewis Committee Report, 1946 in the United Kingdom, it did not incorporate a right of appeal against Court-Martial decisions. The prevailing view was that the review conducted by the Judge Advocate General provided a sufficient safeguard against injustice.

The principal justification advanced for resisting appellate reform was the perceived need to preserve discipline through the speedy administration of military justice. It was argued that a prolonged appellate process would adversely affect operational efficiency by keeping service personnel away from their military duties.

A significant turning point came with the decision of the Supreme Court in Lt. Col. Prithi Pal Singh Bedi v. Union of India,[450] which exposed several deficiencies in the military justice system and highlighted the need for greater procedural safeguards. The judgment, reflecting developments already taking place in the United Kingdom and the United States, became an important catalyst for reform. Subsequently, the Supreme Court observed in 1990[451] that although the Army Act did not mandate the recording of reasons by Courts-Martial, the practice was desirable in the interests of fairness and transparency.

Responding to these concerns, Parliament enacted the Army (Amendment) Act, 1992, requiring Courts-Martial to record reasons in support of their findings. However, the long-standing recommendation for the creation of an appellate forum remained unimplemented.

The movement towards reform gained momentum with the 169th Report of the Law Commission of India (1999),[452] which

---

450 Lt. Col Prithi Pal Singh Bedi, *supra* note73 at p 442 (the Court observed that, 'winds of change blowing over the country have not permeated the closed and sacrosanct precincts of the Army' the Court further held that the absence of even one appeal with power to review evidence, legal formulation, conclusion and adequacy or otherwise of punishment was a distressing and glaring lacuna in the laws relating to the Armed Forces and urged the Government to take steps to provide for at least one judicial review in service matters).

451 SN Mukherjee v. Union of India, 1990 (4) SCC, 594.

452 LawCommissionofIndia,REP.NO.169,AmendmentofArmy,Navyand Air Force Acts (Apr. 1999), *available at* http://lawcommissionofindia.nic.in/101-169/Report169.pdf (Accessed on 23.02.2012).

strongly recommended the establishment of an Armed Forces Appellate Tribunal. The Commission proposed a specialised forum comprising both judicial and military members, including retired senior officers and retired judges of the higher judiciary, thereby combining military expertise with judicial independence.

The demand for an appellate body was further reinforced by the Parliamentary Standing Committee on Defence, which in its reports of 2003 and 2004–2005 urged the Government to expedite the establishment of a dedicated appellate forum, drawing inspiration from similar institutions functioning in countries such as the United Kingdom, France, Germany, Sweden, and Russia.

These developments ultimately paved the way for the creation of the Armed Forces Tribunal, marking the first major structural reform of the Indian Military Justice System and providing service personnel with a long-awaited statutory right of appeal against Court-Martial decisions.

ARMED FORCES TRIBUNAL ACT, 2007

A major milestone in the evolution of the Indian Military Justice System was the establishment of the Armed Forces Tribunal (AFT). In September 2005, the Union Cabinet approved the proposal of the Ministry of Defence for the creation of a specialised tribunal to adjudicate service matters and hear appeals arising from Court-Martial decisions.[453] This culminated in the enactment of the Armed Forces Tribunal Act, 2007, which received Presidential assent on 25 December 2007.

---

453 Jha, *supra* note 62 at 265.

The Tribunal was vested with jurisdiction to adjudicate appeals against findings, orders, and sentences of Courts-Martial. It was also granted original jurisdiction over a wide range of service matters, including pay, pension, promotion, appointment, retirement benefits, and other service-related disputes.[454] However, matters relating to transfers, postings, and leave were excluded from its jurisdiction. Significantly, Summary Court-Martial cases involving sentences of less than three months' imprisonment were also excluded from the appellate jurisdiction of the Tribunal.

The AFT possesses wide appellate powers. The Tribunal can remit or mitigate or commute a sentence if it is unjust, illegal or excessive or even enhance the punishment awarded by the Court-martial.[455] Under this Act, the conviction by the Court-martial can be quashed and a retrial by Court-martial ordered by the Tribunal.[456] The Tribunal shall have the power to punish for contempt.[457] All applications before the Tribunal have to be decided expeditiously.[458] All appeals from the decision of the Tribunal directly lies with the Supreme Court of India, with the leave of the Tribunal.[459]

Notwithstanding these significant reforms, certain limitations continue to affect the effectiveness of the Tribunal. One of the

---

454 Armed Forces Tribunal Act 2007 (AFT, 2007), § 3 (Service matter's is defined in section 3).

455 AFT 2007, § 15(6).

456 AFT 2007, § 16.

457 The procedure followed in contempt process shall be according to the Code of Civil Procedure 1908.

458 AFT 2007, § 23 (The Act does not have any laid down time frame for deciding an application or appeal).

459 AFT 2007, § 30.

principal concerns is the exclusion of Summary Court-Martial cases involving imprisonment of less than three months, despite the serious consequences such proceedings may have on the liberty, reputation, and future livelihood of service personnel. Concerns have also been expressed regarding the absence of a comprehensive legal aid mechanism for indigent service personnel and the restrictions on the grant of bail in certain categories of offences.[460]

Another frequently highlighted deficiency is the limited enforcement mechanism available to the Tribunal, particularly in matters involving implementation of its orders. Consequently, while the establishment of the AFT marked a substantial advance in providing an appellate remedy to service personnel, it did not fully address the broader concerns relating to independence, impartiality, and accountability within the military justice system.[461]

Further reform efforts gained momentum in 2015 when the Ministry of Defence constituted a Committee of Experts under the leadership of the late Shri Manohar Parrikar. The Committee recommended several measures, including the creation of a permanent Court-Martial structure, reduction of the influence of the Convening Authority, greater professional training for Judge Advocate General officers, and restricting the use of Summary Courts-Martial to exceptional circumstances. Although many of these recommendations remain unimplemented, they represent an important step towards modernising military justice in India.

---

460 AFT, 2007, § 15(3).

461 Jha, *supra* note 62 at 275.

The appointment of the Chief of Defence Staff in 2019 has further renewed discussions on comprehensive military justice reform, including the possibility of a unified code applicable to all three Services. Such reforms have the potential to enhance consistency, fairness, and public confidence in the administration of military justice in India.

Comparative Overview of Military Justice Reforms in the United Kingdom, United States, and India

Aspect	United Kingdom	United States	India
Historical Basis	Mutiny Act 1689, Service Discipline Acts	British Articles of War 1774, UCMJ 1951	Army Act 1950, Navy Act 1957, Air Force Act 1950
Major Reform Trigger	European Convention on Human Rights and Findlay v. United Kingdom	Constitutional scrutiny, Congressional reforms, concerns over command influence	Lt. Col. Prithi Pal Singh Bedi and Law Commission recommendations
Independent Prosecuting Authority	Service Prosecuting Authority (SPA), independent of chain of command	Special Trial Counsel and independent military prosecutors	No independent prosecuting authority; prosecution remains within military hierarchy
Convening Authority Influence	Significantly reduced after Armed Forces Act 1996	Gradually reduced but not completely eliminated	Continues to exercise substantial influence

Selection of Court Members	Independent Court Administration System	Convening Authority retains role subject to safeguards	Convening Authority selects Court-Martial members
Status of Military Judges	Independent Judge Advocates outside chain of command	Military Judges exercise significant authority	No permanent military judiciary; Courts-Martial remain ad hoc
Standing Military Courts	Yes	Yes	No
Right to Legal Representation	Fully recognized	Fully recognized	Available in Courts-Martial but absent in Summary Court-Martial proceedings
Right to Elect Trial	Available in summary proceedings	Accused may reject Summary Court-Martial and opt for higher Court-Martial	No comparable right in SCM proceedings
Appellate Structure	Summary Appeal Court, CMAC, Supreme Court	Courts of Criminal Appeals, CAAF, Supreme Court	Armed Forces Tribunal and Supreme Court

Appeal Against Summary Proceedings	Yes	Limited review available	Punishments below three months generally excluded from AFT jurisdiction
Protection Against Unlawful Command Influence	Structural safeguards substantially reduce risk	Explicit statutory prohibition under Article 37, UCMJ	No express statutory prohibition
Application of Human Rights Standards	Strong influence of ECHR and Human Rights Act 1998	Constitutional due process protections and judicial oversight	Constitutional protections apply, but broad exceptions remain
Victim-Centric Reforms	Strengthened through modern legislation	Major reforms under NDAA 2022 and Special Trial Counsel system	Limited reforms
Current Reform Trend	Independence, transparency, unified system	Reduced command influence and enhanced prosecutorial independence	Incremental reforms centered mainly on the Armed Forces Tribunal

The comparative analysis demonstrates a clear global trend towards enhancing the independence and impartiality of military justice systems. Both the United Kingdom and the United States have progressively reduced command influence, strengthened judicial and prosecutorial independence, expanded appellate remedies, and increased procedural safeguards for accused service personnel. In contrast, while India has made notable progress through the establishment of the Armed Forces Tribunal, significant structural reforms within the Court-Martial system remain outstanding. The comparative experience of these jurisdictions suggests that military discipline and fair trial guarantees can coexist within a modern military justice framework.

CONCLUSION

Military justice systems across the world have undergone sustained scrutiny and reform in an effort to reconcile the demands of military discipline with the requirements of fairness, independence, and due process. The experiences of the United Kingdom and the United States demonstrate a clear movement towards strengthening judicial independence, limiting command influence, expanding procedural safeguards, and enhancing the rights of accused service personnel.

In the United Kingdom, reforms initiated after the decision in *Findlay v. United Kingdom* transformed the military justice system by reducing the role of the Convening Authority, establishing an independent prosecutorial structure, creating standing courts, and strengthening appellate review. The Armed Forces Act, 2006 introduced a unified system of service law for all three Services, while subsequent legislation, including the Armed Forces Act, 2021, further strengthened both the Service Justice System and the protection afforded to service personnel and veterans.

Armed Forces personnel in India may have certain rights abrogated by the Parliament but the farmers of Indian

Constitution could not have intended to deprive them of their Fundamental Rights. "At the time when we are questioning whether animals have rights, we must be compelled to ensure that the people who protect our country are not deprived of their rights"[462] The Hon'ble Supreme Court of India has also held:

'It is fallacy to regard Fundamental Rights as a gift from the State to its citizens. Individual possess basic Human Rights independently of any Constitution by reasons of basic fact that they are members of human race. These Fundamental Rights are important as they possess intrinsic value.'[463]

The Supreme Court in a case[464] commented that right to Fair Trial is a basic Fundamental Right not only under Indian Constitution but also under International Treaties. In another case it held that access to justice is a Human Right.[465] It is high time that Indian Military jurisprudence catches up with its counterparts around the world and gives dignity to its citizen servicemen by affording them a Fair Trial.

The United States has likewise undertaken a gradual but significant transformation of its military justice system.

---

462 *Id. at* 124.

463 M Nagraj v. Union of India, AIR, 2007, SC 71. *also cited* in, *See* Jha, *supra* note 62, at 296.

464 DP Agarwal v. BD Agarwal (2003) 6 SCC 230 (at Para 38 the Court commented: 'any procedure which comes in the way of the party in getting a fair trial would be violative of Article 14 of the Constitution of India. The right to fair trial by an independent and impartial Tribunal is part of Article 6(1) of the European Convention for the Protection of Human Rights and Fundamental Freedoms, 1950'), *also cited* in, Jha, *supra* note 62, at 298.

465 Arunima Baruah v Union of India, (2000) 6SCC 120. *also cited* in, Jha, *supra* note 62, at 296.

Beginning with the Uniform Code of Military Justice in 1951 and continuing through the Military Justice Acts of 1968 and 1983, as well as the recent reforms of 2019 and the National Defense Authorization Act, 2022, there has been a consistent effort to enhance due process, strengthen judicial oversight, reduce command influence, and increase prosecutorial independence. Although concerns regarding the independence and impartiality of Courts-Martial continue to be debated, the direction of reform has been unmistakably towards greater accountability and fairness.

A comparative analysis of these developments reveals a common trend: increasing emphasis on the independence of adjudicators, greater access to legal representation, expansion of appellate remedies, reduction of command control over judicial processes, and the establishment of institutional safeguards designed to ensure fair trial standards. These reforms reflect the growing influence of constitutional principles, international human rights norms, and contemporary notions of justice.

In contrast, reforms within the Indian Military Justice System have been comparatively limited. The establishment of the Armed Forces Tribunal was undoubtedly a significant milestone, providing service personnel with a long-awaited appellate remedy against Court-Martial decisions. However, many of the structural concerns that have been addressed in other jurisdictions—such as the concentration of powers in the Convening Authority, the absence of permanent military courts, limited judicial independence, and inadequate procedural safeguards in certain forms of military trials—continue to persist.

The framers of the Indian Constitution never intended that members of the Armed Forces should be deprived of their fundamental rights merely because they serve the nation. The Supreme Court of India has repeatedly affirmed that fundamental rights are not a gift of the State but inherent human rights possessed by every individual by virtue of being human. It has further recognised that the right to a fair trial is a fundamental constitutional guarantee and that access to justice is itself a human right.

The comparative experience of the United Kingdom and the United States demonstrates that military discipline and fair trial guarantees are not mutually exclusive. Rather, an independent and impartial military justice system strengthens confidence, legitimacy, and morale within the Armed Forces. It is therefore imperative that Indian military jurisprudence continues its journey of reform and evolves in a manner that preserves discipline while ensuring that citizen servicemen are afforded the dignity, fairness, and justice that the Constitution promises to every individual.

CHAPTER 09

The Military Justice System Through the Eyes of Those Who Serve

> *"If we are to believe that joining the Armed Forces means embracing a completely different set of laws, then we must ask: does that also mean we accept a surrender of our basic rights—rights that would be protected under the Constitution for every other citizen?"*
>
> **- A Serving Officer**

"Justice delayed is justice denied" is a well-known legal maxim. However, the concerns surrounding the Indian Military Justice System extend far beyond questions of delay. The preceding chapters examined the system through constitutional provisions, statutory frameworks, judicial pronouncements, comparative reforms, and the concept of unlawful command influence. Yet, an equally important question remains: how is the system perceived by those who live and work within it?

The Armed Forces Tribunal (AFT) was envisioned as a significant step towards modernising military justice and providing service personnel with an effective appellate remedy. While the Tribunal has undoubtedly ushered in an important phase of reform, concerns continue to be expressed regarding the broader administration of military justice, particularly in relation to fair trial guarantees, due process, judicial independence, and the rights of service personnel. These concerns become especially significant when viewed against developments in military justice systems across other democratic jurisdictions.

In order to better understand these issues, views were sought from serving and retired members of the Armed Forces. The exercise was neither simple nor straightforward. Many potential participants were reluctant to share their views, while others preferred not to discuss issues relating to military justice. Nevertheless, valuable insights were obtained from 34 retired officers, 80 serving officers of varying ranks, and 69 Personnel Below Officer Rank (PBOR), representing different branches of the Armed Forces.

Although the study initially relied on a questionnaire, it soon became apparent that many respondents were either hesitant or unable to provide detailed responses through written questionnaires alone. Consequently, structured interviews incorporating focused and close-ended questions were also conducted. This approach allowed for a more meaningful exploration of participant perspectives and experiences.

The responses revealed several recurring themes concerning awareness of military law, constitutional rights, discipline and justice, judicial independence, fairness of procedures, and the need for institutional reform. Perhaps the most striking finding was the significant disparity in awareness and understanding of military justice across different ranks and services. These findings, discussed in the following sections, provide an empirical perspective on many of the issues examined throughout this study and offer a rare insight into how the Military Justice System is perceived by those who serve within it.

The Knowledge Gap: A Tale of Three Wings

Picture a young lieutenant, fresh from training, armed with theoretical knowledge of military law but uncertain how to apply it in practice. Contrast this with a veteran airman confidently navigating grievance mechanisms and institutional forums to voice concerns. This disparity in awareness emerged as one of the most striking findings of the study.

Younger serving officers, many of whom had studied military law during their training, often admitted that their understanding remained largely theoretical. While familiar with legal provisions, they lacked the experience and confidence required to navigate the practical complexities of the Military Justice System.

The disparity was even more pronounced among Personnel Below Officer Rank (PBOR), particularly in the Army. While Air Force and Navy personnel generally demonstrated greater awareness of their legal rights, aided by comparatively transparent grievance mechanisms and reporting platforms, many Army PBOR remained unfamiliar with even basic legal safeguards available to them. Awareness was largely confined to clerical staff, personnel who had undergone legal training, or those who had previously been involved in disciplinary proceedings.

The findings reveal a significant gap in legal awareness across the Services. They also highlight the need for greater dissemination of information regarding military law and constitutional rights, particularly among PBOR, who constitute the backbone of the Armed Forces. Strengthening such awareness would contribute significantly towards a more transparent and equitable justice system.

The Blindspot in Military Service

"If we surrender our uniforms, do we also surrender our rights?"

This question, posed by a serving officer, captures one of the most significant findings of the study. Approximately 94% of respondents stated that they joined the Armed Forces without any meaningful understanding of how military service could affect the exercise of their constitutional rights, particularly under Article 33 of the Constitution.

As one officer from a military family observed, *"Only those of us who grew up with it or studied law had any inkling of what we were agreeing to."* This sentiment was echoed by many respondents who stated that they were never formally informed of the legal limitations that accompany military service.

Among retired officers and PBOR, only a small number of JAG officers demonstrated a clear understanding of the constitutional and statutory framework governing military service. For most respondents, enlistment was motivated by patriotism, duty, and a desire to serve the nation, with little attention paid to the legal implications of military life.

Another officer reflected:

"If we are to believe that joining the Armed Forces means embracing a completely different set of laws, then we must ask: does that also mean we accept a surrender of our basic rights—rights that would be protected under the Constitution for every other citizen?"

Many respondents admitted that awareness of these issues came only much later in their careers. A JAG officer summarized the situation succinctly:

"The system assumes knowledge where there is none. These young soldiers, driven by patriotism, sign away rights they do not even know they have."

The findings reveal a serious informational deficit within the Armed Forces regarding constitutional rights and military law. While service personnel willingly accept restrictions necessary for military discipline, the study suggests that many do so without fully understanding the extent or implications of those restrictions.

The Discipline–Justice Tightrope

The question whether the Military Justice System exists primarily to maintain discipline or to administer justice revealed a significant divide in perception among respondents.

Approximately 63% of respondents believed that the primary purpose of the Military Justice System is the maintenance of discipline. This view was particularly prevalent among officers, who emphasized that military effectiveness depends upon obedience, cohesion, and an unbroken chain of command.

As one officer explained:

"In times of war, every decision is a matter of life and death. Orders must be followed without hesitation. That is the essence of military discipline. Without it, we would not be able to face the enemy or maintain operational effectiveness."

For many officers, discipline was viewed not merely as an organizational requirement but as a moral necessity essential to operational success.

PBOR respondents, while acknowledging the importance of discipline, frequently expressed concern that the system sometimes prioritised authority over fairness. One respondent observed:

"We understand that discipline is key, but it should come from respect, not fear. When a Commanding Officer is fair, discipline comes naturally."

Several respondents felt that punishments were at times disproportionate to the offences committed and that the system often emphasized compliance at the expense of justice.

A smaller but influential group argued that discipline and justice are not competing values but mutually reinforcing principles. As one senior officer stated:

"Justice is the foundation of true discipline. If the system is unjust, morale will suffer. And when morale falters, so does discipline."

The findings suggest that while discipline remains central to military life, many respondents believe that its legitimacy ultimately depends upon the fairness and credibility of the justice system through which it is enforced.

Weaknesses and Defects in the Military Justice System

When asked to identify weaknesses within the Military Justice System, respondents offered sharply contrasting perspectives.

A number of retired officers, particularly those familiar with military legal processes, defended the existing framework. They argued that the self-contained nature of military justice, including mechanisms such as the Court of Inquiry and Summary of Evidence, remains essential for maintaining discipline and operational effectiveness.

As one retired JAG officer remarked:

"The Military Justice System is tailored to address the distinctive needs of the military. It cannot—and should not—be compared to civilian law. In remote areas, where there is no access to civilian courts, our system is essential for maintaining order."

However, a larger group of respondents expressed concern regarding the concentration of authority within the system, particularly the powers exercised by the Convening Authority. Many believed that personal biases and command influence could affect the administration of justice.

PBOR respondents were especially critical of Summary Court-Martial proceedings, where cases are often concluded rapidly. One respondent stated:

"We have seen trials conducted in just a few hours and were given no meaningful opportunity to prepare a defence. Sometimes it feels as if the outcome has already been decided."

Concerns were also raised regarding legal representation. Several respondents believed that military-appointed defence officers often lacked sufficient legal expertise, while the cost of engaging civilian counsel remained beyond the means of many service personnel.

Many PBOR further expressed the desire for greater representation of personnel from their own rank within the adjudicatory process, arguing that such individuals would better appreciate the practical realities and challenges faced by junior servicemen.

Should Military and Non-Military Offences Be Dealt with Differently?

The issue of whether military courts should continue to exercise jurisdiction over non-military offences generated considerable debate.

Approximately 66% of respondents favoured the transfer of peacetime non-military offences to the civilian criminal justice system while retaining military jurisdiction during wartime and operational deployments.

As one officer observed:

"In wartime everything is different. The system must be unified. But in peacetime, separation is necessary to ensure fairness."

At the same time, approximately 21% of officers believed that the existing Military Justice System was fully capable of dealing with both military and civil offences, provided that adjudication remained independent, impartial, and free from undue influence.

Need to Revamp the Military Justice System: A Call for Change

Perhaps the most significant finding of the study was the overwhelming support for reform. Approximately 83% of respondents agreed that the Military Justice System requires substantial changes.

A serving Colonel remarked:

"The Indian Military Justice System is in dire need of transformation. It should not remain an instrument of the executive but must evolve to reflect the values of fairness and due process."

A retired JAG officer similarly argued:

"We must bring the Military Justice System in line with contemporary legal standards. The powers of Commanding Officers should be redefined so that they are exercised only where necessary for maintaining discipline. Justice and fairness must take precedence."

The findings demonstrate that respondents do not reject the Military Justice System itself. Rather, they seek a system that continues to preserve discipline while incorporating stronger safeguards for fairness, transparency, judicial independence, and due process.

Looking Forward

The responses reveal a shared belief that while discipline remains indispensable to military effectiveness, the Military Justice System must evolve to meet contemporary standards of fairness, transparency, and accountability. The challenge lies not in recognising the need for reform but in implementing changes that preserve operational discipline while safeguarding the rights of those who serve.

The study ultimately reflects a growing aspiration among service personnel for a justice system that is both effective and fair—one that maintains discipline without compromising the principles of justice that the Armed Forces exist to defend.

The JAG Dilemma: Balancing Expertise and Experience in Military Justice

"The courtroom was tense as the young officer stood awaiting his fate. Across from him sat senior military officers entrusted with

deciding his future, guided by the only legally trained person in the room—the Judge Advocate. In that moment, a fundamental question emerged: would legal principles prevail, or would military hierarchy and command influence shape the outcome?"

The role of the Judge Advocate General (JAG) Branch emerged as one of the most debated issues during the study. While respondents generally agreed that legal expertise must play a greater role in military trials, they were divided on how such expertise should be incorporated without undermining the military character of the justice system.

A recurring concern was whether civilian legal professionals, despite their legal competence, could fully appreciate the unique demands of military service. As one senior officer observed:

"How can a civilian lawyer truly understand the pressures of military life?"

This sentiment reflected a broader belief that military justice requires not only legal proficiency but also an understanding of military discipline, operational realities, and command responsibilities. The challenge, therefore, lies in balancing legal expertise with military experience.

The Role of JAG Officers in Court-Martial Proceedings

A substantial majority of respondents supported a greater adjudicatory role for JAG officers in Court-Martial proceedings. More than half of both serving and retired officers believed that only those formally trained in military law possess the expertise necessary to ensure fair and legally sound outcomes.

As one General remarked:

"Soldier lawyers have an advantage over soldier citizens because of their proficiency in dealing with legal matters. Matters of law should be handled and presided over by this section of the Armed Forces to ensure any accused person is treated fairly."

Support for this view was particularly strong among senior officers, with 67 serving officers and 30 retired officers favouring a greater judicial role for JAG officers. Respondents argued that legally trained officers are better equipped to interpret military law objectively and reduce the risk of decisions being influenced by command preferences or institutional pressures.

However, a minority of respondents expressed reservations. Approximately 8% argued that while JAG officers should play a significant role in military trials, adjudicatory responsibilities should not be concentrated exclusively within a single branch. One Brigadier suggested that legal members should be drawn from different corps and services to prevent excessive institutional influence and preserve balance within the system.

An even smaller group opposed the proposal entirely, warning that excessive concentration of authority within the JAG Branch could itself create opportunities for bias or misuse of power. As one General Officer cautioned:

"Too much power in one authority is dangerous. There is no guarantee that it would not be misused."

Despite these concerns, the overwhelming majority favoured granting JAG officers greater authority in determining legal issues during Court-Martial proceedings.

The Case for an Independent JAG Branch

Perhaps the strongest consensus revealed by the study concerned the institutional independence of the JAG Branch. Approximately 92% of respondents supported placing the JAG Branch outside the regular military chain of command and under the Ministry of Defence.

Respondents believed that judicial independence is essential to maintaining confidence in military justice. Many argued that JAG officers should be insulated from command pressures so that legal decisions are guided solely by law rather than considerations of hierarchy, career progression, or institutional influence.

One Air Force Sergeant explained:

"For those undergoing legal proceedings, it is critical to feel that the system is just and fair. Knowing that those who judge our cases are well-versed in the law—without being influenced by superiors—would instil greater trust in the process."

According to respondents, an independent JAG Branch would enhance both the credibility and legitimacy of military justice by reinforcing the perception that trials are conducted impartially and free from external influence.

Striking the Balance

The findings reveal a clear desire for greater legal expertise within the Military Justice System while preserving the practical understanding that comes from military service. Respondents largely favoured a strengthened role for legally trained JAG officers but simultaneously recognised the risks associated with concentrating excessive authority within any single institution.

The central challenge, therefore, is not whether legal expertise should play a greater role in military justice, but how to integrate that expertise while maintaining operational understanding, institutional balance, and public confidence in the fairness of the system. The future effectiveness of military justice may well depend upon successfully reconciling these competing considerations.

Power and Process: The Convening Authority Controversy

A day in a civilian courtroom. The judge not only presides over the trial but also selects the jury, appoints the prosecutor, decides whether the case should proceed, and retains the authority to review the outcome. Such a concentration of power would raise serious concerns regarding judicial independence. Yet, many respondents perceived the role of the Convening Authority within the Military Justice System in a similar light.

The role of the Convening Authority (CA) emerged as one of the most debated aspects of the Military Justice System. While respondents acknowledged the necessity of command authority in maintaining discipline, many questioned whether the concentration of powers vested in the Convening Authority is compatible with the principles of fairness, impartiality, and judicial independence.

One respondent succinctly captured the concern:

"How can we ensure fairness when the judge and prosecutor answer to the same commanding officer?"

The responses reveal an enduring tension between military discipline and judicial independence—a tension that lies at the heart of contemporary debates on military justice reform.

The Convening Authority and Judicial Independence

The majority of respondents expressed concern that the Convening Authority's role in initiating and overseeing Court-Martial proceedings compromises judicial independence. Among 114 serving and retired officers and 29 PBOR respondents, approximately 68% believed that the involvement of the Convening Authority undermines the independence of the Court-Martial process.

A retired JAG officer observed:

"One of the fundamental tenets of the legal system is that the prosecutor, the adjudicator, and the awarder of punishment should be separate. To merge all three functions into one authority not only goes against the spirit of the Rule of Law but is also unconstitutional."

Even respondents who recognised the necessity of command authority stressed that such authority should operate within clearly defined limits. As a Wing Commander of the Indian Air Force remarked:

"The Commanding Officer must have authority to maintain discipline, but this power should not be misused where due process or the rights of soldiers are compromised."

Notably, approximately 32% of respondents either declined to answer or expressed uncertainty, suggesting that awareness of the legal implications of the Convening Authority's role remains uneven.

Influence on Court Members

A second area of concern related to the potential influence exercised by the Convening Authority over Court Members themselves. Approximately 68% of respondents believed that the relationship between the Convening Authority and the Members of the Court-Martial could consciously or unconsciously affect judicial decision-making.

One retired Colonel recounted an occasion when, after being appointed Presiding Officer of a Court-Martial, the Convening Authority remarked that the accused should be "made an example of." Although no direct instruction was given, the observation raised concerns regarding the subtle pressures that may arise within a hierarchical organisation.

A minority of respondents (22%) maintained that Court Members are capable of acting independently unless explicit instructions are issued by the Convening Authority. Nevertheless, the findings suggest that many respondents perceive the mere possibility of command influence as sufficient to undermine confidence in the impartiality of proceedings.

Influence on Findings and Sentences

Concerns regarding command influence extended beyond the composition of the Court-Martial to the outcome of proceedings themselves. Approximately 71% of respondents believed that the Convening Authority possesses the ability to influence findings and sentences, either directly or indirectly.

Several respondents referred to instances where favourable findings were reconsidered, punishments revised, or proceedings directed for reconsideration. A retired JAG officer stated:

"When a court is directed to reassemble, it is clear that the verdict will now align with the Convening Authority's wishes."

For many respondents, such powers create the perception that judicial outcomes remain vulnerable to command preferences, thereby diminishing confidence in the fairness of the system.

A smaller group (19%) disagreed, arguing that Court Members remain capable of independent decision-making despite the institutional authority of the Convening Authority, while 10% remained undecided.

Accountability and Restriction of Powers

The issue of accountability emerged as a recurring concern throughout the responses. Many participants questioned why a functionary exercising such extensive authority remains largely insulated from legal scrutiny or institutional accountability.

One officer remarked:

"A person with limited legal knowledge and understanding should not hold the power to decide the fate of an accused individual."

A substantial majority of respondents—approximately 80%—favoured restricting the powers of the Convening Authority. Most proposed retaining the Convening Authority's role in initiating investigations and convening proceedings while transferring responsibility for judicial and legal decisions to legally qualified authorities.

A senior JAG officer suggested:

"The Convening Authority's role should be limited to initiating a Court of Inquiry. If the matter proceeds to trial, the selection

of court members and all legal decisions should fall within the exclusive domain of the legal branch."

Only a small minority (4%) opposed any reduction in the Convening Authority's powers, arguing that strong command authority remains indispensable to maintaining discipline and operational effectiveness.

Balancing Discipline and Judicial Independence

The findings reveal a widespread perception that the concentration of authority in the hands of the Convening Authority poses challenges to judicial independence, transparency, and accountability. At the same time, respondents recognised that command authority remains an essential component of military discipline and operational effectiveness.

The challenge identified by respondents is therefore not the elimination of command authority, but its recalibration. The overwhelming view was that discipline and justice are not mutually exclusive objectives. Rather, an effective Military Justice System must preserve command responsibility while ensuring that legal decisions remain independent, impartial,

The Summary Court-Martial: Swift Justice or Rushed Judgment?

"A young soldier stands before his Commanding Officer, facing a Summary Court-Martial. Within a matter of hours, a proceeding that may affect his liberty, livelihood, and future will be concluded. The question that arises is whether speed and discipline can coexist with fairness and due process."

The Summary Court-Martial (SCM) remains one of the most debated features of the Indian Military Justice System. Designed to provide swift disciplinary action, particularly in operational environments, it is viewed by many as an essential mechanism for maintaining order and discipline. At the same time, respondents repeatedly questioned whether the procedural safeguards available in SCM proceedings are sufficient when the consequences may include detention, dismissal from service, or lasting damage to a soldier's career.

Survey Overview

The survey included both officers and Personnel Below Officer Rank (PBOR), with approximately 77% of respondents belonging to the Indian Army and the remaining 23% drawn from the other Services. PBOR constituted the majority of respondents, while officers accounted for approximately 40% of the sample. The questions focused on legal representation, procedural fairness, the powers of the Commanding Officer, and the future of the SCM system.

The Need for Legal Representation

One of the strongest findings of the study was the overwhelming support for legal representation during SCM proceedings. Approximately 91% of respondents favoured the presence of legal counsel, arguing that proceedings capable of resulting in loss of liberty or livelihood should not take place without legal assistance.

A retired JAG officer observed:

"Convictions in a Summary Court-Martial, which often result in the loss of liberty and livelihood, should not be valid without legal

counsel. The adjudicators frequently lack sufficient legal knowledge, and such trials can lead to irreversible consequences."

Many PBOR respondents expressed frustration regarding their inability to adequately prepare a defence. Several reported receiving only limited time to respond to allegations, while simultaneously lacking the educational background, legal knowledge, or resources necessary to challenge the proceedings effectively.

A minority of respondents (9%) considered legal representation unnecessary for minor offences, arguing that the primary purpose of SCM is the swift disposal of relatively less serious disciplinary matters.

Should Soldiers Have a Choice?

The question of whether a soldier should be permitted to choose between SCM and a regular Court-Martial generated mixed responses. Approximately 75% of respondents opposed granting such a choice, largely on the ground that operational efficiency and military discipline require a mechanism for the rapid disposal of minor offences.

A smaller group argued that the right to elect a regular Court-Martial should be available whenever the accused believes that the seriousness of the allegations warrants fuller procedural safeguards. For these respondents, the right to a fair trial outweighed considerations of administrative convenience.

SCM and Fundamental Rights

Perhaps the most significant concern raised by respondents related to the impact of SCM proceedings on fundamental rights.

More than 91% believed that the current system can adversely affect basic rights, particularly where the accused is denied adequate time to prepare a defence, call witnesses, or challenge evidence.

Respondents frequently referred to the long-term consequences of SCM punishments, including dismissal from service and the resulting stigma that may affect future employment opportunities. Many argued that procedures capable of producing such outcomes should incorporate stronger safeguards and greater procedural fairness.

A smaller group of respondents maintained that the unique requirements of military discipline justify a simplified procedure for minor offences. As one retired General remarked:

"The goal of the military justice system is not only to maintain discipline but also to uncover the truth swiftly. Any delay can undermine operational effectiveness."

Retention or Reform?

The responses revealed support for reform rather than complete abolition. Approximately 53% of respondents favoured retaining SCM while limiting its use to minor disciplinary matters and relatively minor punishments. More serious allegations carrying the possibility of dismissal, imprisonment, or severe career consequences were considered more appropriate for trial by a regular Court-Martial.

At the same time, 38% of PBOR respondents favoured abolishing SCM altogether, viewing it as an inherently unfair process that places excessive authority in the hands of Commanding Officers.

The Powers of the Commanding Officer

The role of the Commanding Officer in SCM proceedings generated considerable debate. While some respondents emphasised that strong command authority is indispensable to military discipline, others argued that concentration of investigative, prosecutorial, and adjudicatory powers within a single authority creates an unacceptable risk of unfairness.

A retired Colonel remarked:

"The Commanding Officer is central to maintaining order in the army. His authority ensures that soldiers adhere to rules and regulations."

Conversely, another officer who had presided over SCM proceedings observed:

"Many times, I was under pressure to conclude the SCM proceedings within a short time frame, which often made it difficult to ensure fairness. Serious charges should always be handled by Court-Martial."

Approximately 53% of respondents favoured restricting the powers of the Commanding Officer by limiting SCM jurisdiction to minor offences while requiring serious cases to be referred to a regular Court-Martial.

An Institution at a Crossroads

The findings reveal that respondents do not reject the principle of Summary Court-Martial. Rather, they question whether its present form adequately protects the rights of accused personnel. The dominant view was that SCM should remain available as a disciplinary tool for minor infractions but should be accompanied by stronger procedural safeguards, greater access to legal assistance, and clearer limits on the powers of Commanding Officers.

The debate ultimately reflects a broader challenge confronting military justice: how to preserve discipline and operational effectiveness while ensuring that those who serve are not deprived of the fundamental guarantees of fairness and due process.

Fair Trial and Due Process of Law

"A soldier stood before his Commanding Officer, accused of a minor infraction. Without legal representation, with little time to prepare, and uncertain of the outcome, he clung to a single hope—that he would at least be heard. In that moment, fairness was not merely about the verdict; it was about the opportunity to present a defence and be judged through a process perceived as just."

The concept of a fair trial emerged as the central concern underlying almost every issue examined during the study. Whether discussing the powers of the Convening Authority, the role of the JAG Branch, the operation of Summary Court-Martial proceedings, or the independence of adjudicators, respondents repeatedly returned to the same question: does the Military Justice System provide sufficient safeguards to ensure fairness and due process?

The findings reveal significant differences in perception between officers and Personnel Below Officer Rank (PBOR). While many officers viewed military justice through the lens of discipline and operational necessity, a substantial number of PBOR respondents expressed concerns regarding fairness, transparency, and the protection of individual rights.

Does the Citizen-Soldier Receive a Fair Trial?

The notion of a fair trial was familiar to most officers but considerably less understood among many PBOR respondents. After being informed of the essential elements of a fair trial—including adequate opportunity to prepare a defence, legal representation, impartial adjudication, and the ability to challenge evidence—participants were asked whether such standards were being observed within the Military Justice System.

Approximately 37% of PBOR respondents believed that military trials, particularly Summary Court-Martial proceedings, were significantly influenced by the Commanding Officer, thereby compromising fairness. One respondent stated:

"Once I understood what a fair trial is supposed to look like, I can confidently say we do not get one in Summary Court-Martial. We have no legal representation, cannot properly present evidence, and are given insufficient time to prepare our defence. Sometimes we are pressured into confessing simply to avoid harsher charges."

For many PBOR respondents, the absence of procedural safeguards created a perception that outcomes were often predetermined rather than independently adjudicated.

A smaller group, comprising approximately 21% of respondents, believed that although the Military Justice System differed from civilian criminal justice, it nevertheless delivered fairness within its own framework. A retired JAG officer observed:

"Military justice is distinct from civilian law. The civilian justice system prioritises individual liberty, whereas military justice must ensure discipline and operational readiness. If the Commanding Officer acts impartially, the process can still be fair within the military context."

Similarly, a serving Brigadier remarked:

"A soldier's service requires certain sacrifices, including restrictions on rights that civilians enjoy. The justice system must therefore prioritise discipline, even where some procedural protections available in civilian courts are limited."

The responses illustrate the continuing tension between two competing perspectives: one emphasising procedural fairness and individual rights, and the other prioritising discipline and operational effectiveness.

Acceptance of Adverse Outcomes When Due Process is Followed

One of the more encouraging findings of the study was the broad agreement that adverse outcomes are generally accepted when due process is perceived to have been followed.

Across all ranks, respondents indicated that they were more willing to accept an unfavourable verdict if they believed that the proceedings had been fair, transparent, and impartial. As one retired General remarked:

"When due process is properly followed, soldiers are far more likely to accept the outcome, even when it goes against them."

Several respondents nevertheless acknowledged that operational realities may limit the extent of procedural safeguards available in military settings. One senior officer explained:

"When units are deployed in remote areas with limited access to civilian institutions, Summary Court-Martial proceedings become necessary for maintaining discipline. While they may not provide

the same procedural safeguards as civilian courts, they fulfil an important operational requirement."

The responses suggest that dissatisfaction often arises not from the outcome itself, but from a perception that the process was unfair.

Independence and Impartiality of Adjudicators

Concerns regarding the independence of adjudicators emerged as another recurring theme. A substantial number of respondents believed that military adjudicators, particularly in Summary Court-Martial proceedings, may be influenced—directly or indirectly—by the Convening Authority or Commanding Officer.

One participant observed:

"The Convening Authority has too much power. It is difficult for those presiding over proceedings to remain completely unaffected by that influence. This inevitably raises doubts regarding the fairness of the outcome."

For these respondents, the issue was not necessarily actual interference but the perception that adjudicators operate within a hierarchical structure where independence can never be fully assured.

Interestingly, a minority of respondents, particularly from the Indian Navy, expressed greater confidence in the impartiality of military adjudicators. They attributed this to the greater accountability imposed upon Commanding Officers, who may face legal consequences if proceedings are later found to be unjust. Several respondents noted that Naval Commanding

Officers routinely seek legal advice before initiating disciplinary proceedings, thereby reducing the likelihood of arbitrary action.

Fairness, Discipline and the Way Forward

The findings reveal that perceptions of fairness within the Military Justice System remain deeply divided. While many respondents accept that military justice cannot replicate every safeguard available in civilian courts, there is widespread agreement that the system must provide sufficient procedural protections to inspire confidence among those subject to it.

The study further demonstrates that discipline and fairness are not mutually exclusive objectives. Respondents repeatedly indicated that they were willing to accept even adverse outcomes when they believed that the process was impartial, transparent, and consistent with due process. Ultimately, confidence in military justice depends not merely upon the punishment imposed, but upon the belief that every serviceman has been afforded a genuine opportunity to be heard and judged fairly.

The Need for Reform in Military Justice: The Path Forward

The findings of this study reveal a clear and recurring concern across ranks and services: while military discipline remains indispensable to operational effectiveness, the present Military Justice System is perceived by many respondents as falling short of contemporary standards of fairness, transparency, and due process.

One of the most significant concerns identified during the study relates to the concentration of authority within the military justice framework, particularly the role of the Convening Authority and the limited procedural safeguards available in Summary Court-Martial proceedings. Many respondents believed that these features create a perception of bias and undermine confidence in the independence and impartiality of military adjudication.

The responses also highlighted a noticeable divide between officers and Personnel Below Officer Rank (PBOR). While many officers viewed military justice primarily through the lens of discipline and operational necessity, PBOR respondents were more likely to express concerns regarding legal representation, access to procedural safeguards, and protection of individual rights. The findings suggest that lower-ranking personnel often feel particularly vulnerable within a system that they perceive as hierarchical, opaque, and difficult to challenge.

Across the survey, several recurring themes emerged as priority areas for reform:

1. **Judicial Independence and Impartiality** – Respondents repeatedly emphasized the need to insulate adjudicators from actual or perceived command influence and to strengthen the independence of military judicial institutions.
2. **Legal Representation** – The absence of legal counsel, particularly in Summary Court-Martial proceedings, was widely regarded as inconsistent with the principles of fairness and due process.
3. **Transparency and Accountability** – Many respondents sought clearer procedures, greater awareness of legal rights, and increased accountability for those exercising judicial authority.

4. **External Oversight** – A significant number of participants favoured stronger mechanisms of review and oversight to enhance public confidence in the administration of military justice.
5. **Legal Awareness and Education** – The study revealed substantial gaps in awareness, particularly among younger officers and PBOR personnel, regarding legal rights, remedies, and procedural safeguards.

At the same time, respondents did not advocate abandoning the military justice system or weakening military discipline. Rather, the overwhelming sentiment was that discipline and justice should reinforce one another. A system perceived as fair, transparent, and impartial ultimately strengthens discipline by enhancing trust in the institution and encouraging voluntary compliance with its decisions.

The voices gathered through this research reflect neither hostility towards military authority nor rejection of military discipline. Instead, they reveal a desire for a justice system that combines operational effectiveness with the fundamental principles of fairness, accountability, and due process. The challenge for future reform lies not in choosing between discipline and justice, but in ensuring that both objectives coexist within a framework that commands the confidence of those who serve under it.

The findings of this study therefore suggest that reform of the Indian Military Justice System is not merely desirable but increasingly necessary. By incorporating greater judicial independence, stronger procedural safeguards, meaningful access to legal representation, and enhanced transparency, the system can evolve to meet the legitimate expectations of the citizen-soldier while continuing to preserve the discipline essential to military service.

Ultimately, the legitimacy of any justice system rests not only upon its ability to punish wrongdoing but upon its ability to convince those subject to it that justice has been administered fairly. For the men and women who dedicate their lives to the defence of the nation, nothing less should suffice.

CHAPTER 10

Justice in Uniform: Discipline, Dignity and the Citizen-Soldier

INTRODUCTION

> *"Men and women in the Armed Forces do not leave constitutional safeguards and judicial protection behind when they enter military service. A member of the Armed Forces is entitled to equal justice under law not as conceived by the generosity of a commander but as written in the Constitution."* [466]
>
> **– Justice Ginsburg**

When soldiers enlist, they enter a profession unlike any other. They voluntarily submit themselves to a unique legal regime that governs not only their professional conduct but, in many respects, their personal liberty, livelihood, and future. Unlike ordinary citizens, they do not choose the justice system under which they will be tried, nor do they fully comprehend the extent to which military law will influence their lives. Their primary purpose is to serve and defend the nation. Yet, in doing so, they become subject to a system where the demands of discipline and the rights of the individual must constantly be balanced against one another.

466 *Weiss v. United States supre* note 135 at p. 194 (Ginsburg J., concurring).

This reality presents a fundamental paradox. No Armed Forces can function without discipline, obedience, and operational readiness. Discipline remains the cornerstone of military effectiveness and the foundation upon which national security rests. At the same time, members of the Armed Forces do not cease to be citizens merely because they wear a uniform. They continue to possess inherent human dignity and remain beneficiaries of the constitutional promise of equality, fairness, and the rule of law. The challenge for every military justice system is therefore not whether discipline should prevail over rights, or rights over discipline, but how both can coexist within a framework that commands legitimacy and public confidence.

As Lord Chief Justice Hewart famously observed:

"Justice should not only be done, but should manifestly and undoubtedly be seen to be done."[467]

This principle assumes even greater significance within the military environment, where judicial processes operate within a rigid hierarchical structure. A justice system may be legally sound, yet if those subject to it perceive it as lacking independence, impartiality, or fairness, confidence in the institution inevitably suffers. Discipline imposed through a process perceived as arbitrary generates resentment; discipline enforced through a process perceived as fair generates trust and legitimacy.

The Indian Military Justice System was inherited substantially from the colonial framework of the British Indian Army Act of 1911 and continues to retain many of its command-centric characteristics. Although significant developments such as the establishment of the Armed Forces Tribunal have

467 *R v Sussex Justices, supra* note 10.

improved access to appellate remedies, concerns regarding judicial independence, procedural fairness, unlawful command influence, Summary Court-Martial proceedings, and the concentration of authority within the military chain of command continue to attract scrutiny. These concerns are neither unique to India nor recent in origin. Military justice systems across the world have undergone extensive reforms over the past century in an effort to reconcile the requirements of military discipline with evolving constitutional and human rights standards.

This study has examined these issues through multiple perspectives. It has analysed the constitutional framework governing military justice, evaluated the statutory provisions of the Armed Forces Acts, examined the concept of fair trial and due process, explored the problem of unlawful command influence, studied reforms undertaken in the United Kingdom and the United States of America, and considered the perceptions of serving and retired military personnel through empirical research. Collectively, these chapters reveal a system that continues to perform an essential disciplinary function but which also faces significant challenges in its quest to achieve complete independence, impartiality, and procedural fairness.

The findings of this research demonstrate that discipline and justice are not competing objectives. On the contrary, they are mutually reinforcing principles. A military justice system that is perceived as fair, transparent, and independent strengthens morale, promotes confidence in command, and enhances institutional legitimacy. Conversely, a system perceived as arbitrary or influenced by extraneous considerations risks undermining the very discipline it seeks to preserve.

The purpose of this concluding chapter is therefore twofold. First, it synthesizes the principal findings emerging from the doctrinal, comparative, and empirical components of the study. Secondly, it proposes reforms aimed at strengthening the Indian Military Justice System while preserving the operational effectiveness and disciplinary requirements of the Armed Forces. The objective is not to weaken command authority, but to ensure that military discipline derives its legitimacy from justice administered according to law.

As Martin Luther King Jr. observed, "*Injustice anywhere is a threat to justice everywhere*" (King, 1963).[468]

For the citizen-soldier who stands ready to defend the Constitution, the expectation of justice is neither a privilege nor a concession. It is an essential component of the rule of law itself.

MAJOR FINDINGS OF THE STUDY

Finding I

The Indian Military Justice System Continues to Remain Predominantly Command-Centric

One of the principal findings emerging from this study is that the Indian Military Justice System continues to be predominantly command-centric in both structure and operation. While the maintenance of discipline remains the primary objective of military law, the administration of military justice continues to be closely intertwined with the chain of command. The concentration of authority within the hands of the Convening

468 King, M.L. Jr. (1963) *Letter from Birmingham Jail*. Birmingham, Alabama, 16 April 1963.

Authority and the Commanding Officer creates a system in which the executive exercises substantial influence over judicial processes.

The research revealed that the Convening Authority occupies a central position at almost every stage of the military justice process. From the initiation of proceedings and framing of charges to the constitution of Courts-Martial and confirmation of findings, the Convening Authority exercises powers that extend far beyond those ordinarily associated with disciplinary administration. Such concentration of authority creates both actual and perceived risks to the independence and impartiality of military adjudication.

The empirical findings of this study further demonstrated that a significant number of respondents viewed the extensive powers of the Convening Authority as one of the major weaknesses of the present system. Participants repeatedly expressed concern that adjudicators functioning within the military chain of command may consciously or unconsciously align their decisions with the perceived expectations of superior authorities. Even in situations where no direct interference occurs, the hierarchical nature of military service creates an appearance of influence capable of undermining confidence in the fairness of proceedings.

The study does not suggest that Convening Authorities routinely misuse their powers or deliberately interfere with the administration of justice. Indeed, military commanders require substantial disciplinary powers to maintain operational effectiveness, cohesion, and combat readiness. However, the existence of extensive discretionary authority without corresponding institutional safeguards inevitably raises concerns regarding accountability and transparency. As Lord Acton famously observed, "Power tends to corrupt and absolute power corrupts absolutely."[469] The issue therefore is not merely the exercise of authority, but the perception created when authority remains concentrated without adequate checks and balances.

Comparative analysis undertaken in this study demonstrates that other democratic jurisdictions have progressively reduced the direct involvement of commanders in judicial functions. Reforms in the United Kingdom and the United States have sought to separate prosecutorial, adjudicatory, and administrative functions, thereby reducing both actual and perceived command influence while preserving military discipline. The Indian Military Justice System, however, continues to retain several command-centric features inherited from its historical antecedents.

The findings of this research therefore indicate that while command authority remains indispensable to military discipline, its extensive role in the administration of military justice creates persistent concerns regarding independence, impartiality, and public confidence. The challenge for future reform lies not in weakening command responsibility, but in establishing a more appropriate balance between the legitimate requirements of discipline and the equally important demands of justice, fairness, and accountability.

---

469 Acton, J.E.E.D. (1887) *Letter to Bishop Mandell Creighton, 5 April 1887*. In: Figgis, J.N. and Laurence, R.V. (eds.) (1907) *Historical Essays and Studies*. London: Macmillan, pp. 504–506.

Finding II

Judicial Independence and Impartiality Remain Areas of Concern

An independent and impartial adjudicatory process is the cornerstone of every credible justice system. The present study finds that despite various procedural safeguards introduced over time, concerns regarding the independence and impartiality of military adjudicators continue to persist within the Indian Military Justice System. These concerns arise not necessarily from proven instances of interference, but from the structural relationship that exists between those responsible for administering justice and the military chain of command within which they function.

The empirical research conducted during this study revealed that a substantial number of respondents perceived the existing structure as vulnerable to actual, perceived, or potential influence. Serving and retired personnel alike expressed reservations regarding a system in which adjudicators, prosecutors, defending officers, and legal advisers remain part of the same hierarchical organization. Many respondents felt that the dependence of officers on superior authorities for postings, promotions, confidential reports, and career advancement creates circumstances in which complete judicial independence may be difficult to achieve.

Particular concern was expressed regarding the position of Court-Martial members, who are appointed for specific trials and continue to remain within the command structure before, during, and after the proceedings. Unlike judges in civilian courts, they do not enjoy fixed tenure, institutional independence, or complete separation from executive authority. Consequently, even where adjudicators act with utmost integrity and impartiality, the appearance of dependence may undermine public confidence in the fairness of the proceedings.

The issue of perceived impartiality assumes special significance in military justice. As Lord Chief Justice Hewart famously observed:

"Justice should not only be done, but should manifestly and undoubtedly be seen to be done".[470]

This principle applies with equal force to military tribunals. The legitimacy of any justice system depends not only upon the fairness of its decisions but also upon the confidence of those subject to its jurisdiction. Where a reasonably informed observer perceives that adjudicators may be influenced by command considerations, confidence in the system is inevitably weakened, irrespective of whether actual influence exists.

The comparative analysis undertaken in this study demonstrates that many democratic jurisdictions have progressively sought to strengthen judicial independence within their military justice systems. Reforms in the United Kingdom and the United States have increasingly insulated judges and prosecutors from command influence by creating independent prosecutorial structures, enhancing judicial tenure, and expanding procedural safeguards. These reforms were motivated by the recognition that military discipline is strengthened rather than weakened when justice is administered through institutions that are demonstrably independent and impartial.

470 *R v Sussex Justices, supra* note 10.

The findings further indicate that concerns regarding judicial independence are closely linked with perceptions of unlawful command influence, the limited role of legally qualified personnel in decision-making, and the absence of complete separation between executive and judicial functions. These concerns do not necessarily imply that military justice is incapable of delivering fair outcomes. Rather, they highlight the need to strengthen institutional safeguards so that fairness is not only achieved but is also visibly apparent.

Accordingly, this study finds that while the Indian Military Justice System continues to perform an essential disciplinary function, questions regarding judicial independence and impartiality remain among the most significant challenges confronting the administration of military justice today. Addressing these concerns is critical to enhancing confidence in the system and ensuring that the citizen-soldier perceives military justice as both fair and legitimate.

Finding III

Legal Expertise and the Role of the Judge Advocate General Require Strengthening

A recurring theme throughout this study has been the tension between military experience and legal expertise in the administration of military justice. While military discipline and operational understanding remain indispensable to the functioning of the Armed Forces, the increasing complexity of modern legal principles has heightened the need for greater legal expertise within military adjudicatory processes. The findings of this study indicate that the present structure does not sufficiently integrate legal expertise into decision-making at all levels of military justice.

Unlike civilian courts, where legally trained judges determine questions of law and procedure, Courts-Martial in India continue to be adjudicated by military officers who may possess considerable professional and operational experience but often lack formal legal training. Although the Judge Advocate General (JAG) provides legal advice to the Court, such advice is advisory in nature and does not bind the adjudicators. Consequently, the final determination of guilt, innocence, and punishment remains with officers who are not necessarily trained in the principles of criminal jurisprudence, evidence, sentencing, or constitutional law.

The empirical findings of this research revealed significant support for increasing the role of legally qualified personnel in military trials. A majority of respondents, particularly among senior serving and retired officers, expressed the view that legal matters should be adjudicated or supervised by officers possessing specialised legal knowledge. Many participants believed that the presence of legally trained personnel would enhance both the fairness of proceedings and confidence in the administration of justice. At the same time, respondents also emphasised the importance of preserving an understanding of military culture, operational realities, and the unique demands of service life.

This apparent tension reflects a broader challenge confronting military justice systems worldwide. The question is not whether military experience should be replaced by legal expertise, but how the two can be harmonised. Military justice requires adjudicators who understand both the realities of command and the requirements of law. Comparative developments in the United Kingdom and the United States demonstrate a gradual movement towards increasing the role of legally qualified judges while retaining military participation in the adjudicatory process. Such reforms have sought to ensure that legal decisions are guided by professional legal standards without losing sight of the unique context within which military discipline operates.

The study also identified concerns regarding the institutional position of the Judge Advocate General's Branch. A substantial majority of respondents favoured greater independence for the JAG organisation and expressed the view that legal officers should be insulated, as far as practicable, from influences arising from the ordinary chain of command. The underlying concern was not that legal officers routinely act improperly, but rather that public confidence in military justice is strengthened when legal advisers are perceived to function independently and impartially.

The findings further reveal that legal expertise assumes particular importance in cases involving serious criminal offences, complex evidentiary issues, constitutional rights, and questions of sentencing. In such cases, the absence of a legally determinative role for qualified legal professionals may create uncertainty regarding the consistency and predictability of outcomes. The study therefore highlights the need to ensure that legal principles are applied with the same degree of rigour that would ordinarily be expected in any system entrusted with determining questions affecting personal liberty, professional reputation, and, in some cases, life itself.

Accordingly, this research finds that while military experience remains an essential component of military justice, the growing demands of fairness, due process, and constitutional accountability require a stronger and more visible role for legal expertise within the system. The challenge for future reform lies in achieving an appropriate balance between military knowledge and legal competence so that the administration of justice commands both professional respect and public confidence.

Finding IV

Summary Court-Martial Continues to Raise Significant Due Process Concerns

One of the most consistent findings emerging from this study relates to the Summary Court-Martial (SCM) system and its compatibility with contemporary notions of fairness, due process, and natural justice. While the Summary Court-Martial was originally conceived as a mechanism for maintaining discipline in exceptional circumstances, particularly in operationally challenging environments, concerns persist regarding the adequacy of procedural safeguards available to the accused. The findings indicate that the SCM remains one of the most contentious aspects of the Indian Military Justice System.

The rationale underlying the SCM is neither difficult to understand nor entirely without merit. Armed Forces units may be deployed in remote locations, border areas, counter-insurgency environments, or operational theatres where access to regular judicial institutions is limited or impracticable. In such circumstances, commanders require the ability to deal expeditiously with misconduct that threatens discipline, cohesion, and operational effectiveness. The need for swift disciplinary action has therefore historically been viewed as an essential element of military command.

However, the study reveals that concerns arise not from the existence of summary procedures themselves, but from the concentration of functions within a single authority and the limited procedural protections available to the accused. Under the existing framework, the Commanding Officer performs multiple roles within the process, including the initiation of proceedings, assessment of evidence, adjudication, and imposition of punishment. This combination of investigative, prosecutorial, and adjudicatory functions creates a perception that the accused is not afforded the same degree of procedural protection ordinarily associated with the principles of natural justice.

The empirical findings of this research reinforce these concerns. A substantial number of respondents, particularly among Personnel Below Officer Rank (PBOR), expressed reservations regarding the fairness of SCM proceedings. Many participants highlighted the absence of legal representation, limited opportunities to prepare a defence, difficulties in presenting evidence, and the lack of meaningful appellate review. Several respondents perceived the process as heavily influenced by command authority, leading to doubts regarding its independence and impartiality.

The study further reveals a noticeable divergence in perceptions between senior officers and lower-ranking personnel. While many senior officers viewed the SCM as an indispensable disciplinary tool necessary for maintaining operational effectiveness, a significant number of PBOR respondents regarded it as the least fair component of the Military Justice System. This divergence itself is noteworthy, as it reflects differing experiences of the same institution depending upon one's position within the military hierarchy.

Comparative analysis undertaken in this study demonstrates that military justice systems in several democratic jurisdictions have progressively expanded procedural safeguards even within summary proceedings. Reforms in the United Kingdom, for example, have enhanced the rights of accused personnel to elect trial by Court-Martial and to seek appellate review of summary decisions. Such developments reflect a broader recognition that efficiency and discipline need not be achieved at the expense of procedural fairness.

As Justice Felix Frankfurter aptly observed:

"The history of liberty has largely been the history of observance of procedural safeguards."[471]

The principle is particularly relevant in the military context, where the consequences of disciplinary proceedings may extend beyond immediate punishment to affect career progression, reputation, livelihood, and personal liberty.

Accordingly, this study finds that although the Summary Court-Martial continues to serve an important disciplinary function, it remains the aspect of the Military Justice System most frequently associated with concerns regarding due process and fairness. The challenge for future reform lies in preserving the operational utility of summary procedures while ensuring that the rights of the citizen-soldier are protected through adequate procedural safeguards consistent with constitutional principles and contemporary standards of justice.

471 Frankfurter, F. (1938) *The Public and Its Government*. New Haven: Yale University Press.

Finding V

The Armed Forces Tribunal Has Strengthened Appellate Justice but Has Not Fully Addressed Trial-Level Deficiencies

One of the most significant developments in the evolution of the Indian Military Justice System has been the establishment of the Armed Forces Tribunal (AFT) under the Armed Forces Tribunal Act, 2007. The creation of the Tribunal marked a historic departure from the traditional military justice framework by introducing, for the first time, an independent appellate forum for service personnel aggrieved by findings and sentences of Courts-Martial. The study finds that the establishment of the AFT has substantially enhanced access to justice for members of the Armed Forces and represents a major step towards aligning military justice with constitutional principles and contemporary standards of judicial review.

Prior to the establishment of the Tribunal, service personnel convicted by Courts-Martial had no independent statutory right of appeal. Their remedies were largely confined to petitions and reviews within the military hierarchy, raising concerns regarding the absence of an external appellate mechanism. The creation of the AFT therefore addressed a long-standing deficiency in the Military Justice System by providing service personnel with an independent judicial forum empowered to examine findings, sentences, and service-related grievances.

The study reveals that the Armed Forces Tribunal has played an important role in strengthening accountability within military justice. Through its appellate jurisdiction, the Tribunal has subjected Court-Martial proceedings to greater judicial scrutiny and has provided an effective mechanism for correcting legal errors, procedural irregularities, and instances of disproportionate punishment. The availability of appellate review has significantly improved confidence in the justice system by assuring service personnel that military decisions are not beyond independent examination.

However, the findings of this research also indicate that the establishment of the AFT has not fully resolved concerns relating to the fairness of proceedings at the trial stage. The Tribunal functions primarily as an appellate body and therefore addresses deficiencies only after they have occurred. Structural concerns relating to judicial independence, unlawful command influence, Summary Court-Martial procedures, and the limited role of legally qualified adjudicators continue to arise at the initial stages of the justice process. In this sense, the Tribunal operates more as a corrective mechanism than as a preventive safeguard.

The empirical findings suggest that while respondents generally welcomed the existence of the AFT, many viewed it as only a partial solution to deeper structural issues. Several participants expressed the view that access to appellate review, though essential, cannot substitute for fairness at the first instance. A system that relies excessively on appellate correction may still impose considerable financial, professional, and emotional burdens upon individuals who have already undergone a flawed trial process.

The study also identifies certain limitations in the existing framework governing the Tribunal. Concerns have been expressed regarding delays in implementation of Tribunal orders, the restricted jurisdiction over certain categories of Summary Court-Martial proceedings, and the continued absence of complete parity with appellate mechanisms available in civilian criminal justice systems. These concerns do not diminish the importance of the Tribunal but demonstrate that the process of military justice reform remains incomplete.

The study further notes that concerns relating to the structure and functioning of military justice have not gone unnoticed within the defence establishment itself. In 2015, under the leadership of the late Shri Manohar Parrikar, then Raksha Mantri, a Committee of Experts was constituted to examine litigation, grievance redressal mechanisms, and broader issues concerning military justice reform. The Committee submitted an extensive report containing numerous recommendations aimed at enhancing fairness, transparency, and accountability within the military justice system. Significantly, it recommended the establishment of permanent infrastructure for Courts-Martial at designated military stations in order to reduce the potential for command influence and strengthen the independence of military adjudication. The Committee also advocated measures to improve grievance redressal, decentralise decision-making, and modernise aspects of military justice administration. While several administrative initiatives were subsequently undertaken, many of the broader structural reforms remain unrealised. Nevertheless, the Parrikar Committee represented one of the most important official acknowledgements that military justice in India required progressive reform consistent with contemporary principles of fairness and accountability. (Chhina, 2015; Chhina, 2015a).[472]

472 Chhina, M.A.S. (2015) 'Defence Ministry sets up committee to suggest measures to reduce litigations of personnel', *The Indian*

The comparative analysis undertaken in this study further illustrates that mature military justice systems have increasingly focused not only upon appellate safeguards but also upon improving fairness, independence, and procedural protections at the trial stage itself. The experience of the United Kingdom and the United States suggests that effective appellate institutions function most successfully when supported by robust safeguards during investigation and trial.

As Justice Krishna Iyer observed:

"A fair trial is the first imperative of the dispensation of justice."[473]

This principle underscores the reality that appellate review, however important, cannot entirely compensate for deficiencies occurring at the initial stages of adjudication.

Accordingly, this study finds that the Armed Forces Tribunal represents one of the most progressive reforms in the history of Indian military justice and has significantly enhanced access to appellate justice. Nevertheless, the existence of an appellate forum alone cannot fully address concerns relating to fairness, independence, and due process at the trial level. Meaningful reform therefore requires attention not only to appellate mechanisms but also to the foundational structures through which military justice is initially administered.

Express, 17 July,; Chhina, M.A.S. (2015a) 'Committee on reduction in defence litigation submits report to Parrikar', *The Indian Express*, 24 November.

473 *Zahira Habibullah Sheikh v State of Gujarat* (2004) 4 SCC 158.

Finding VI

Discipline and Fair Trial Are Complementary Rather Than Competing Objectives

Perhaps the most significant finding emerging from this study is that military discipline and fair trial rights should not be viewed as competing objectives. Discussions on military justice have traditionally been framed as a conflict between the requirements of discipline and the protection of individual rights. The findings of this research demonstrate that such a dichotomy is both artificial and misleading. Rather than undermining discipline, a fair and impartial system of justice strengthens military effectiveness by promoting confidence, legitimacy, and institutional trust.

Throughout the study, it became evident that the primary justification advanced for retaining command-centric features within the Military Justice System is the need to preserve discipline and operational readiness. Undoubtedly, discipline remains the bedrock of military effectiveness. No Armed Forces can function without obedience to lawful authority, cohesion within the ranks, and the ability to respond swiftly to operational demands. However, the evidence gathered through doctrinal analysis, comparative examination, and empirical research indicates that discipline derives its enduring legitimacy from the perception that authority is exercised fairly, transparently, and in accordance with law.

One of the most striking findings of the field research was that a majority of respondents, irrespective of rank, expressed a willingness to accept even unfavourable outcomes if they were satisfied that the process leading to those outcomes had been fair. Participants repeatedly emphasised that what generated dissatisfaction was not necessarily punishment itself, but the perception that proceedings lacked transparency, independence, or adequate procedural safeguards. This observation reinforces the principle that confidence in the process is often as important as confidence in the outcome.

The study further demonstrates that fairness and due process serve important institutional functions within the Armed Forces. A justice system perceived as impartial enhances morale, strengthens confidence in command, and promotes respect for lawful authority. Conversely, where decisions are perceived as arbitrary or influenced by extraneous considerations, trust in the institution is weakened and discipline itself may suffer. The objective of military justice should therefore be not merely the punishment of wrongdoing, but the maintenance of discipline through procedures that command legitimacy among those subject to them.

The debate surrounding military justice in India is, at its core, a constitutional one. Article 33 of the Constitution empowers Parliament to restrict or abrogate certain Fundamental Rights of members of the Armed Forces to ensure the proper discharge of their duties and the maintenance of discipline. However, neither the Constitution nor Parliament has defined the precise limits of the concept of discipline. Consequently, the balance between military necessity and individual rights has largely evolved through legislation, judicial interpretation, and institutional practice.

The findings of this study indicate that while certain restrictions upon rights may be justified by the unique demands of military service, such restrictions cannot extend to the complete denial of fairness, impartiality, and due process. Members of the Armed Forces remain citizens of India and do not cease to be entitled to the protection of law merely because they wear a uniform. The purpose of military justice must therefore be to reconcile the legitimate demands of discipline with the equally important obligation to protect the rights and dignity of the citizen-soldier.

The research further reveals that the right to a fair trial forms an essential component of the Rule of Law. Access to justice is not confined merely to the existence of courts or appellate forums; it also encompasses the principle of legality, whereby decisions affecting life, liberty, livelihood, and reputation are made in accordance with established legal norms rather than arbitrary discretion. Respondents repeatedly expressed the view that confidence in the Military Justice System would increase significantly if adjudicatory processes were perceived as independent, impartial, and insulated from undue influence. The findings therefore support the proposition that procedural fairness is not incompatible with military discipline but is, in fact, one of its most important sources of legitimacy.

An equally significant observation emerging from the study is that service personnel are more willing to accept adverse outcomes when they believe that the process leading to those outcomes has been fair. This finding reinforces the broader jurisprudential principle that due process is not merely a procedural formality but a substantive guarantee of justice. Where individuals are afforded a meaningful opportunity to be heard before an impartial authority applying established legal principles, the legitimacy of the outcome is enhanced even when the decision operates against their interests.

The comparative experience of jurisdictions such as the United Kingdom and the United States further reinforces this conclusion. Over the past several decades, both jurisdictions have progressively strengthened judicial independence, reduced the scope for command influence, enhanced procedural safeguards, expanded rights of legal representation, and developed robust appellate mechanisms. These reforms reflect a growing recognition that modern military justice must preserve discipline while simultaneously adhering to contemporary standards of fairness, accountability, and respect for individual rights.

As Justice Ruth Bader Ginsburg observed:

"Men and women in the Armed Forces do not leave constitutional safeguards and judicial protection behind when they enter military service" (*Weiss v. United States*, 1994, p. 194).

The findings of this study strongly support this principle. The protection of procedural rights, access to independent adjudication, and adherence to due process are not obstacles to military discipline. Rather, they are essential elements of a justice system that seeks to maintain discipline through legitimacy rather than through the mere exercise of authority.

Accordingly, this research concludes that the future development of the Indian Military Justice System should not be guided by a perceived choice between discipline and justice. The true challenge lies in harmonising both objectives within a framework that inspires confidence among service personnel, respects constitutional values, and preserves the operational effectiveness of the Armed Forces. In a democratic society governed by the Rule of Law, the strength of military discipline ultimately rests upon the confidence of the citizen-soldier that justice will be administered fairly, independently, and according to law.

Recommendations for Reform

The findings of this study demonstrate that the objective of reform should not be to weaken military discipline, but to strengthen its legitimacy by ensuring that disciplinary processes are perceived as fair, impartial, and consistent with constitutional principles. The following recommendations seek to strike a balance between the operational requirements of the Armed Forces and the rights of the citizen-soldier.

A. Constitutional Awareness and Legal Education

The study revealed a significant gap in awareness regarding military law and the constitutional implications of military service. It is therefore recommended that all personnel, at the time of recruitment and throughout their careers, be educated regarding their rights, duties, and obligations, particularly those affected by Article 33 of the Constitution. Such awareness would enable service personnel to better understand the legal framework within which military discipline operates.

Further, military law should occupy a more prominent place in professional military education. Periodic refresher courses in military law should be conducted for officers, particularly those likely to perform adjudicatory functions. Consideration may also be given to introducing Military Law as an elective or specialised subject within civilian law schools, thereby fostering greater understanding of military justice among future lawyers, judges, and policymakers.

B. Reform of the Court-Martial System

The administration of military justice should reflect a clearer distinction between disciplinary matters and criminal offences. Minor disciplinary infractions affecting unit administration and good order may continue to be dealt with by Commanding Officers. However, offences of a criminal nature carrying serious consequences for liberty, livelihood, or reputation should be investigated, prosecuted, and adjudicated by legally qualified authorities.

The role of the Convening Authority should be substantially curtailed once cognisance of an offence has been taken. Thereafter, responsibility for legal evaluation, framing of charges, prosecution, and post-trial review should rest with independent legal authorities. Such reforms would reduce both actual and perceived unlawful command influence while preserving the Commanding Officer's responsibility for discipline.

Court-Martial members should be selected through a transparent and objective process. Consideration may be given to random selection from an approved panel of qualified officers, taking into account service experience, educational qualifications, integrity, and suitability for judicial responsibilities. Any decision to exclude a selected member should be recorded in writing and be subject to review.

The conduct of Court-Martial proceedings should be placed under greater legal supervision. The role of legally qualified officers should be strengthened to ensure that decisions are based upon established legal principles, procedural fairness, and consistent application of military law.

C. Strengthening the Independence of the Judge Advocate General's Branch

The study consistently identified the need for greater institutional independence of the Judge Advocate General's Branch. Consideration should therefore be given to restructuring the JAG Branch so that it functions with a greater degree of autonomy from the ordinary chain of command while remaining accountable within an appropriate statutory framework.

To ensure fairness and avoid conflicts of interest, the legal functions of investigation review, prosecution, defence representation, and judicial support should be institutionally separated. Such separation would promote objectivity, strengthen confidence in military justice, and align the Indian system more closely with contemporary international practices.

Post-trial review of findings, sentencing, and legal errors should also be undertaken by legally qualified authorities independent of the Convening Authority. This would ensure consistency, transparency, and accountability in the administration of military justice.

D. Establishment of Permanent Military Courts

One of the most significant reforms recommended by this study is the gradual transition from ad hoc Courts-Martial towards a system of Permanent Military Courts. Such courts should possess a stable institutional structure, clearly defined jurisdiction, and adequate safeguards to ensure independence and impartiality.

Permanent Military Courts should function under an independent administrative framework and be insulated from undue influence arising from the ordinary chain of command.

Members should be selected on the basis of legal qualifications, experience, competence, and integrity, and should enjoy an appropriate degree of tenure protection.

The offices of investigation, prosecution, defence, and adjudication should be institutionally separated within this structure. Such separation would strengthen public confidence in military justice and reduce the risk of actual or perceived bias.

Judges and members of Permanent Military Courts should be subject to appropriate accountability mechanisms for misconduct, bias, or failure to discharge their judicial duties. Independent review procedures may be established for this purpose.

E. Reform of Summary Court-Martial Proceedings

The Summary Court-Martial system emerged during the course of this research as one of the most controversial aspects of military justice. While concerns were raised regarding its compatibility with Articles 14 and 21 of the Constitution, the practical realities of military service indicate that some form of summary disciplinary mechanism may continue to be necessary, particularly in remote and operational environments.

Accordingly, Summary Court-Martial jurisdiction should be restricted to minor offences, primarily disciplinary or administrative in nature, carrying proportionate punishments. Serious criminal offences should ordinarily be referred for trial by a regular Court-Martial.

The accused should have the right to legal representation from the earliest stage of proceedings. Where operational circumstances make physical access to counsel difficult, adequate facilities should be provided to ensure meaningful legal consultation.

To minimise perceptions of bias, the Commanding Officer of the accused should not ordinarily conduct the proceedings once formal cognisance of the offence has been taken. Consideration may be given to assigning such cases to an independent officer outside the immediate chain of command of the accused.

Procedural safeguards, including the right to present evidence, call witnesses, receive legal assistance, and challenge adverse material, should be strengthened. Decisions resulting in significant penalties should be subject to meaningful judicial review.

F. Legislative Reform and Periodic Review

The study also highlights the need for continuous review of military law. Certain provisions of the Army Act, Air Force Act, and Navy Act employ broad and open-ended language which may create uncertainty regarding the scope of criminal liability. Provisions relating to conduct prejudicial to good order and military discipline, or conduct unbecoming, should be periodically reviewed to ensure clarity, certainty, and consistency with modern principles of criminal jurisprudence.

A permanent mechanism for review of military justice legislation may therefore be established. Such a body, comprising military professionals, legal experts, academics, and representatives of relevant institutions, should periodically examine the operation of military justice and recommend amendments in light of constitutional developments, comparative jurisprudence, and evolving operational requirements.

The military justice system should also be subjected to periodic independent review, preferably every five years, to assess its effectiveness, fairness, and compatibility with contemporary standards of due process and human rights.

These recommendations do not seek to dilute military discipline. Rather, they seek to strengthen it by ensuring that the administration of justice within the Armed Forces is transparent, accountable, constitutionally compliant, and worthy of the confidence of the citizen-soldier whom it serves.

Scope for Future Research

The present study has examined the Indian Military Justice System through the prism of discipline, constitutional rights, fair trial standards, unlawful command influence, and comparative developments in the United Kingdom and the United States. While the research has identified significant structural and procedural concerns, it has also revealed several areas that warrant further scholarly inquiry.

A major area requiring future research concerns the doctrine of unlawful command influence within the Indian context. While extensive scholarship exists in jurisdictions such as the United States, the concept remains relatively underexplored in India. Detailed empirical and doctrinal studies examining the extent to which command influence affects investigations, prosecutions, adjudication, and sentencing would contribute significantly to the development of Indian military jurisprudence.

Further research may also examine the feasibility of establishing a unified military justice code applicable to all three Services. The appointment of the Chief of Defence Staff and the increasing emphasis on jointness and theatre commands provide an opportunity to reconsider whether a common code, similar to the Uniform Code of Military Justice in the United States or the unified system introduced in the United Kingdom, would enhance efficiency, consistency, and fairness.

The functioning of the Armed Forces Tribunal presents another important field of inquiry. Studies may be undertaken to assess its effectiveness as an appellate forum, the implementation of its decisions, the impact of its judgments on military justice reform, and the challenges arising from its existing jurisdictional limitations.

The role and institutional structure of the Judge Advocate General's Branch also merit further examination. Comparative research may explore models adopted by other democratic jurisdictions regarding prosecutorial independence, judicial tenure, legal aid, and the separation of investigative, prosecutorial, defence, and adjudicatory functions.

Future studies may additionally focus on the operation of Summary Court-Martial proceedings. Empirical research involving a larger sample of serving personnel across ranks and Services could provide valuable insights into perceptions of fairness, access to legal representation, and the practical impact of summary procedures on discipline, morale, and operational effectiveness.

The findings of this study also suggest the need for interdisciplinary research combining law, military sociology, psychology, leadership studies, and organisational behaviour. Such research could examine how perceptions of justice influence morale, cohesion, trust in command, combat effectiveness, and institutional legitimacy within the Armed Forces.

An important area for future research concerns the substantive provisions of military law themselves. Certain provisions, such as Section 45 (Unbecoming Conduct) and Section 63 (Act Prejudicial to Good Order and Military Discipline) of the Army Act, 1950, and their corresponding provisions in the Air Force Act, 1950 and the Navy Act, 1957, are framed in broad and general terms. While such provisions provide commanders with flexibility to address a wide range of conduct that may adversely affect discipline and military effectiveness, their breadth also raises important questions concerning certainty, uniformity of application, and the scope of discretion vested in military authorities.

Future research may therefore undertake a detailed doctrinal and comparative analysis of these provisions to examine whether greater legislative precision is desirable while continuing to preserve the unique requirements of military discipline and operational effectiveness. Such studies may draw upon constitutional principles, comparative military jurisprudence, and evolving standards of criminal law to assess whether the existing provisions strike an appropriate balance between disciplinary necessity and legal certainty.

It is further suggested that a broader review of military offences contained in the Army Act, Air Force Act, and Navy Act be undertaken to identify provisions that may benefit from clarification, modernisation, or harmonisation. Such research could contribute towards progressive reform of military law and may ultimately assist in updating the relevant statutory framework while preserving the ethos, traditions, and operational requirements of the Armed Forces.

The present research does not claim to provide the final word on military justice reform. Rather, it seeks to contribute to an ongoing dialogue concerning how a modern democratic State may best reconcile the imperatives of military discipline with the rights and dignity of the citizen-soldier. It is hoped that future scholarship will build upon these findings and continue the process of developing a Military Justice System that is both operationally effective and constitutionally robust.

Concluding Thoughts

Military justice occupies a unique position within any democratic society. It exists at the intersection of two powerful and sometimes competing imperatives: the necessity of maintaining discipline within the Armed Forces and the obligation of the State to uphold the rule of law. Unlike civilian justice systems, military justice is required to function within an environment where obedience, cohesion, operational readiness, and national security are matters of paramount importance. Yet, those who serve within this system remain citizens, entitled to dignity, fairness, and the protection of law.

This study began with a simple but fundamental question: whether the existing Military Justice System adequately balances the requirements of discipline with the right of the citizen-soldier to a fair trial. The answer that emerges is neither wholly critical nor wholly celebratory. The Indian Military Justice System has served the nation for decades and has contributed significantly to maintaining discipline within one of the world's largest and most professional armed forces. However, the research demonstrates that important questions remain regarding judicial independence, command influence, procedural safeguards, legal representation, and the perception of fairness among those who are subject to the system.

The comparative experiences of the United Kingdom and the United States illustrate that military justice systems are neither static nor immune from reform. Both jurisdictions have progressively adapted their systems to reflect evolving constitutional values, human rights standards, and expectations of procedural fairness. Importantly, these reforms have not weakened military discipline. Rather, they have strengthened public confidence in military institutions by ensuring that justice is not only done but is seen to be done.

The findings of this study suggest that India stands at a similar point of evolution. The establishment of the Armed Forces Tribunal represented a significant milestone in providing an independent appellate mechanism for service personnel. Likewise, the recommendations of the Committee of Experts constituted under the leadership of the late Shri Manohar Parrikar demonstrated official recognition that aspects of military justice require modernisation. Yet much remains to be done if the system is to fully reflect contemporary constitutional expectations and international best practices.

The field research undertaken as part of this study revealed a recurring theme across ranks, services, and experiences. Service personnel are prepared to accept even adverse outcomes when they believe that the process leading to those outcomes is fair. What they seek is not preferential treatment, but confidence that decisions affecting their liberty, livelihood, reputation, and careers are made independently, impartially, and according to law. This insight may well represent the most important lesson of the entire study.

Military discipline and fair trial rights should not be viewed as opposing forces. Discipline derives its strength from legitimacy, and legitimacy is sustained through fairness. A justice system perceived as transparent, independent, and accountable is more likely to command respect than one that relies solely upon authority. In this sense, the protection of procedural rights is not a threat to discipline but one of its strongest foundations.

The Indian Constitution recognises the unique position of the Armed Forces through Article 33, permitting restrictions on certain rights in the interest of discipline. However, the Constitution does not contemplate the abandonment of justice. The citizen who dons the uniform does not surrender the core values that the Constitution seeks to protect. The challenge, therefore, is not to choose between discipline and justice, but to ensure that both coexist in a manner that strengthens the Armed Forces and the democratic values they are sworn to defend.

As military operations become increasingly complex and as expectations of accountability continue to evolve, the Military Justice System must evolve as well. Reform should not be viewed as criticism of the institution but as a reflection of its strength and maturity. A professional military deserves a professional justice system—one that inspires confidence among service personnel, commands respect from society, and remains faithful to the principles of fairness and the rule of law.

Ultimately, the true measure of a Military Justice System lies not merely in its ability to punish misconduct, but in its capacity to deliver justice while preserving discipline. A nation that entrusts its soldiers with the defence of constitutional values must ensure that those same values are reflected in the system of justice to which they are subject. The citizen-soldier stands at the heart of this balance. Ensuring that he or she receives both discipline and justice is not simply a legal obligation; it is a moral imperative for a democratic republic governed by the rule of law.

Bibliography

PRIMARY SOURCES

Statutes and Rules

- Air Force Act, 1950.
- Armed Forces Tribunal Act, 2007.
- Army Act, 1950.
- Army Rules, 1954.
- Constitution of India, 1950.
- Navy Act, 1957.

International Instruments

- American Convention on Human Rights, 1969.
- European Convention for the Protection of Human Rights and Fundamental Freedoms, 1950.
- International Covenant on Civil and Political Rights, 1966.
- Universal Declaration of Human Rights, 1948.

Official Reports and Manuals

- Law Commission of India, 169th Report on Amendment of the Army, Navy and Air Force Acts (1999).
- Manual of Military Law (MML), Vol. III.
- United States Department of Defence, Report to the Honourable Wilber M. Brucker, Secretary of the Army: Good Order and Discipline in the Army.

- Basic Principles on the Independence of the Judiciary (1985).
- International Commission of Jurists, International Principles on the Independence and Accountability of Judges, Lawyers and Prosecutors, Practitioners' Guide No. 1 (2007).

SECONDARY SOURCES

Books

- Austin, Granville, Working a Democratic Constitution: A History of the Indian Experience, Oxford University Press, New Delhi, 1999.
- Chandrachud, Abhinav, Due Process of Law, Eastern Book Company, New Delhi, 2011.
- Dicey, A.V., Introduction to the Study of the Law of the Constitution, 10th ed., Macmillan & Co., London, 1885.
- Frankfurter, Felix, The Public and Its Government, Yale University Press, New Haven, 1938.
- Jain, M.P., Indian Constitutional Law, Wadhwa & Company, Nagpur, 2005.
- Jha, U.C., The Military Justice System in India: An Analysis, LexisNexis Butterworths Wadhwa, Nagpur, 2009.
- Kumar, Brig Nilendra, Court-Martial and Military Matters, Manas Publications, New Delhi, 2000.
- Kumar, Major General Nilendra, Case Studies on Military Law, Universal Law Publishing Co. Pvt. Ltd., New Delhi.
- Lederer, Frederic L. and Hundley Zeliff, Barbara, Court-Martial Procedure.

- Oberoi, Major J.L., Military Law and Writs, SAAR Printers, Chandigarh, 2007.
- Oberoi, Major J.L., Questions Answered on Military Law, Paradise Printers, Chandigarh, 2003.
- Sen, Amartya, The Idea of Justice, Allen Lane, London, 2009.
- Sharma, Col. G.K. and Jaswal, Col. M.S., Study and Practice of Military Law, Deep & Deep Publications Pvt. Ltd., New Delhi, 2010.
- Sharma, O.P., Military Law in India, M.N. Tripathi Pvt. Ltd., Bombay, 1990.
- Singh, M.P., The Indian Army Under the East India Company, Sterling Publishers Pvt. Ltd., New Delhi, 1976.
- Walker, Janet, Military Justice: From Oxymoron to Aspiration, 1994.

Journal Articles and Book Chapters

- Alleman, Lindsy Nicole, 'Who is in Charge and Who Should Be? The Disciplinary Role of the Commander in Military Justice Systems', Duke Journal of Comparative and International Law, 2006.
- Becker, Thomas G., 'Games Lawyers Play: Pre-Preferral Delay, Due Process, and the Myth of Speedy Trial in the Military Justice System', Air Force Law Review, Vol. 45, 1998.
- Fidell, Eugene R., 'A World-Wide Perspective on Change in Military Justice', Air Force Law Review, Vol. 48, 2000.
- Fidell, Eugene R. and Sullivan, Dwight H. (eds.), Evolving Military Justice, Naval Institute Press, Annapolis, Maryland, 2002.

- Jordash, Wayne and Scott, Martin, 'Due Process and Fair Trial Rights at the Special Court for Sierra Leone', Leiden Journal of International Law, Vol. 23, 2010.
- Lederer, Frederic L. and Hundley Zeliff, Barbara, 'Needed: An Independent Military Judiciary—A Proposal to Amend the Uniform Code of Military Justice', William & Mary Bill of Rights Journal, 1994.
- Lyon, Ann, 'After Findlay: A Consideration of Some Aspects of the Military Justice System', in Evolving Military Justice, 2002.
- Maiese, Michelle, 'Procedural Justice', in Guy Burgess and Heidi Burgess (eds.), Beyond Intractability, University of Colorado, 2004.
- Nicholas, Louis B., 'The Justice of Military Justice', William & Mary Law Review, Vol. 12, No. 3, 1971.
- Rant, J.W., 'The British Courts-Martial System: It Ain't Broke, But It Needs Fixing', Military Law Review, Vol. 152, 1996.
- Rowlinson, Simon P., 'The British System of Military Justice', Air Force Law Review, Vol. 52, 2002.
- Schlueter, David A., 'The Court-Martial: An Historical Survey', Military Law Review, Vol. 87, 1980.
- Schlueter, David A., Military Criminal Justice: Practice and Procedure, LexisNexis, United States, 2004.
- Tyler, Tom R., 'What Is Procedural Justice? Criteria Used by Citizens to Assess the Fairness of Legal Procedures', Law and Society Review, Vol. 22, No. 1.

Reports, Lectures and Institutional Publications

- Center for Democracy and Governance, Handbook on Fighting Corruption, U.S. Agency for International Development, 1999.

- Icelandic Human Rights Centre, The Right to Due Process.
- Lawyers Committee for Human Rights, What Is a Fair Trial? A Basic Guide to Legal Standards and Practice, 2000.
- Morris, Lieutenant Colonel Lawrence J., 'This Better Be Good: The Courts Continue to Tighten the Burden in Unlawful Command Influence Cases', The Army Lawyer, 1998.
- Oyewole, Olubunmi, Corruption: Challenge to Good Governance and Development in Nigeria, 2010.
- Sen, Justice D.M., 'The Relationship of Military Law and Discipline with the Judicial System of the Country', United Services Institution of India, New Delhi, 1982.

Online Sources and Commentary

- Bhanu, P.N., 'Analysis on 169th Law Commission Report – Amendment of Army, Navy and Air Force Acts', 2023.
- Chhina, M.A.S., 'Defence Ministry Sets Up Committee to Suggest Measures to Reduce Litigation of Personnel', The Indian Express, 2015.
- Chhina, M.A.S., 'Committee on Reduction in Defence Litigation Submits Report to Parrikar', The Indian Express, 2015.
- Nath, Chandra C.P., 'Time to Put Court-Martial on Trial', Broad mind, 2011.
- Singh, Navdeep, 'Military Justice Reform – Developments and Challenges', 2023.

Unpublished Thesis

- Newhouse, Claire, Summary Proceedings Within the Australian Military Justice System: How and Why Are They Inherently Unjust?, Unpublished Honours Thesis, Faculty of Law, The Australian National University, 2005.

www.ingramcontent.com/pod-product-compliance
Lightning Source LLC
LaVergne TN
LVHW090303210926
848480LV00001B/108